Deborah Wallrabenstein
Sounds of a New Generation

Lettre

Für Tata

Deborah Wallrabenstein completed her dissertation project at the department of Jewish studies at the University of Basel. She has studied at the Universities of Heidelberg and Massachusetts. Currently she is Deputy Head of Communications at the University Children's Hospital Basel, Switzerland.

Deborah Wallrabenstein

Sounds of a New Generation
On Contemporary Jewish-American Literature

[transcript]

This book is the revised version of a dissertation which was submitted to and published at the University Library of Basel, Switzerland in November 2016.

Bibliographic information published by the Deutsche Nationalbibliothek
The Deutsche Nationalbibliothek lists this publication in the Deutsche Nationalbibliografie; detailed bibliographic data are available in the Internet at http://dnb.d-nb.de

© 2017 transcript Verlag, Bielefeld

All rights reserved. No part of this book may be reprinted or reproduced or utilized in any form or by any electronic, mechanical, or other means, now known or hereafter invented, including photocopying and recording, or in any information storage or retrieval system, without permission in writing from the publisher.

Cover layout: Maria Arndt, Bielefeld
Printed and bound in Great Britain by Marston Book Services Ltd, Oxfordshire
Print-ISBN 978-3-8376-3986-5
PDF-ISBN 978-3-8394-3986-9

Content

Acknowledgment | 7

Introduction | 9

1 Generations on the Move | 19
1.1 Generation and Socialization | 26
1.2 Family and Intertext | 30
1.3 Various Sounds – Who is writing an   y? | 38
1.4 Chapter Conclusion | 42

2 Contemporary Jewish American   erature | 47
2.1 A Short History of Jewish-American Li rature | 47
2.2 Overview of Jewish-American Literature in the 20th Century | 51

3 The Past of *Shtetl* and Family | 61
3.1 Jonathan Safran Foer – Everything is Illuminated | 65
3.2 Dara Horn – The World to Come | 75
3.3 Chapter Conclusion | 84

4 New Beginnings | 91
4.1 Shalom Auslander – Foreskin's Lament | 95
4.2 Deborah Feldman - Unorthodox | 107
4.3 Allegra Goodman – The Family Markowitz | 120
4.4 Lisa Schiffman – Generation J | 125
4.5 Gideon Lewis-Kraus – A Sense of Direction | 133
4.6 Chapter Conclusion | 144

5 The New 'Russian-Jewish-American' Literature | 147
5.1 David Bezmozgis – Natasha and Other Stories | 154
5.2 Gary Shteyngart – The Russian Debutante's Handbook | 159
5.3 Ellen Litman – The Last Chicken in America | 163
5.4 Anya Ulinich - Petropolis | 171
5.5 Chapter Conclusion | 181

Conclusion | 187

Bibliography | 191

Acknowledgment

Writing this book would not have been possible without the tremendous support of so many people.

First of all I would like to thank my PhD advisor Prof. Dr. Alfred Bodenheimer. For the past 12 years he has always encouraged and supported me, ever since I was an undergrad at the University of Heidelberg. With his cool-headed and humorous nature, Alfred has guided me through highly difficult phases during the dissertation process. I would also like to thank my second advisor Prof. Dr. Olga Gershenson.

Special gratitude goes to Dr. Celia Zwillenberg for her trust and the generous financial support from the Lutz Zwillenberg Scholarship. Without this scholarship this book would probably not exist.

I would also like to thank my dear colleagues at the Centre for Jewish Studies in Basel. Our lunch breaks in the garden were wonderful and will always remain a special memory of mine.

Finally, and most importantly, I want to thank my family, my friends and my husband for never losing patience with me, for bringing me back down to earth, and being there when needed.

Basel, June 2017

Introduction

In the beginning of Elie Wiesel's *The Gates of the Forest* we find a parable about the great Rabbi Israel Baal Shem Tov:

> When the great Rabbi Baal Shem-Tov
> saw misfortune threatening the Jews
> it was his custom
> to go into a certain part of the forest to meditate.
> There he would light a fire,
> say a special prayer,
> And the miracle would be accomplished
> And the misfortune averted.
>
> Later, when his disciple,
> the celebrated Magid of Mezritch
> had occasion for the same reason, […]
> he would go to the same place in the forest
> and say: "Master of the Universe, listen!
> I do not know how to light the fire,
> but I am still able to say the prayer."
> And again the miracle would be accomplished.
>
> Still later,
> Rabbi Moshe-Leib of Sasov,
> in order to save his people once more,
> would go into the forest and say:

"I do not know how to light the fire,
I do not know the prayer,

but I know the place
and this must be sufficient."
It was sufficient and the miracle was accomplished.

Then it fell to Rabbi Israel of Rizhyn
to overcome misfortune. [...]
"I am unable to light the fire
and I do not know the prayer;
I cannot even find the place in the forest.
all I can do is to tell the story,
and this must be sufficient."
And it was sufficient.[1]

This short and concise parable about Rabbi Baal Shem Tov reflects very well the central issue that seems to have befallen Jewish-American literature. While the majority of the Jewish immigrants in the early 20th century were still very familiar with Jewish traditions and rites, and their children's generation likewise had noticeable points of contact with Judaism through their parents, a third generation seems to have grown whose relation to the Jewish heritage is rather precarious. It is the writing of this young generation, born in the 70s and 80s of the last century that I seek to talk about in this thesis.

In 1977, author and literary critic Irving Howe wrote his infamous dictum that predicted the end of Jewish-American literature:

My own view is that American Jewish fiction has probably moved past its high point. Insofar as this body of writing draws heavily from the immigrant experience, it must suffer a depletion of resources, a thinning out of materials and memories. Other than in books and sentiment, there just isn't enough left of that experience.[2]

---

1 Wiesel, Elie. Foreword. *The Gates of the Forest*. New York: Schocken Books, 1982.
2 Howe, Irving. Ed. Introduction. *Jewish-American Stories*. New York: A Mentor Book, 1977. 16.

Accordingly, Howe was of the opinion t... Jewish-American literature would run out of topics to talk about, be... all future generations of authors would lack the experience of immi... n to and assimilation with the American society. Howe has been co... cted many times and long been proven wrong by the continuous outp... Jewish-American writing.[3] However, in this thesis I want to focus on h... ophecy, because it predicts that the death of Jewish themes in America... rature will occur precisely now, in the phase of post-immigration and ... t-assimilation. As it turns out, however, the opposite has occurred wh... y the third generation after immigration has made it their business ... unlike the previous two

---

[3] The list of refutations of Howe's prediction is ... and it can simultaneously be understood as state of the art of scholarly d... ssions about contemporary Jewish-American fiction. For a selection of influential authors and titles see: Zakrzewski, Paul. Ed. *Lost Tribe. Jewish Fiction from the Edge.* New York: HarperCollins Publishers Inc., 2003; Bukiet, Melvin Jules, and David G. Roskies. Eds. *Scribblers on the Roof.* Contemporary American Jewish Fiction. New York: Persea Books, 2006; Rubin, Derek. Ed. *Promised Lands. New Jewish American Fiction on Longing and Belonging.* Amsterdam: Amsterdam University Press, 2010. Further literature on the most recent output of Jewish-American fiction with a focus on the topic of Israel includes: Furman, Andrew. *Israel through the Jewish-American Imagination. A Survey of Jewish-American Literature on Israel 1928-1995.* Albany: State University of New York Press, 1997. Michael P. Kramer and Hana Wirth-Nesher and their contributors offer texts about Jewish female writers, Jewish-American poetry, and Hebrew literature in: Kramer, Michael P., and Hana Wirth-Nesher. Eds. *The Cambridge Companion to Jewish American Literature.* Cambridge: Cambridge University Press, 2003. Victoria Aarons discusses religious topics in contemporary literature in: Aarons, Victoria. *What Happened to Abraham? Reinventing the Covenant in American Jewish Fiction.* Newark: University of Delaware Press, 2005. Janet Burstein Handler discusses, among other things, the second generation's dealing with the Holocaust and exile in: Handler Burstein, Janet. *Telling Little Secrets. American Jewish Writing since the 1980s.* Madison: The University of Wisconsin Press, 2006. Finally, the writing of recent Jewish immigrants to the US from the former Soviet countries is dealt with in Rosenfeld, Alvin H. Ed. The Writer Uprooted. Contemporary Jewish Exile Literature. Bloomington: Indiana University Press, 2008.

generations – to revive the Jewish heritage in American writing. Interestingly, despite his pessimism, Irving Howe had seen this twist coming, however he brushed it off as a kind of last upheaval before the final collapse:

There remains, to be sure, the problem of "Jewishnessness" [sic] and the rewards and difficulties of definition it may bring us. But this problem, though experienced as an urgent one by at least some people, does not yield a thick enough sediment of felt life to enable a new outburst of writing about American Jews. It is too much a matter of will and nerves, and not enough shared experience. Besides, not everything which concerns or interests us can be transmuted into imaginative literature.[4]

As accomplished in other places before, this thesis is another attempt at refuting this latter skepticism of Howe. Indeed, the question of Jewishness, which is exactly the question raised with fervor by the third generation after immigration, offers enough shared experience and enough imaginative material for Jewish-American literature to be fully alive today.

There is a simple cultural dynamic of immigration underlying the differences between these three generations that has been described by cultural historian Marcus Lee Hansen as "the almost universal phenomenon that what the son wishes to forget the grandson wishes to remember."[5] This must be explained: When Jewish immigrants arrived in America throughout the first half of the 20th century, the habits and customs they brought with them from the countless *shtetls* in the Eastern European Pale of Settlement were still intact, including religious practices and the Yiddish language. These immigrants tried to make a living, mostly in poor and cramped places like the Lower East Side of New York and other urban conglomerates. However, to get a start in American society, most of them were willing to give up much of their traditional life and religious customs like the Shabbat and also the Yiddish language. Moreover, the literature

---

4   Howe, Irving. Ed. Introduction. *Jewish-American Stories*. New York: A Mentor Book, 1977. 16.

5   Hansen, Marcus Lee. "The Problem of the Third Generation Immigrant." *American Immigrants and their Generation. Studies and Commentaries on the Hansen Thesis after Fifty Years*. Eds. Kivisto, Peter, and Dag Blanck. Urbana: University of Illinois Press, 1990. 192-193.

published by immigrants dealt with escaping the Old World and making it in the New World.

By the time the second generation was born, the first to be born in America, many families had already succeeded in making a moderate to successful living, could even afford to move to the suburbs (e.g., of New Jersey), and took pride in sending their children off to institutions of higher education. However, as it turned out, these children – the second generation – soon developed the desire to become completely assimilated into American society, to get rid of their marginality and to be perceived no longer as Jewish immigrants and foreigners. Many were ashamed of their homes and the customs that were still upheld there and tried to shed as much as possible what had linked them to their Jewish heritage. Accordingly, the literature of this second generation reflects on this struggle for assimilation and the tension felt between the alleged anchor of a Jewish home and family and the promises of dissolving into mainstream American society. However, a new generation – the third generation – has recently entered the stage of Jewish-American literature, and as Hansen has implicated, this generation has tried to recover as much of their Jewish heritage as possible. What has been cast away, ignored or hidden by the previous generation is now deliberately being explored again. These younger Jewish writers, born in the 1970s and 80s, have begun taking an interest in their Jewish heritage again and have focused on exploring and expressing their heritage.

The reason, it seems, why young Jewish-American authors seem to feel comfortable again with exploring their Jewish heritage instead of hiding it, is because unlike the preceding generations they finally feel naturalized as Americans. Assimilation is no longer their aim; they have been born without question as Americans and do not perceive of any significant differences between their non-Jewish-American peers. Indeed, one could say, they set out to reestablish such differences, by looking for a clearer sense of what it means to be *Jewish*-American. The writer Nessa Rapoport strongly confirms my assumption in describing the feeling of her generation: "Having won our place in American culture, we are beginning to be confident enough to reclaim Jewish culture [...]."⁶ In his 2009 article "Rise of the New Yiddishists," the journalist David Sax has pointed to this re-affirmative trend and argued that there is a "newfound ethnic pride that has revitalized Jewish literature in America."⁷ According to Sax, the mantra of the previous generation was: "We're Jews, we hate it, but we can't escape it."⁸ However, the rising young Jewish writers of the next generation seem to have a completely different approach to their identity: "Our generation is secure enough in their Americanism to be hungry for a more clearly defined sense of self."⁹ Again, Sax seems to confirm my impression that the new curiosity for matters of Judaism and Jewishness of contemporary American writers is based on their natural and primary sense of being American and being integrated into American society.

The argument that I propose in this thesis is that we can look at these young Jewish-American writers as one literary generation, not only because most of them are the grandchildren of immigrants and roughly the same age, but rather exactly because their stories share the common ground of exploring their Jewish heritage and dealing with the question of what being Jewish-American means to them.

I will not try to provide answers to complex questions such as what it means to be Jewish, or try to provide definitions of terms such as Jewishness,¹⁰ Judaism and Jewish-American. Instead, I will stay focused on showing that the writing of this young generation is centered on dealing

---

6   Rapoport, Nessa. "Summoned to the Feast." *Writing Our Way Home. Contemporary Stories by American Jewish Writers.* Eds. Solotaroff, Ted and Nessa Rapoport. New York: Schocken Books, 1992. xxx.
7   Sax, David. "Rise of the New Yiddishists." *Vanity Fair,* April 2009. 16 June 2015.
8   Ibid.
9   Ibid.
10 Irving Howe writes about the term Jewishness: "When one speaks of Judaism or the Jewish religion, it is to invoke a coherent tradition of belief and custom; when one speaks of 'Jewishness,' it is to invoke a spectrum of styles and symbols, a range of cultural memories, no longer as ordered or weighty as once they were yet still able to affect experience." In: Howe, Irving. Introduction. *Jewish-American Stories.* New York: A Mentor Book, 1977. 10.

with such terms and questions, regardless of which – if any – answers they find. As Sara R. Horowitz puts it:

The best of contemporary Jewish American fiction seeks to complicate a foreshortened and simplified discussion about Jewish identity and Jewishness in our time. In looking at America's Jewish question, they opt to explore the in-betweenness, the shifting borders, rather than to resolve them by engraving the borderlines.[11]

As Horowitz points out, it would be beside the point to seek answers to questions of Jewish identity in this thesis, because the authors I am dealing with complicate these question themselves and show us that there *are* no clear-cut definitions; rather, the debate is in a constant state of flux. In the following chapters and subchapters, I will expand on these initial thoughts on generations in Jewish-American writing and discuss the various current groups of writers and their divergent approaches. I will try to subsume them under one roof, calling them 'one generation' of authors, even though not all of them seem to be members of one generation in one or the other sense. Neither are all of these authors the exact same age, nor are all of them third generation in terms of immigration history. Also the literature from all these authors is as diverse and heterogeneous as their own backgrounds. However, they all seem to belong to one single generation in sharing the same curiosity about which Hansen is speaking, a curiosity about what makes them Jewish and what this means, no matter whether the answers are to be found in the past, present or future. The single texts discussed in this dissertation might sound diverse as individual pieces, however, they harmonize in this common aspect of curiosity.

In the first chapter of this thesis I will therefore elaborate on my argument and develop my own definition of the term 'generation.' I will also argue that questions like whether a single literary work is fictitious or autobiographic are not important, because I look at all these stories collectively and subsume them under the umbrella of one generation speaking to us.

---

11 Horowitz, Sara R. "Mediating Judaism: Mind, Body, Spirit, and Contemporary North American Jewish Fiction." *AJS Review* 30.2 (Nov. 2006): 253.

In the second chapter of this thesis I will provide a very brief and rough overview of the respective histories of Jewish immigration to America and of Jewish-American literature in the 20th century. I feel this is necessary because my overall argument of a third generation of Jewish writing in America is largely embedded within this historical, sociological and cultural background.

The following chapters will each deal respectively with one thematic 'sub-trend' as 'layers' within the work of this current generation of young Jewish-American writers. Each chapter looks at a number of exemplary literary works in order to highlight both the sub-themes and the overall argument of how these texts comprise a new generation of Jewish-American writing. During my early research, I noticed that many works by current Jewish-American writers seemed not only to share certain motives but also sounded similar with regard to an overarching new curiosity in everything Jewish. I kept looking for these sounds in further readings and found an abundance. Naturally, the corpus of current Jewish-American literature is vast, so the final choice of texts was at my discretion. This was on purpose, because – as I will continue to argue – the voice of a single text or author is not the matter at question, but rather the harmonious combination of their multiple sounds. However, in choosing the single texts, I have made an effort to strike a balance between female and male writers in each chapter, to ensure that my choice of texts can be considered a representative profile in terms of gender.

In chapter 3, called 'The Past of Shtetl and Family,' I will discuss how in both Jonathan Safran Foer's *Everything is Illuminated* and Dara Horn's *The World to Come*, young protagonists try to reestablish some link to their Jewish heritage by unraveling their family's European past. Particularly, the *shtetl,* as a place of former Jewish habitation and nostalgic desire, seems to play an important role in this regard, as it becomes creatively reimagined and fictionally resurrected in Foer's novel. In Dara Horn's novel, on the other hand, it is a single object, namely a lost and retrieved Chagal painting that triggers a series of events leading the young protagonists back into the European past of their family.

The next chapter, called 'New Beginnings,' looks at a number of literary statements from this new generation that seem to be very diverse and even contradictory at first glance. I will call the sub-group of authors/protagonists in this chapter 'searchers,' 'detachers,' and 'self-shapers,' because unlike in the previous chapter, the stories presented here do not return to the past or to the family, but rather try to craft something completely new, which in some cases even means breaking away from the family. Both Shalom Auslander's *Foreskin's Lament* and Deborah Feldman's *Unorthodox* are classical coming of age stories about two young Jewish-Americans who struggle to break away from their ultra-orthodox families and communities, in order to live a secular life. In contrast to these stories of perceived escape and liberation from the orthodox world, there is Allegra Goodman's *The Family Markowitz*, which includes a story of return from secular life to orthodox observance. This is the inversion of the previous two stories, and yet, both cases share the fact that a young Jewish person chooses to take a different path than their family and the community they grew up in and to independently craft their own new Jewish identity. The last two stories presented in this chapter – Lisa Schiffman's *Generation J*, and Gideon Lewis-Kraus' *A Sense of Direction* – are about journeys that are taken in order to find and explore the Jewish heritage and self. In particular, Schiffman sets out on a series of almost absurd experiments in order to find an answer to the pressing question of what being a Jewish-American means. Lewis-Kraus, on the other hand, rather seems to stumble upon the question of Jewishness coincidentally during the trips he is taking across the world. All these stories discussed in this 4th chapter are indeed very multifaceted approaches by young Americans dealing with their Jewish heritage. Nevertheless, they all describe a completely new path being taken and a new Jewish identity being crafted and shaped.

Finally, in the last chapter of my thesis I will test both my overall argument and Hansen's three-stage theory about the cultural dynamic of immigration by applying them to the literary works of my third focus group: the new immigrants from the former Soviet Union who came to North America in the 1970s and 1980s. Specifically, this last group of contemporary Jewish writers in America seems to stick out because unlike the other subgroups whose stories may differ in content, this group has a completely different biography. Unlike their American same-age peers, they were not born in America and are certainly not yet "secure enough in their Americanism" as implied by David Sax.[12] In other words, my very basic sociological assumptions do not apply to this group, which begs the question of whether their experiences as young Jews in America still share a common ground with their larger generation or whether they must rather be compared to the earlier immigrants of the 20th century. I will argue that this sub-group still belongs to the same new generation of Jewish American writing, however adding a completely new and different texture. Their experience is different, and yet their literary material is part of what makes the new Jewish-American literature distinct from what has been written before. The newly arrived immigrants from the former Soviet Union – like their American born peers – ask questions about Jewish identity, about what being Jewish and being American means. Obviously, their answers turn out to be very different.

---

12 Sax, David. "Rise of the New Yiddishists." *Vanity Fair*, April 2009. 16 June 2015.

1 Generations on the Move

> "What the son wishes to forget
> the grandson wishes to remember"
> HANSEN, MARCUS LEE. "THE PROBLEM
> OF THE THIRD GENERATION IMMIGRANT."
> 195.

What do I mean when talking about the 'third generation' of Jewish-American writers? In general, one can define the term generation historically, culturally and biographically.

In the context of this thesis it is seemingly clear what 'culturally' means – all authors I am going to present and analyze consider themselves to be Jewish; more precisely I am focusing on young authors with their roots based in Eastern European Jewry. However, I will later need to return to this question of a generation in terms of culture when specifying my own approach, because I will argue that the matter is indeed more complex than just saying all authors in this group are young and Jewish. But let us first turn to other concepts of the term 'generation.' Biographically speaking, I am focusing on third generation Jewish-American authors, who are the grandchildren of immigrants. This aspect will have to be watered down to some extent, in order to keep such authors in the picture, who are not personally, let us even say biologically, the grandchildren of immigrants, but who grew up along and together with a peer group of 'immigrant-grandchildren,' and thus belong to this 'generation' at least by sharing their age. If, for example, an immigrant came to the U.S. in the 1920s, their children grew up in the 1950s or 1960s. In my argument, the children of these children would be considered third generation Jewish-Americans. However, in combining both historical/biographical and social concepts of the term generation to the group of authors that I am looking at, I will make the concession of including such authors who are not technically speaking the grandchildren of immigrants but who happen to be of the same age at the same time. Obviously this brings the cultural definition of generation back into the game and as promised, I will return to this aspect later. But let us first focus on what I call general cultural dynamics of immigration.

With every wave of immigration to the United States, the new citizens started from scratch, no matter whether they were old or young, male or female; immigration marked the zero hour. It does not matter for the sake of my argument whether this immigration took place due to pogroms at the turn of the century or later because of the Holocaust, because the cultural dynamic of immigration seems to be similar and maybe universal in each case. Whenever Jewish immigrants came to the U.S. a certain dynamic can be observed:[1] The first generation of European immigrants came to America knowing and well aware that they were newcomers and thereby outsiders. They had to handle the new culture, acquire the language and simply struggle to survive by doing any kind of labor offered. These immigrants neither could nor actually tried to get rid of their heritage. They remained in their place, wishing for their children and grandchildren to have a better life in the new world than they had lived back in the Old World. Probably the most popular examples of first generation accounts, both from a male and female point of view are Henry Roth's *Call it Sleep* from 1934, about the life of the immigrant boy David Schearl, growing up on the Lower East Side of Manhattan, and Mary Antin's autobiography *The Promised Land* from 1912, in which she describes the struggles of her life as an immigrant in the slums of Boston.[2]

The second generation, the first to be born in the New World, had to fight a different battle, a battle with itself. The American historian Marcus Lee Hansen describes this very precisely:

---

1 A similar if not identical cultural dynamic of immigration can probably be observed for any other cultural group, e.g., Asian, Italian, or German immigration. However, I will only focus on the group of Jewish-Americans without diving deeper into the general principles of US-immigration or the specifics of other cultural groups.

2 A more detailed description of the literature by the first and second generations of Jewish-American authors will be provided in chapter 2.2.

The sons and daughters of the immigrants were really in a most uncomfortable position. They were subjected to the criticism and taunts of the Native Americans and to the criticism and taunts of their elders as well. [...] Life at home was hardly more pleasant. Whereas in the schoolroom they were too foreign, at home they were too American. [...] when the sons and daughters refused to conform, their action was considered a rebellion of ungrateful children for whom so many advantages had been provided. [...] How to inhabit two worlds at the same time was the problem of the second generation. [...] That problem was solved by escape. [...] He [the son] wanted to forget everything: the foreign language that left an unmistakable trace in his English speech, the religion that continually recalled childhood struggles, the family customs that should have been the happiest of all memories.[3]

Accordingly, the second generation saw their heritage as an obstacle which they tried to overcome, a stain that needs to be hidden in order to blend in. They tried to fully assimilate into American society. And this dynamic of the second generation seems to be universal at different historical points in time, no matter whether born as a child of Eastern European immigrants in the 1920s or growing up as a child of Holocaust survivors later in the 1950s, these children shared a similar experience. The 1954-born author Lev Raphael talks about his first generation parents in Derek Rubin's essay collection *Who We Are. On Being (and Not Being) a Jewish American Writer*:

So it's no wonder that when friends or acquaintances in junior high or high school made anti-Semitic jokes or remarks, I never challenged them. Being Jewish was somehow shameful to me, and being the child of Holocaust survivors was beyond shame – it was not even a topic to think about, let alone discuss.[4]

---

3   Hansen, Marcus Lee. "The Problem of the Third Generation Immigrant." *American Immigrants and their Generation. Studies and Commentaries on the Hansen Thesis after Fifty Years*. Eds. Peter Kivisto and Dag Blanck. Urbana and Chicago: University of Illinois Press, 1990. 192-193.
4   Lev, Raphael. "Writing Something Real." *Who We Are. On Being (and Not Being) a Jewish American Writer*. Ed. Rubin, Derek. New York: Schocken Books, 2005. 194.

Similarly, the Nobel Prize winning author Saul Bellow who was born in 1915 as a son of Russian Jewish immigrants and grew up in Chicago, has been quoted by Derek Rubin:

For I thought of myself as a Midwesterner and not a Jew. I am often described as a Jewish writer; in much the same way one might be called a Samoan astronomer or an Eskimo cellist or a Zulu Gainsborough expert.[5]

Despite being born 40 years apart, obviously both authors feel similarly about their Jewishness. It is something not to be mentioned, to be overcome and left behind. Precisely this similarity in attitude towards the cultural heritage of the immigrant parent generation is what I would call the typical if not universal cultural dynamic of the second generation.

But when the third generation of Jewish-Americans appears, something very different happens. One would assume that there would be yet an increase of denial for their heritage, that the third generation would do anything just to finally get rid of the "Old World" in their life. But actually the complete opposite occurs. As the subtitle of this chapter suggests, the prevailing cultural dynamic of the third generation is nicely summarized in Hansen's words, that "what the son wishes to forget the grandson wishes to remember."[6] This theory by Hansen is exactly what I managed to find in the writings of third generation Jewish-American authors. Also Adam Meyer sees similarities in the writings of Michael Chabon, Allegra Goodman, Tova Reich, and Rebecca Goldstein in this regard:

---

5   Bellow, Saul. "Starting Out in Chicago." *Who We Are. On Being (and Not Being) a Jewish American Writer.* Ed. Rubin, Derek. New York: Schocken Books, 2005. 5.

6   Hansen, Marcus Lee. "The Problem of the Third Generation Immigrant." *American Immigrants and their Generation. Studies and Commentaries on the Hansen Thesis after Fifty Years.* Eds. Kivisto, Peter and Dag Blanck. Urbana and Chicago: University of Illinois Press, 1990. 195.

[They] confirm sociologist Marcus Lee Hansen's theory of third generation return, the idea that grandsons will want to remember parts of their grandparents' lives that the fathers have wanted to forget, in this case their Jewishness."[7]

The third generation, accordingly, tries to refer back to their Jewish roots, but there is no increased desire for belonging to the 'new' society anymore. These young people are part and parcel of the American society which their parents tried so desperately to crack into. For these young Jewish-Americans, being assimilated into American culture is not even a question, it is the state they find themselves born into. There is no question of belonging. Naturally, they are an integral part of American society. But while being American is not an issue for them any longer, there comes a time for retrieving their place in another culture, namely their Jewish heritage.

Again it is Marcus Lee Hansen who describes the third generation and their point of view:

As a broad generalization it may be said that the second generation is not interested in and does not write any history. That is just another aspect of their policy of forgetting. Then, however appears the "third generation." They have no reason to feel any inferiority when they look about them. They are American born. Their speech is the same as that of those with whom they associate.[8]

Hansen continues to elaborate on his theory which he first developed in 1937 and which was originally observed in third generation accounts of the American Civil War (reports of grandchildren of Civil War-witnesses).[9] He

---

7 Meyer, Adam. Abstract. "Putting the 'Jewish' Back in 'Jewish American Fiction': A Look at Jewish American Fiction from 1977 to 2022 and an Allegorical Reading of Nathan Englander's 'The Gilgul of Park Avenue.'" *Shofar. An Interdisciplinary Journal of Jewish Studies* 22.3 (2004): 104.

8 Hansen, Marcus Lee. "The Problem of the Third Generation Immigrant." *American Immigrants and their Generation. Studies and Commentaries on the Hansen Thesis after Fifty Years*. Eds. Peter Kivisto and Dag Blanck. Urbana and Chicago: University of Illinois Press, 1990. 196.

9 The fact that Hansen has never actually talked about the specifics of Jewish immigration and is instead talking about a general phenomenon which he first

believes that the third generation tends to write about events that have occurred two generations earlier. They are the ones who want to know more about their family history and their heritage:

> They do not have the same reasons or complexes that encourages the second [generation] to make a complete break. They are as American as any of their neighbors. There is no accent in speech caused by the intermingling of two tongues. No feeling of inferiority troubles them in the presence of persons of Mayflower or Knickerbocker descent. They have a healthy curiosity to know something of the family saga.[10]

Hansen's observation of the third generation is fully confirmed by Binnie Kirshenbaum, a contemporary Jewish-American writer:

> The concept of the shiksa goddess, popularized by Philip Roth and Woody Allen so that every Jewish boy wanted one and Jewish girls were bobbing their noses and dying their hair blond in order to pass, has fallen out of favor. Jewish girls are, I'm pleased to say, once again considered hot. My generation is travelling to Prague and to Kraków and Berlin. Looking for what? We can ask. For what got lost along the way to America, what was lost on the way to becoming American? Has the shame of being "too Jewish" eased into a shame at having been self-loathing? And we are writing about that search, the longing. We're attaching ourselves to the world of our grandparents. The literary theme of alienation in America has taken a new (re)turn.[11]

Kirshenbaum accordingly confirms that her generation – the third generation – returns to embrace the world of their grandparents, their

---

observed in Civil War remembrance and then applied to immigration, is yet another indicator that indeed the cultural dynamic of immigration seems to be universal, independent of historical point in time and cultural group.

10 Hansen, Marcus Lee. "Who Shall Inherit America?" *American Immigrants and their Generation. Studies and Commentaries on the Hansen Thesis after Fifty Years.* Eds. Kivisto, Peter and Dag Blanck. Urbana: University of Illinois Press, 1990. 209.

11 Kirshenbaum, Binnie. "Princess." *Who We Are. On Being (and Not Being) a Jewish American Writer.* Ed. Rubin, Derek. New York: Schocken Books, 2005. 224-225.

European descent and their Jewishness. Similarly Rachel Kadish, a grandchild of Holocaust survivors, reports about the curiosity for the past in her own writings:

> In my early twenties, every line I wrote seemed to lead back to the Holocaust. [...] While I've to see this documented, I believe this to be a phenomenon of the grandchildren of Holocaust survivors: We are compulsive story gatherers. [...] They [grandparents] tell their grandchildren the stories they didn't want to impose on their own children, but don't now wish to take to the grave. And we grandchildren, freed from our parents' need to protect their own parents in those immediate postwar years, ask and ask and ask.[12]

In pointing to universal dynamics of third generation authors and to similarities in their perspectives, I hope to be far from equalizing third generation accounts of the Holocaust with all other third generation writing. I realize that the struggle of the post-traumatized descendants of Holocaust survivors can be of greater despair and necessity than the accounts of other third generations. Nevertheless, the writings of Holocaust-survivors' grandchildren are part of the spectrum of (current) Jewish-American literature that I am describing and clearly share typical features of third generation writing. In conclusion, I would in general agree with Hansen's theory, about the distinctive curiosity of the third generation. Writers of this generation/these generations try to return to their family's cultural roots and redevelop an interest in what their own parents have rather tried to forget or even deny, namely the stories, lives and ways of their own parents. Quintessentially, I have tried to outline the typical cultural dynamics of first, second and third generations after immigrating to the United States and hinted at how this dynamic is reflected in the history of Jewish-American literature.

---

12 Kadish, Rachel. "The Davka Method." *Who We Are. On Being (and Not Being) a Jewish American Writer*. Ed. Rubin, Derek. New York: Schocken Books, 2005. 288-289.

1.1 GENERATION AND SOCIALIZATION

What do I mean by the frequent use of the term 'generation'? So far I have been speaking about first, second and third generations with regard to a family's immigration history. However, if my argument is centered on the assumption that there is a certain 'generation' of American Jewish authors that can be considered one collective group, the use of the term 'generation' must be further specified. So what exactly is a generation? Although in sociological research it is often pointed out that there is no clear definition of this term,[13] I would like to discuss some possible approaches. One classic definition of the term would be that it points to a contemporary community of people who experienced and processed certain events in their lives in a similar or even the same way. This community is also more or less the same age and happens to share the same values and lifestyles. Because this group of people grew up under similar or the same conditions of socialization, what binds them together is considered a collective experience.[14] The German historian Ulrike Jureit explains that people of the same age have a specific way of thinking, feeling and acting, and thus feel connected to one another.[15] Accordingly, I would argue, that the same applies to literature, namely that there are authors forming a literary generation bound by similar experience. In an interview with the literary magazine *Akzente,* the German author W.G. Sebald uses the term *Zeitheimat*[16] when speaking about the time when he was born and raised, more precisely the years after 1945. Sebald explains that when watching documentaries about that time, he gets the feeling of a shared identity, a

---

13 See amongst others: Bude, Heinz. "Qualitative Generationenforschung." *Qualitative Forschung. Ein Handbuch.* Eds. Flick, Uwe et al. Reinbek bei Hamburg: Rowohlt Verlag, 2010. 188; Weisbrod, Bernd. "Generation und Generationalität in der neueren Geschichte." *Aus Politik und Zeitgeschichte 8. Bundeszentrale für politische Bildung.* (2005): 16 June 2015; Jureit, Ulrike. *Generationenforschung.* Göttingen: Vandenhoeck & Ruprecht, 2006. 10.

14 See: Jureit, Ulrike. *Generationenforschung.* Göttingen: Vandenhoeck & Ruprecht, 2006. 7-8.

15 Ibid. 8.

16 Although it is generally hard to translate compound words from German into English, I will give it a try: 'home in time.'

common origin from which the writing of his generation stems. Speaking for his own generation (children of postwar Germany), the author Sebald confirms that the writing of individuals who share a certain experience in growing up will somehow be connected and accordingly share certain features and scopes.[17]

W.G. Sebald's use of the term *Zeitheimat* and his explanation are connected to historical-social theories that regard generations as social categories, which reflect social similarities due to collective experiences and a shared upbringing.[18] The entire field of research on 'generation' was initiated and is to this day dominated by Karl Mannheim and his formative essay "Das Problem der Generationen," published in 1928.[19] In this essay, Mannheim states that a generation is not only formed by the 'objective' affiliation to a group of people of the same age, but also, and this is even more essential, by the subjective affiliation to a community of shared experiences.[20] A generation constitutes itself only out of a pool of shared experiences and the resulting behavior and actions. Marc Szydlik and Harald Künemund also define the term social generation on the basis of common experiences which are typical for a group of people roughly born at the same time. However, because the main constituent of a generation are such shared experiences that result in common values and life styles, the term is not even restricted to a certain age group.[21] In other words,

---

17 See: Hage, Volker. "Interview with W.G. Sebald." *Akzente. Zeitschrift für Literatur.* Ed. Krüger, Michael. München: Carl Hanser Verlag, 2000. 35-36.

18 See: Höpfinger, François. *Generationenfrage - Konzepte, theoretische Ansätze und Beobachtungen zu Generationenbeziehungen in späteren Lebensphasen.* Lausanne: Réalités Sociales 1999. 10.

19 Mannheim, Karl. *Wissenssoziologie. Auswahl aus dem Werk.* Ed. Wolff, Kurt H. Berlin: Luchterhand Verlag, 1964.

20 Liebau, Eckart. "Generation – ein aktuelles Problem?" *Das Generationenverhältnis. Über das Zusammenleben in Familie und Gesellschaft.* Ed. Liebau, Eckart. München: Juventa Verlag, 1997. 22.

21 See: "Dieser *gesellschaftliche Generationenbegriff* zielt auf Gemeinsamkeiten aufgrund gleicher oder benachbarter Geburtsjahrgänge im Sinne von generationstypischen Erfahrungen und – möglicherweise als Konsequenz – gemeinsamen Werte oder Lebensstilen, nicht aber auf Altersgruppen." In:

everybody who shares some basic experiences – no matter at what age – can belong to a generation.

But there is another important factor which should not be underestimated, namely the historical constellation. A shared kind of upbringing and common experiences do not occur in a neutral non-historical time and place, but always have a concrete historical context at any given time, as in the case of Sebald, who found the experiences of his generation largely based on the conditions of postwar-Germany. This should lead us to the insight that concrete historical constellations, in other words, what has been happening at a certain place at a certain time, come to be part of the specific experiences of a generation.

It happens that the current generation of Jewish-Americans, born and raised during the late 20th century, have grown up at a time predominately characterized by economic prosperity, domestic peace, and a general spirit of liberal-mindedness cherishing individualism and free self-fulfillment. However, the common experiences that form a social generation are not restricted to a similar upbringing at a certain societal and cultural time, but might also be coined by sudden and drastic marking events, e.g., wars. The terrorist attacks of September 11, 2001 might be such an incisive experience formative of the sentiments of a generation (of authors). Indeed, the author Dara Horn points out that "there emerged a heightened sense of Jewish identity because of 9/11," in an article on the new way of writing about Jewish life in the U.S.[22] Other factors might be the abundance of travel opportunities, e.g., reflected in the increasing popularity of birth right programs that have sent thousands of young American Jews to travel to Israel to let them learn more about their culture. It might be that the combination of all these stimuli in the noughties has created a new approach to define Jewish life in America. While this hypothesis might be speculative until some further historical distance will allow for retrospective verification, it remains an accepted thesis in social science that certain events or experiences leave an imprint on a group of people,

---

Künemund, Harald and Marc Szydlik Eds. *Generationen. Multidisziplinäre Perspektiven.* Wiesbaden: VS Verlag für Sozialwissenschaften, 2009. 10.

22 Sax, David. "Rise of the New Yiddishists." *Vanity Fair,* April 2009. 16 June 2015.

resulting in common attitudes, habits, and life styles that form a 'new' generation that is distinguishable from previous ones.

In his seminal essay, Mannheim also states that within the context of one generation various subunits can coexist.[23] Especially against the background of my thesis, this is an important note, since I would like to show that different approaches to Jewish life coexist in America within one generation of Jewish-American writing. To illustrate his argument, Mannheim refers to the coexistence of two youth movements in the 1800s, namely the romantic-conservative vs. the liberal-rationalistic youth.[24] Accordingly, Mannheim's theory can be adapted to my definition of different sub-groups within the contemporary generation of Jewish-American writing. Thinking about Shalom Auslander[25] and his brutally honest depiction of the experiences of a child and young adult in an orthodox community, and comparing these accounts with Dara Horn's[26] almost mystical stories about families and their heritage, it is obvious that they write from different angles. However, I would argue that they still share a generational unity. More precisely, it is important to elaborate on what Karl Mannheim meant when talking about subunits of a generation. For specification, he introduced the three terms *Generationslagerung* (generational layers), *Generationszusammenhang* (generational connection) and *Generationseinheit* (generational unit). The term *Generationslagerung* (generational layers) simply refers to a cohort of people who are born more or less at the same time and in the "same historical-social space."[27] Belonging to this generational layer constitutes the basic condition under which a generation can develop. It then requires a generational connection (*Generationszusammenhang*), namely the experience of a shared fate.[28] Within such a generation (formed by layer and connection), separate units (*Generationseinheiten*) can exist and the members of each unit are closely

---

23 Mannheim, Karl. *Wissenssoziologie. Auswahl aus dem Werk.* Ed. Wolff, Kurt H. Berlin: Luchterhand Verlag, 1964. 547.
24 Ibid. 543.
25 See more about Shalom Auslander's *Foreskin's Lament* in chapter 4.1.
26 See more about Dara Horn's *The World to Come* in chapter 3.2.
27 Mannheim, Karl. *Wissenssoziologie. Auswahl aus dem Werk.* Ed. Wolff, Kurt H. Berlin: Luchterhand Verlag, 1964. 542.
28 Ibid. 542.

connected, because they share the same way of dealing with their respective *zeitgeist*.[29] This means that a generational connection is created by a shared fate, which may then result in different generational units. These units within a generation are sub-strata of how the common fate is dealt with. The units may be oppositional, but still share a common prevailing mood.[30] My own definition of a current generation of Jewish-American writing, finally, is based on this sociological definition of the term 'generation' as coined by Karl Mannheim. In simple terms my argument is that the current generation is *layered* by their common upbringing during the late 20th century. They are *connected* by their heightened sense of curiosity towards their Jewish heritage. And finally, under this common roof of a generation of writing, separate *units* can be found, namely diverging approaches of how to deal with this common curiosity.

1.2 FAMILY AND INTERTEXT

In comparison to the social definition of a generation, the genealogical definition of the term generation seems to be obvious. Here we talk about the classic break down of family members: grandchildren, children, parents, and grandparents as the generational sequence of family members. The affiliation with one generation stays constant and clear for each family member.[31] However, it must be added that while the affiliation with one generation remains constant for the individual, the role of each generation evolves over time, parents becoming grandparents, children becoming parents, etc. Accordingly, the role of each generation changes both in terms of family and historical perspective. Moreover, children are constantly born, thus complicating the question of an overarching generation (i.e., of cousins) even within a single family. The larger the family is, the more complicated it becomes to define one such generation. Therefore, Marc

---

29 Ibid. 542.
30 See: Mannheim, Karl. "Das Problem der Generationen." *100(0) Schlüsseldokumente der deutschen Geschichte im 20. Jahrhunderts*. Bayerische Staatsbibliothek. 15 June 2015. 313.
31 See: Künemund, Harald and Marc Szydlik. Eds. *Generationen. Multidisziplinäre Perspektiven*. Wiesbaden: VS Verlag für Sozialwissenschaften, 2009. 9.

Szydlik and Harald Künemund point out in *Generationen. Multidisziplinäre Perspektiven* that it is rather difficult to define a generation only based on the affiliation to a certain family line.[32] This problem of fuzziness with the genealogical definition of a generation makes it a rather inaccurate method. Nevertheless, the genealogical definition of a generation is commonly used in day to day life but also in the field of family sociology, since it is the simplest way of categorizing different groups of people. Because of an increased life expectancy, diverse and modern ways of living, complex and open family situations, etc., one could argue that the entire concept of 'family' is now in flux, and along with it tumbles the whole genealogical construct of a generation. It is often less clear even within a single family who belongs to which generation. To give a simple example: Uncles/aunts and nephews can be of the same age, thus complicating the question to which family generation they belong. However, the genealogical approach to generations is still often used in the pedagogical and psychoanalytic area. Ulrike Jureit argues in *Generationenforschung* that the family remains a point of origin and also a reference point, from which everything else evolves, like the passing of social skills or educational background.[33] Jureit also points out that the term family can be seen as a cornerstone of a person's identity.[34] Family is a fundamental part in one's biography. This psychoanalysis of family background and identity also exists in connection to authors and literature. Such constellations are often revealed in reviews and critical reception: In his book *Philip Roth & Söhne*, Manuel Gogos writes about the fact that contemporary Jewish-American authors such as Binnie Kirshenbaum are often connected to intellectual relatives like Philip Roth or Saul Bellow.[35] It is not surprising that similarly, Shalom Auslander's memoir *Forskin's Lament* is often regarded as the

---

32 Ibid. 9.
33 See: Jureit, Ulrike. *Generationenforschung*. Göttingen: Vandenhoeck & Ruprecht, 2006. 10.
34 Ibid. 11.
35 See: Gogos, Manuel. *Philip Roth & Söhne. Zum jüdischen Familienroman.* Hamburg: Philo, 2005. 27-28. In an article from a German Jewish newspaper Jüdische Allgemeine Wochenzeitung, the author was connected to Saul Bellow being her "intellectual grandfather," Philip Roth and Erika de Jong being her "intellectual parents."

contemporary and up-to-date version of Philip Roth's classic novel *Portnoy's Complaint* from 1969. By looking at the titles of these two texts, a connection is clearly visible. There are several more examples for Jewish-American writers to be presented as a large family, such as in Mark Schechner's approach:

[D]er zeyde (Saul Bellow), die bubbe (Cynthia Ozick), the prosperous, erratic, high-achieving sons and daughters, from Philip Roth, the eldest, down to the brat of the month [...].[36]

Genealogical categories, in other words, create an order in terms of a literary legacy. Accordingly, texts should not be regarded as completely separated pieces of art, but each text can also be seen as an altered version or a sequel of one or more former texts, the pieces of work that seem to be its 'parental- or grandparental' generation. This means that a text, regardless of how unique and new it may appear, always originates from a genealogical series of previous texts. Hereby the 'new' text always, whether explicitly or not, carries some essence of the prior text within itself.[37]

This notion of a 'genealogy of texts' which I have just tried to evoke is more commonly known as the concept of intertextuality. The concept of intertextuality, in short, describes the fact that all literary texts are based on prior texts. This includes immediate quotes, direct or indirect references, as well as invocations of styles, which are used consciously or unconsciously by the author. One could even argue that intertextuality is completely independent of the author – who might not even know that a certain other text reverberates in his own work, but depends only on the reader's perception and recognition. Yet it would be more radical to assume that there is an intertextuality utterly independent of both the author's and the reader's knowledge of any textual predecessors, an intertextuality in the

---

36 Schechner, Mark. "Is This Picasso, or Is It the Jews? A Family Portrait at the End of History." *Tikkun Magazine*, 1 Nov. 1997.

37 See also: Müller Nielaba, Daniel. "Die alten grossen Meister. Generationsfolge als literarische Ursprungserzählung." *Generationen. Multidisziplinäre Perspektiven*. Eds. Künemund, Harald and Marc Szydlik, eds. Wiesbaden: VS Verlag für Sozialwissenschaften, 2009. 145.

sense of a general reverberation of thought. Even the mere genre classification of a text – be it a novel, an autobiography or a short story, already implies its vicinity to other texts. In *Intertextualität. Formen, Strukturen, anglistische Fallstudien*, Ulrich Broich and Manfred Pfister point out that "each text is a reaction to prior texts, while again those are reactions to others, etc. [...]."[38] This general assumption of a relatedness of texts goes back to antiquity and has been revived by theories of originality and creativity in the 18th century.[39] The actual term 'intertextuality' which was coined by Julia Kristeva in 1967 is still a valid approach for literary text analysis. Intertextuality describes the relation between one text and others, and the three elements of literary studies – text, audience and author – are being debated in the field of intertextuality.[40] In 2002 Julia Kristeva stated:

> My concept of intertextuality thus goes back to Bakhtin's dialogism and Barthes' text theory. At that time, I contributed by replacing Bakhtin's idea of several voices inside an utterance with the notion of several texts within a text.[41]

Like films tend to borrow images, quotes or simply themes from other films, also literary texts use different motifs and themes from other texts, sometimes unintentionally, but often well aware of this method. Let me give an example: A possibly intentional use of reference to an older text can be found in Steve Stern's *The Frozen Rabbi* from 2010. Already on the first page of the book, we participate in the young protagonist's attempt to have sexual 'intercourse' with a piece of meat because he has read about this in a "scandalous novel"[42] from the sixties, which he stole from his parents. We certainly know what he is talking about – Philip Roth's classic

---

38 Broich, Ulrich and Manfred Pfister. Eds. *Intertextualität. Formen, Funktionen, anglistische Fallstudien*. Tübingen: Max Niemeyer Verlag, 1985. 11-12.
39 See: Berndt, Frauke and Lily Tonger-Erk. *Intertextualität. Eine Einführung.* Berlin: Erich Schmidt Verlag, 2013. 7.
40 See: Ibid. 9.
41 Kristeva, Julia. "'Nous deux' or a (Hi)story of Intertextuality." *Romanic Review* 93.1-2. (2002): 8.
42 Stern, Steve. *The Frozen Rabbi*. Chapell Hill: Algonquin Books of Chapel Hill, 2010. 1.

novel *Portnoy's Complaint*, in which the homonymous hero gets intimate with a piece of raw liver. Another form of intertextuality can be seen in the aforementioned title *Foreskin's Lament* by Shalom Auslander which is clearly a reference again to Roth's omnipresent *Portnoy's Complaint*.

These examples hint at a possibly conscious reference to a previous text, with Roth's *Portnoy's Complaint* figuring as an arch-text of Jewish-American literature. But it is important to stress that Julia Kristeva's original thesis is based on the assumption of prior texts also being interwoven into new texts unconsciously:

> Each text is build up by mosaics of quotes, each text is an absorption and transformation of another text. Instead of the term intersubjectivity, the term intertextuality steps in and the poetic language can be read as at least double.[43]

This means that no text ever stands alone, it is always at least *double* in the sense that other texts inescapably remain constituting parts of its context, no matter whether the author consciously refers to these texts or not. Even if not on purpose, older texts are always and immanently absorbed in the creation of a new text, and there exists a continuum of texts, each being both a recreation and transformation of all previous. From this point of view, a literary text cannot be seen as an autonomous piece of art but as a crossing point of intertextual and intellectual impacts. Similarly Roland Barthes, for whom each text is a "chambre d'échos,"[44] wrote about intertextuality in his renowned essay "The Death of the Author:" "The text is a netting of quotes from various cultural sources" and "[...] is composed by multifaceted writings, which originate from different cultures which enter a dialogue, mimic and question each other."[45] Barthes, accordingly, stresses the concepts of dialogism and mimicry as basic principles of intertextuality. This kind of mimicry that results in a dialogue between a text and its predecessors could well be observed in the afore-mentioned

---

43 Kristeva, Julia. "Bachtin, das Wort, der Dialog und der Roman." *Literaturwissenschaft und Linguistik. Ergebnisse und Perspektiven*. Ed. Ihwe, Jens. Frankfurt am Main: Athenäum Verlag, 1972. 348. Translation by myself.
44 Barthes, Roland. *Über mich selbst*. München: Matthes und Seitz, 1978. 81.
45 Barthes, Roland. "Der Tod des Autors." *Texte zur Theorie der Autorschaft*. Eds. Jannidis, Fotis et al. Stuttgart: Reclam, 2000. 190-192. Translation by myself.

examples of Shalom Auslander and Steve Stern, whose texts respond to Roth's previous text through mimicry.

So far I have depicted the concept of intertextuality as a neutral phenomenon or even a positive and appreciable aspect of all literature. But from an author's perspective the entire concept can also be perceived as a looming threat. Will my text be an original or a cheap copy of something else? Every author knows that the reception of their text always comes in package with comparing the latest piece to a prior body of texts. Naturally, no author wants his/her work to appear inferior to its predecessors. Probably to show off one's knowledge of world literature, literary allusions and bows to former texts are very common, but as said, there remains the additional fact that texts can be connected to other texts, even if this connection is not intended by the author. However, deliberate references to former texts – to classics, written by intellectual 'fathers' and 'mothers' – are not employed to make the new text look small or less original, but rather to put the new text in line with great previous literature which is obviously the ultimate accolade for an author. As long as they avoid immediate and complete plagiarism, but rather create witty homages and references to prior texts, younger authors do not have to worry about their reputation. Rather, this is about creating a sense of tradition as Frauke Berndt and Lily Tonger-Erk describe in *Intertextualität*.[46]

The American literary critic Harold Bloom presented his own theory as an answer to the concept of intertextuality in 1973. His work *The Anxiety of Influence. A Theory of Poetry* states that authors always fear the influence of prior authors and try to escape from this influence. All poets, driven by their pursuit for originality, try to free themselves from prior poets or literary idols. Bloom compares this pursuit with the classical oedipal complex in which the son tries to 'kill' his intellectual father:

Poetic Influence – when it involves two strong, authentic poets, – always proceeds by a misreading of the prior poet, an act of creative correction that is actually and necessarily a misinterpretation.[47]

---

46 See: Berndt, Frauke and Lily Tonger-Erk. *Intertextualität. Eine Einführung.* Berlin: Erich Schmidt Verlag, 2013. 64.
47 Bloom, Harold. *The Anxiety of Influence. A Theory of Poetry.* New York: Oxford University Press, 1975. 30.

By introducing a psychoanalysis of intertextuality, Bloom basically states that it is fear that drives young writers and thereby the whole history of literature.[48] According to Bloom, the quality of a text can be measured by the energy which is used to replace or push aside prior texts:

Poetic history, in this book's argument, is held to be indistinguishable from poetic influence, since strong poets make that history by misreading one another, so as to clear imaginative space for themselves.[49]

To provide an example of what Bloom might be referring to, I would return once more to Steve Stern's *The Frozen Rabbi* in which – as stated above – the allusion to *Portnoy's Complaint* is made by an initially equally pubescent boy copulating with a piece of raw meat. However, unlike Roth's Alexander Portnoy, Stern's protagonist Bernie Karp does not continue his struggle into adolescence along the trajectories of assimilation and sexual desire, but soon his focus is radically transformed to religious curiosity about orthodox Judaism and Jewish mysticism. This could be the kind of deliberate misreading then – transforming the classic story of desire and assimilation into a story of religious return – that Bloom has in mind. A new text can certainly acknowledge its predecessors, however it has to deviate significantly, has to break somehow with the former, in order to stand on its own.

Ultimately, Bloom comes to the same conclusion as Kristeva and Barth, "that there are no texts, but only relationships between texts."[50] However, he seems to conclude on a somewhat less enthusiastic note than Kristeva and Barthes and places the authors' fear, their anxiety of influence, and their creative struggle to overcome their predecessors by misinterpreted transformation at the center of this relativism. While Bloom is talking about the single poet here, I would argue that the same concept of 'overcoming the predecessors' applies to collectives as well. This should bring us back

---

48 See: Berndt, Frauke and Lily Tonger-Erk. *Intertextualität. Eine Einführung*. Berlin: Erich Schmidt Verlag, 2013. 70.
49 Bloom, Harold. *The Anxiety of Influence. A Theory of Poetry*. New York: Oxford University Press, 1975. 5.
50 Bloom, Harold. *A Map of Misreading*. New York: Oxford University Press, 1975. 3.

once more then to the concept of a generation. While we have come to understand how a generation is defined in sociological terms, I can now make an attempt at introducing a cultural definition. Fittingly, Heinz Bude argues that "generations are determined by differences from other generations."[51] Consequently, a new generation of authors would not only share some common literary interests, motifs, etc. but also commonly break with a previous idiom. Bloom's psychoanalysis of Kristeva's and Barthes' rather neutral and relativistic concept of intertextuality shows us that indeed we could call the group of young Jewish authors whom I will be dealing with in this thesis a new generation *because* they so obviously transform and change the hitherto prevailing canon of Jewish-American literature.

In this subchapter I have tried to show how current Jewish-American authors are often regarded as intellectual children and grandchildren of a previous group of authors. I have thereby tried to link the term 'generation' with poststructuralist theories of intertextuality as well as with Bloom's psychoanalytic modification of these theories. While some literary allusions, e.g., to Roth's *Portnoy's Complaint* in recent works of literature seem to be deliberate, others are rather indirect in the sense of a general intellectual continuum of inescapable intertextuality. In Bloom's psychoanalytic terms, a new generation of authors has to break with its predecessors and aggressively transform the previous literary material in order to create something genuinely new. Both the concept of intertextuality and Bloom's psychoanalytic transformation seem to fit with my overall argument, that there exists a distinguishable new generation of Jewish-American authors, trying to do things in a different manner than previous generations. In order to foster this argument that the current group of Jewish-American authors can be called a generation because they collectively break with the idiom of a preceding generation, a concise description of the previous canon of Jewish-American literature, and especially a definition of the two previous generations will be provided in chapter 2.2.

---

51 Bude, Heinz. "Qualitative Generationenforschung." *Qualitative Forschung. Ein Handbuch.* Eds. Flick, Uwe et al. Reinbek bei Hamburg: Rowohlt Verlag, 2010. 190.

1.3 Various Sounds – Who is Writing Anyway?

By defining a generation of literature in terms of intertextuality, I have touched upon another question, namely the question of authorship. In this subchapter I would therefore like to raise the question of whether it is of any importance or interest at all who exactly is writing. Especially with regard to intertextuality, we have come close to a kind of nihilism with regard to the author. If every single text embodies an entire intellectual continuum of other texts, the actual author of a given text is reduced to – in Bloom's words – a mere transformer of previous literary material.

However, I want to weaken the role of the single author even more, namely in the framework of my overall argument, that we are dealing with the collective sound of a new generation of Jewish-American writing in which single voices are subsumed. Before diving deeper into the question about the role of the single author with regard to such concepts as autobiography and autofiction, I would like to dwell on the term 'sound' as opposed to the term 'voice' for a moment.

While the term voice is too strongly tied to the individual, the term sound is more fitting to my argument. We are dealing with a new generation of Jewish-American writing which is 'sounding' different than the previous idiom. The 'voices' of single texts may be quite different from one another, even disagreeing, yet, in some way they all contribute to an overall new sound. Also with regard to Mannheim's theory of generational units, the term sound seems to be a useful and suitable expression. As Mannheim argues, a generation can be built of different units that are taking different approaches and yet belong to the same generational connection. The term sound similarly suggests that within one generation there can be different kinds of single voices which are ultimately contributing to the same harmonious collective sound. I am thus borrowing from musicological terminology: A musical chord is built of single tones – each coming with their own timbre[52] – that are combined to form a harmony of collective sounds. 'Timbre' is what makes particular tones different from another, even when they have the same pitch and loudness. Much can be said about the single tone, the single voice and its distinctive timbre. However, after joining a chord, the single tone acquires new

---

52 In German "Klangfarbe."

meaning. In retrospect it must be interpreted as part of a harmony. I am thus trying to look at single texts with less regard to the interpretation of their single voice and rather try to present them as part of a bigger picture, namely in the larger frame of what I perceive as a new sound of curiosity in Jewish-American writing.

My argument is that an entire new generation of authors is expressing itself in current Jewish-American writing – as I will show in my selected texts. Ostensibly, one could raise the question then, how single works of literature can be representative of a new generation of authors and how these authors are connected to their texts. Some of the texts that I will analyze in the following chapters claim to be autobiographic while others are fictional. One might assume that autobiographies are better suited to support my overall argument that we are dealing with the sentiments of a new generation of writers. In the case of an autobiography the text can easily be tied to an author and thus to their generation. Eventually I will come to the conclusion, however, that the exact narrative constellation does not matter at all for my overall argument. It does not matter whether the texts of my choice are branded as autobiographies – thereby seemingly obtaining some authentic credibility about representing a generation's thinking, or whether we are dealing with fiction, because after all it is the content of what is being told that distinguishes the topics of earlier generations. Nevertheless, I would like to provide a theoretical framework in this sub-chapter in order to argue that there is a flowing transition between autobiography and fiction thus rendering all differentiation between these concepts arbitrary and redundant.

When speaking about autobiographies or what we might define as such, we must keep in mind a certain agreement between the readers and the composer of a narrative which Philippe Lejeune has called the 'autobiographical pact.' It states that the composer of the text vouches for its truthfulness. Even though the account might not be exact, the author pledges for the effort. According to Lejeune, an autobiography is a "retrospective narrative of an actual person about their own existence, if they put emphasis on their personal life and especially on the history of their personality."[53] Lejeune specifies his definition with several rules, e.g.,

---

53 Lejeune, Philippe. *Der autobiographische Pakt.* Frankfurt am Main: Suhrkamp Verlag, 1994. 14. Translation by myself.

that an autobiography has to be written in prose. Author, narrator and protagonist have to be identical. Furthermore, the narrative has to be retrospective and must deal with an individual life account.[54] According to Oliver Still, autobiographies can be two different things, either a historical document or a classical literary piece of art.[55] According to this concept, historical reality and the subjective perspective of the author/narrator seem to be two separate and oppositional kinds of contents. Similarly, yet less oppositional, Martina Wagner-Egelhaaf defines the autobiography as a traveler between two worlds, namely history and literature.[56] She also states that due to the relatedness of the autobiography with (fictional) first-person narratives, it is to some extent impossible to distinguish between these two spheres. One could thus conclude that the question of whether biographical truth or fiction is speaking to us in literature is neither clearly answered by a text's label (novel, memoir, autobiography) nor is it of any relevance if the question cannot finally be answered.

There are numerous fictional novels disguising as autobiographies and vice versa. Therefore, I would not read Shalom Auslander's *Foreskin's Lament*, which is subtitled "A Memoir," strictly as an autobiographic encounter. Instead I would like to use a term which was introduced in the 1970s by the French critic and author Serge Doubrovsky: autofiction.[57] The

---

54 See: Wagner-Egelhaaf, Martina. *Autobiographie*. Stuttgart: Metzler Verlag, 2005. 6. See also: Lejeune, Philippe. Der autobiographische Pakt. Frankfurt am Main: Suhrkamp Verlag, 1994. 14-19.

55 See: Still, Oliver. *Zerbrochene Spiegel: Studien zur Theorie und Praxis modernen autobiographischen Erzählens*. Berlin: Walter de Gruyter, 1991. 27.

56 See: Wagner-Egelhaaf, Martina. *Autobiographie*. Stuttgart: Metzler Verlag, 2005. 1.

57 See: Gasser, Peter. "Autobiographie und Autofiktion. Einige begriffskritische Bemerkungen." *"...all diese fingierten, notieren, im meinem Kopf ungefähr wieder zusammengesetzten Ichs." Autobiographie und Autofiktion*. Eds. Pellin, Elio, and Ulrich Weber. Göttingen: Wallstein Verlag, 2012. 13-27. 25. Gasser points out: "All writing is more or less autobiographical (which in addition to John M. Coetzee, also Philip Roth and many others would agree with) and all writing, also if obligated to facts, contains traces of fiction." Translated by myself. Alles Schreiben ist, in mehr oder weniger hohem Grade, autobiographisch (was heute neben John M. Coetzee auch Philip Roth und viele andere

term autofiction refers to fictionalized autobiographies and thus combines two seemingly antithetic literary modes – fiction and autobiography. This approach stands in utter contrast to Philippe Lejeune's autobiographical pact, which promises factual accuracy as best as the author can guarantee. In autofiction, even though the real life of the author seems to be presented to the audience, it is never clear with final certainty whether all of the provided information is truthful. Accordingly, novels which describe situations or settings that might be familiar to the author's own life, do not have to be autobiographical, but they can be autofictional. For example, Jonathan Safran Foer's *Everything is Illuminated* seems to contain some truth about the author who has lent his own name to the protagonist. Yet the book is labeled a novel. Vice versa, such a seemingly accurate account as Auslander's 'memoirs' can naturally contain fiction, even be completely fictional. The approach of autofiction will therefore be helpful when looking at several of the narratives discussed in this thesis. I consider not only Shalom Auslander's 'memoirs' and Foer's 'novel,' but also Gideon Lewis-Kraus' *A Sense of Direction* as autofiction, because after all, there is no definite method of differentiating between autobiography and fiction. The best example for autofiction within my thesis might be Gary Shteyngart's *The Russian Debutante's Handbook*, in which the author unquestionably resorts to his experiences as a new immigrant in New York, but when it comes to the protagonist's escapade to the fictional city of Prava, it becomes clear that Shteyngart is combining elements of his own biography with fiction.

Quintessentially, my overall argument of a new generation of Jewish-American writers works well without any distinction between fiction and autobiography. However, parts of my argument about this new generation of writers are built on biographical details concerning, for example, immigration history. The concept of 'autofiction' thus provides a useful tool for connecting author and text while obscuring the relation at the same time, thus underlining the futility of such a differentiation.

---

unterschreiben würden würden), und alles Schreiben, auch das dem Faktischem verpflichtete, enthält fiktionale Spuren.

1.4 Chapter Conclusion

In my thesis I have divided the authors and texts I am dealing with into three groups which will be discussed in the following chapters. Within these groups, the texts I am going to analyze share similar motives, themes or interests. These shared motives reflect a shared body of experiences, not only within each subgroup but also as part of a generation of writers at large – the third generation of Jewish-American writing. While each single voice might be interpreted in multiple ways and be tied closer to what could be called its thematic sub-trend, they are nevertheless all formative of the sound of a new generation, because unlike the preceding generation they share a new curiosity about Jewish heritage. I want to stress again that I will not analyze each author and each thematic sub-trend with regard to their uniqueness but, but rather as part of a generation speaking their mind. I also will not differentiate between autobiographies and fictional prose, but tend to look at all texts as prose which is at best autofictional. Therefore, I would like to agree with the core statement of Roland Barthes' essay "Death of the Author" from 1968, in which he proposed that between the written word and its author there is no deeper relation unless the reader's interpretation of a text wants to.[58] In other words, the individual identities of the respective authors are quite irrelevant for my overall argument. At first sight this might seem to be conflicting with the fact that I am analyzing a certain group of authors whom I call the 'third' generation of Jewish-American writers very much based on biographical aspects. But as I have stated before, I intend to look at their stories as the collective sound of a whole generation (or as one generation sub-stratified into more generational units in the sense of Mannheim's theory) and not so much as individual stories. Therefore, the authors are only 'almost' dead, since they do matter in terms of the bigger picture drawn by a group of people. Furthermore, Barthes states that the reader is the one giving meaning and message to the written word. This clearly states that the intention of an author might be completely different from what readers might find in the respective text afterwards. Michel Foucault elaborated on Barthes' theory, however

---

58 See: Barthes, Roland. "Der Tod des Autors." *Texte zur Theorie der Autorschaft*. Eds. Jannidis, Fotis et al. Stuttgart: Reclam, 2000. 185-193. Translation by myself.

without completely abandoning the term author.[59] In his essay "What is an author?" from 1969 he stated that texts should be read by identifying the topics and themes they are discussing, the discourse they are carrying, and not by asking what the author's purpose might have been. Foucault began his famous statement with a quote from Samuel Beckett, rudely calling out: "Who cares, who's talking".[60] This is exactly the kind of argument I want to make here. I would like to propose that individual authors and single texts should not be examined in isolation, but due to a similar discourse in all of their books, the whole generation should be seen as an 'author' who is telling us about the themes, interests and problems while coming of age and living as young Jews in contemporary America.

In order to return to the question of how to define a generation of writing, finally I would like to suggest a combined sociological and cultural definition. Mannheim's sociological theory of generations is a widely accepted approach to the day. He proposed that especially the imprinting during adolescence is crucial for the formation of a generation.[61] A generation develops if people of about the same age share similar experiences, in other words a similar imprinting. Within this one generation, there are different subunits that each have their own way of dealing with the issues of their times. So what might it be that has commonly imprinted on this group of young Jewish authors whom I am calling a generation? I have hinted at 9/11 before, but I think there is more. There is the fact that they have all spent adolescence during the eighties and nineties of the 20th century, a time when anti-Semitism was on the retreat in America,[62] being Jewish had clearly become just another hyphen, and pop-culture had long come to embrace and very naturally depict Jews as part of the mix. Also growing up in the prosperity of suburban life and a society generally characterized by tolerance and individualism are likely to

---

59 See: Foucault, Michel. "Was ist ein Autor?" *Texte zur Theorie der Autorschaft*. Eds. Jannidis, Fotis et al. Stuttgart: Reclam, 2000. 194-229. Translation by myself.
60 See: Ibid. 198. Translation by myself.
61 See: Jureit, Ulrike. *Generationenforschung*. Göttingen: Vandenhoeck & Ruprecht, 2006. 26.
62 See: Shapiro, Edward S. *A Time for Healing. American Jewry since World War II*. Baltimore: The Johns Hopkins University Press, 1992. 229.

be important in forming a common experience. But there seems to be more, and this brings me back to Hansen's theory about the cultural dynamics of immigration. I think that one determining factor of those Jewish-Americans growing up in the eighties and nineties, is the fact that in terms of immigration history, a large fraction of them, if not the majority, were third generation.

I want to propose a cultural definition of this generation that combines the universal sociological understanding of how generations come into being with the specific historical constellation. It happens that most of the young Jewish-Americans born at the time were third generation immigration-wise. Accordingly, I would argue that this predominance reflects on the writing of the entire generation, even for those writers who themselves may be second or fourth generation immigrants or even newly arrived immigrants from the former Soviet Union. Why should that be so? Because the typical trait of the third generation – according to Hansen – is curiosity, an open-minded return to the roots and a re-embracement of religion and customs. And this exact mindset, I would argue, prevails in the experiences and in the writing of most young American Jews of our time, thereby providing the larger cultural setting even for all those whose individual experiences might have been different in some ways, who might be somewhat older, younger, fourth, fifth, or first generation.

I am neither a sociologist nor a historian qualified to fully describe and generalize on the living conditions of young Jews in America, their upbringing, or in Mannheim's terms, all those factors of society and culture that have imprinted on them to form a generation. However, I can well turn the argument around and argue that these young Jewish authors must belong to a new generation *because* there is something distinct and new in their writing. As clearly as the writings of second generation authors like Philip Roth, Saul Bellow and Bernard Malamud differed from the typical first generation immigrant novels of the 1920s, so too does the contemporary Jewish literature mark a new episode. This new episode is one of predominating curiosity, of searching for roots and attempts at reaffirmation. To me it is nothing but intuitive if not necessary to assume that this new Jewish literature is the sound of a new generation. So after all it is a combination of immigration dynamics and history of Jewish-American literature with sociological theories of generations that lead me to my claim that in the novels I am looking at, we are dealing with a new generation. And this generation is qui tially a third generation in the sense of a cultural dynamic of immigr ue to the predominating tone of curiosity

2 Contemporary Jewish-American Literature

> I was born, I have lived, and I have been made over.
> MARY ANTIN, THE PROMISED LAND, XI.

Certainly Jewish-American literature did not start at the beginning of the 20th century, when the big immigration wave washed thousands of Jewish immigrants ashore in the New World. Because this context is important for my overall argument, in this chapter I would like to provide a rough overview of Jewish immigration to America and of previous Jewish-American literature.

2.1 A SHORT HISTORY OF JEWISH-AMERICAN IMMIGRATION

Generally speaking, Jewish immigration to America is known to have taken place in various waves. Hana Wirth-Nesher and Michael P. Kramer subdivide Jewish immigration into four major waves, a Spanish-Portuguese (1654-1830), a German (1830-1880), an Eastern-European (1880-1924) and a post-Holocaust immigration wave (1940-today),[1] whereupon they

---

[1] Kramer, Michael P. and Hana Wirth-Nesher. "Introduction: Jewish American literature in the making." *The Cambridge Companion to Jewish American Literature*. Eds. Kramer, Michael P. and Hana Wirth-Nesher. Cambridge: Cambridge University Press, 2003. 3.

point out that with each wave, various cultural and religious traditions, customs and languages were transferred to the New World.[2] Jewish immigrants came for different reasons and brought very diverse memories and experiences with them.[3]

1654-1830

The first Jewish settlers in America were the descendants of Sephardic Jews who had to flee the Iberian Peninsula after the Spanish expulsion in 1492. They had travelled through the waystation of a Dutch colony in Brazil and arrived in North America in what was at the time called New Amsterdam in 1654.[4] They settled there, founded Jewish communities, and began to work mostly as merchants and peddlers, to make a living. Towards the end of the 17th century, New York had the largest Jewish population in America, with about one hundred Jews living in the city. These numbers show the early importance of New York City being home for the Jewish population of America. However, they also show that in terms of total numbers, the Jewish community in America did not grow strong before the next large immigration wave.

---

2   Tobias Brinkmann offers another subdivision of the immigration waves, combining them with the history of Jews in Europe and Israel: 1492–1789: Expulsion from Spain and the rise of the Eastern European Diaspora, 1789–1914: Mass migration from Eastern Europe and "Metropolisation," 1914–1948: Expulsion, Shoah and the foundation of Israel. See: Brinkmann, Tobias. "Jewish Migration." *EGO European History Online.* Institut für Europäische Geschichte, 3 December 2010. 29 June 2015.

3   For a more detailed description about Jewish immigration and Jewish life in America, see: Feingold, Henry L. *The Jewish People in America.* Vol. I-V. Baltimore: The Johns Hopkins University Press, 1992.

4   See: Diner, Hasia R. *The Jews of the United States. 1654 to 2000.* Berkeley: University of California Press, 2004. 13. Kramer, Michael P. and Hana Wirth-Nesher. Eds. Chronology. *The Cambridge Companion to Jewish American Literature.* Cambridge: Cambridge University Press, 2003. x.

1830-1880

The next wave of immigration, called the German wave by Wirth-Nesher and Kramer, took place in the middle of the 19th century, when many European Jews emigrated, mostly from German-speaking countries. Famous companies such as Goldman Sachs or Levi-Strauss are living proof of the commercial success of many representatives of this immigration wave. Less than one century after the first Sephardic Jews had arrived in America, they were outnumbered by Ashkenazi Jewish immigrants coming from central and Eastern Europe, who were fleeing from wars and poverty.[5] Jews mostly settled on the east coast, including New York, Rhode Island[6] and the south.[7] By 1880 about 150,000 Jews had emigrated from Europe, driven by poverty and wars, raising the total Jewish population in America to 250,000.[8]

1880-1930

However, it was only then, towards the turn of the 19th century that the huge third wave of Jewish immigration to America, the Eastern-European wave, began. These new immigrants were mostly very poor and many came from the countless shtetls in Galicia, Poland and the Russian Empire. Especially the numerous anti-Semitic pogroms in the late phase of the Russian tsarist rule had led to this exodus. The established Jewish community of New York perceived these newcomers as a threat, because

---

5 See: Diner, Hasia R. *A Time for Gathering. The Second Migration. 1820-1880.* Baltimore: The Johns Hopkins University Press, 1992. 60-85. See also: Diner, Hasia, R. *A New Promised Land. A History of Jews in America.* New York: Oxford University Press, 2000. 6.

6 The Touro Synagogue, named after its cantor Isaac Touro, was built in Newport, Rhode Island in 1763, and is the oldest synagogue in America.

7 See: Diner, Hasia R. *The Jews of the United States. 1654 to 2000.* Berkeley: University of California Press, 2004. 26.

8 Diner, Hasia R. *A New Promised Land. A History of Jews in America.* New York: Oxford University Press, 2000. 38.

they regarded them as uneducated and backward.[9] While the representatives and descendants of the earlier German immigration wave had enjoyed great commercial success and found convenient accommodation in wealthy living quarters such as the Upper East Side of New York, the mostly Yiddish speaking new arrivals started to dwell mainly on New York's Lower East Side, which quickly turned into a packed and spilling Jewish ghetto of New York. As this massive immigration wave from Europe continued between 1880 and 1924, about 25 million immigrants arrived at the harbors of the New World.[10] Of course not all of these immigrants were Jewish. People from all around Europe with various religious and cultural backgrounds came to America in the hope of pursuing a better life. However, by the year of 1925, 4.5 million Jews were living in the United States, scattered around the country.[11] Significantly, by 1927 about 45 percent of American Jews were living in New York, Chicago being among the other American cities with a big Jewish population.[12] By this time, Jews made up 3.6 percent of the total American population.[13] Almost half of the Jewish population of America, in other words, had recently arrived from Galicia and found a new home in the city of New York, mainly on the Lower East Side. These numbers are meant to show how huge this third Jewish immigration wave and how homogenous – to some extent – their

---

9   See: Siebald, Manfred. "Jüdisch-amerikanische Literatur im 20. Jahrhundert zwischen *upward mobility* und *ancestral grief*." *Jüdische Literatur und Kultur in Grossbritannien und den USA nach 1945*. Vol. 3. Ed. Neumeier, Beate. Wiesbaden: Harrassowitz Verlag, 1998. 97.

10 See: Diner, Hasia R. *A New Promised Land. A History of Jews in America*. New York: Oxford University Press, 2000. 42.

11 See: Diner, Hasia R. *A New Promised Land. A History of Jews in America*. New York: Oxford University Press, 2000. 45.

12 See: Diner, Hasia. R. *The Jews of the United States. 1654 to 2000*. Berkeley: University of California Press, 2004. 105. See also: Sorin, Gerald. *A Time for Building. The Third Migration, 1880-1920*. Ed. Feingold, Henry L. *The Jewish People in America*. Baltimore: The Johns Hopkins University Press, 1992. 136-169.

13 Diner, Hasia R. *A New Promised Land. A History of Jews in America*. New York: Oxford University Press, 2000. 69.

experiences had been, which in turn is i̇... ..nt with regard to the stories these ...mmigrant sand their descendants ... ...ontinued to tell.

1930-1950

After the first decades of the 20th centurie... ...wish families, who had lived in big cities such as New York and Chica... ...decided to move westwards and settle in smaller towns or in the suburl... ... big cities, thereby causing yet another major shift in the structures ... ...e Jewish communities in America.[14] In addition, towards the 1... ... the last major Jewish immigration wave was under way, caused ...he Holocaust and Second World War. Many families, who initially ... Europe for Palestine and Israel respectively, immigrated to the Unite... ...tes eventually. By 1947, due to this last Jewish immigration wave ca... ...d by the horrors of the Holocaust, about 5 million Jews were living in America.[15]

2.2 OVERVIEW OF JEWISH-AMERICAN LITERATURE IN THE 20TH CENTURY

There are records of Jewish writers in America dating back as far as the 17th century, for example Judah Monis, who was an Italian Jew of Portuguese decent. He also happened to be the first Jewish faculty member at Harvard College.[16] Just like contemporary literature, early texts by Jewish writers from the 17th or 18th century dealt with topics and themes that were of importance to their community and to American society at the

---

14 See: Diner, Hasia R. *The Jews of the United States. 1654 to 2000.* Berkeley: University of California Press, 2004. 260.

15 See: Kramer, Michael, P. and Hana Wirth-Nesher. Eds. "Chronology." *The Cambridge Companion to Jewish American Literature.* Cambridge: Cambridge University Press, 2003. xiii.

16 See: Kramer, Michael P. "Beginnings and Ends: The Origins of Jewish American Literary History." *The Cambridge Companion to Jewish American Literature.* Eds. Kramer, Michael P. and Hana Wirth-Nesher. Cambridge: Cambridge University Press, 2003. 16.

time. However, I do not want to linger in this distant past and would rather focus on the literature which started to emerge by the end of the 19th century. I am therefore going to point out some of the most important Jewish-American authors and texts of the previous generations, in order to show the main topics Jewish-American literature has dealt with in the 20th century.

Stage I: Immigration

When speaking about the first generation of Jewish writers in North America, amongst others Abraham Cahan[17] (1860-1951), Henry Roth (1906-1995), Anzia Yezierska (1880-1970), and Mary Antin (1881-1949) come to mind. These writers, born in the Old World, were strongly influenced by Yiddish and by European literature. In their writings, they describe the life of immigrants in a new society. It is important to mention that most of their stories reflected many of their own personal experiences as immigrants, as Steven J. Rubin points out:

Autobiography, [...] offered a means of defining an uncertain identity within a new and often alien culture. More important, it provided a vehicle for linking personal history with that of the group – with an entire social process. In recreating the inherent truths of their lives, writers such as Antin and Yezierska recreated the collective truths of their people.[18]

Rubin stresses that these authors chose to speak of their own experiences, because their lives were under transformation, and thereby created a truth that spoke for their entire group and generation. Even though English was not their first language, most of these authors decided to publish in English,

---

17 Cahan first published his work in Yiddish and later changed to English. Other writers – such as Isaac Bashevis Singer (1904-1991) – kept writing in Yiddish. In this short overview, I am focusing on works written in English.

18 Rubin, Steven J. "American-Jewish Autobiography, 1912 to the Present." *Handbook of American-Jewish Literature. An Analytical Guide to Topics, Themes, and Sources.* Ed. Fried, Lewis. New York: Greenwood Press, 1988. 287.

in order to reach a wider audience. However, Ruth R. Wisse perceives certain differences in their writing with regard to language:

Whereas Antin "made herself over" [...] and Cahan accommodated the English reader by treating Yiddish as a foreign language, Yezierska brought the immigrant streets to life by imitating their cacophony and fractured English."[19]

Accordingly, these three authors all used the English language, however choosing different approaches in how to do this. By including aspects of Yiddish to different extents, they either reached out to the foreign readership or rather catered to their own group to different degrees. Similarly, Sanford Sternlicht argues in his article about the Jewish immigrants in New York that each author had his/her own priority to whom he/she was rather preferring to speak:

By choosing to write in English, they signaled that they were reaching out to the greater American public too. Indeed, writing in English contributed to their personal Americanization. They took pride in their mastery of a language with an enormous number of readers. [...] they were writing for their ethnic compatriots and the English-speaking community at the same time. Which audience was prioritized? That was an individual matter for each of the first Jewish American writers.[20]

As Daniel Walden, the founder of the journal *Studies in American Jewish Literature*, points out, it was difficult for new immigrants and their descendants to find their place in the new society. Not only were the mostly poor and uneducated Eastern European Jews treated condescendingly by their gentile environment, but also by their peers, by German Jewish immigrants who had come to America one or two generations earlier and who could already show some respectable economic success compared to

---

19 Wisse, Ruth R. "The Immigrant Phase. American Jewish Fiction from 1900 to 1950." *The Modern Jewish Canon. A Journey Through Language and Culture.* New York: The Free Press, 2000. 272-273.
20 Sternlicht Sanford. "Lower East Side Literature." *Jews and American Pop Culture. Vol. 2. Music, Theater, Popular Art, and Literature.* Ed. Buhle, Paul. Westport: Praeger Publishers, 2007. 213.

their recently arrived Jewish brethren from the Pale of Settlement.[21] Antin's autobiography *The Promised Land* (1912) and Abraham Cahan's novel *The Rise of David Levinsky* (1917) describe these stories about the daily struggles of immigrants in the New World, but also about the Old World and the everyday life of the *shtetl*.[22]

Although published twenty years later, Henry Roth's *Call it Sleep* (1934) might be the most popular of these early accounts of the life as an immigrant in New York. It tells the story of a young boy called David Schearl and his family, who emigrated from Galicia. The novel deals with topics such as poverty in the tenements of the Lower East Side of New York, but also with the general experiences of a young boy growing up with his caring mother and short-tempered father in this inhospitable environment. What is interesting about this literature, according to Sara Horowitz, is the fact that

[…] the fiction of Jewish immigrants and their progeny wrote its way into American and Canadian culture through narratives that captured the process of acculturation by distancing itself from Jewish traditional practices, construed mockingly or nostalgically as relics of a European life left behind.[23]

---

21 See: Walden, Daniel. Ed. *On Being Jewish. American Jewish Writers from Cahan to Bellow*. Greenwich: Fawcett Publications, INC., 1974. 13. See also: Sternlicht, Sanford. *The Tenement Saga. The Lower East Side and Early Jewish American Writers*. Madison: University of Wisconsin Press, 2004. 6-7.

22 In Mary Antin's case, the female point of view is important to her stories. Among other things, she writes about the fact that women and girls were not meant to study the Holy Scripture like men and boys, and only had basic knowledge about the Hebrew language and literature. However, her father had realized how important it is for a woman to be educated and let his daughter learn as much as her brother. See: Antin, Mary. *The Promised Land*. Boston: The Riverside Press Cambridge, 1912. 111-112.

23 Horowitz, Sara R. "Mediating Judaism: Mind, Body, Spirit, and Contemporary North American Jewish Fiction." *AJS Review*, 30 (2006): 231-253. 231. Print. See also: Sternlicht, Sanford. "Lower East Side Literature." *Jews and American Pop Culture. Vol. 2. Music, Theater, Popular Art, and Literature*. Ed. Buhle, Paul. Westport: Praeger Publishers, 2007. 214.

This fact is reflected in Henry Roth's *Call It Sleep*, when a family friend asks the Schearls about the religious customs, and both father and mother amusingly dismiss the question. Significantly, most of these early immigrant novels are stories of success. At the end of a long struggle from the poverty of the *shtetl* and through the poverty of the Lower East Side, comes a commercial breakthrough that leads the way to a better life. This is the typical story, not only in these novels but also of what really happened to most of the immigrant families. However, as Horowitz has pointed out, and as can be seen in the example of the Schearl family in Henry Roth's *Call It Sleep*, these early stories of success came as the result and at the price of abandoning the traditional Jewish practices that had hitherto remained intact for many generations.

Stage II: Americanization

A second spotlight should be put on authors such as Art Spiegelman, Lev Raphael or Philip Roth,[24] the latter humorously called by Lillian Kremer the mentor of the "Roth school of social satire with its cast of stereotypical suburban Jews composed of domineering mothers, ineffectual fathers, pampered daughters and whining sons."[25] As Kremer hints at, these authors of the second generation have dealt with a whole new plate of problems in their texts, such as their position as outsiders in a gentile society.[26] Thomas Friedman offers an accurate description of the motives in the writings of these authors:

---

24 These authors, surely some of the most famous authors of their generation, are just examples. Writers such as Thane Rosenbaum, Melvin Bukiet, Cynthia Ozick, Grace Paley, Jonathan Rosen, etc. are also worth mentioning in this context. However, as this dissertation is about the *third* generation of Jewish-American writers, I will keep this overview brief and focus only on the most prominent examples.

25 Kremer, Lillian S. "Post-alienation: Recent Directions in Jewish-American Literature." *Contemporary Literature* 34.3 (Autumn 1993): 589.

26 See: Dickstein, Morris. "Questions of Identity. The New World of the Immigrant Writer." *The Writer Uprooted. Contemporary Jewish Exile Literature.* Ed. Rosenfeld, Alvin H. Bloomington: Indiana University Press, 2008. 111.

Jewry and Jewish fiction (in print and on screen), well into the seventies, considered its greatest issues to be intermarriage (the lure of the *shiksa*), assimilation, and a sense of "otherness" vis-à-vis gentile neighbors. A Jew (and a Jewish novel) was expected to indicate ethnicity through a special language, featuring Yiddishms and a certain sense of humor, […] an occasional bagel breakfast, […].[27]

Especially the motif of the *shiksa*, the gentile woman, which stands for the gentile and foreign world, as the seducer of the Jewish man, is a major topic in the literature of Philip Roth and can also be found depicted in many films made by Woody Allen throughout the 1960s and 70s. American novelist Binnie Kirshenbaum, born in 1959, writes about the fact that because of Woody Allen's and Philip Roth's depiction of the *shiksa*, Jewish boys and girls were idealizing this type of woman, as a way of passing as a true American.[28] However, the struggle of this generation of writers was not only about fitting into American society, but also being part of American literature per se. As Morris Dickstein notes:

Where their predecessors had been written into the story as ethnic subtexts, they themselves demanded recognition as American writers, very much the way ordinary Jews struggled for inclusion as full-fledged Americans.[29]

The Holocaust was also a main topic in their writings, particularly for children of survivors. Lev Raphael, born 1954 in New York, explains that being Jewish meant something to be ashamed of – as I have cited before – and seemed to be constantly torn between two worlds.

---

27 Friedman, Thomas. "Back to Orthodoxy: The New Ethic and Ethnics in American Jewish Literature." *Contemporary Jewry* 10.1 (1989). 70.
28 Kirshenbaum, Binnie. "Princess." *Who We Are. On Being (and Not Being) a Jewish American Writer.* Ed. Rubin, Derek. New York: Schocken Books, 2005. 224-225.
29 Dickstein, Morris. Morris. "Questions of Identity. The New World of the Immigrant Writer." *The Writer Uprooted. Contemporary Jewish Exile Literature.* Ed. Rosenfeld, Alvin H. Bloomington: Indiana University Press, 2008. 111.

[...] but being Jewish did not seem something they [my parents] were consistently proud of. So it's no wonder that when friends or acquaintances in junior high or high school made anti-Semitic jokes or remarks, I never challenged them. Being Jewish was somehow shameful to me, and being the child of Holocaust survivors was beyond shame – it was not even a topic to think about, let alone discuss.[30]

On the one hand Raphael wants to be loyal to his parents, while on the other hand he tries to blend into the American, non-Jewish society. However, another important aspect mentioned by Raphael here seems to be the silence surrounding the topic of the Holocaust. In most cases, this trauma was too big to be discussed at the dinner table of Jewish-American families, especially in the families of survivors. Obviously, this silence and the trauma that looms behind the silence is therefore passed on to the next generation, and becomes the topic of their works of literature. Like Art Spiegelman in his graphic novel *Maus* (1991), Raphael also deals with the difficult legacy of being a child of Holocaust survivors. Victoria Aarons puts this similarly:

Although without "the cruel history of Europe," [...] those American-born characters, seemingly free from the baggage of the ghetto, nevertheless are haunted by it, haunted by a past they never really know, a past that existed only in the memory of parents and grandparents before them.[31]

However, Saul Bellow and Bernard Malamud, both born in the New World, also come to mind when thinking about literature written by the second generation of authors, even though they are slightly older. Together with Philip Roth, these two writers seem to form the core of Jewish-American

---

30 Lev, Raphael. "Writing Something Real." *Who We Are. On Being (and Not Being) a Jewish American Writer.* Ed. Rubin, Derek. New York: Schocken Books, 2005. 194.

31 Aarons, Victoria. *A Measure of Memory. Storytelling and Identity in American Jewish Fiction.* Athens: The University of Georgia Press, 1996. 13. Quote within quote: Paley, Grace. "The Immigrant Story." *Enormous Changes at the Last Minute.* New York: Farrar Straus Giroux, 1986. 171.

literature.[32] In Saul Bellow's *The Adventures of Augie March* (1953) the protagonist declares right at the beginning of the novel: "I am an American, Chicago born."[33] This sentence can be seen as the mission statement of the second generation. The fact that March is American, even born in the New World, stands above all. It becomes clear then, that for this second generation, the most important process is what can be called 'Americanization' and what is more commonly referred to as assimilation. The stories of these writers of the second generation more or less all seem to deal with the struggle of losing the immigrant-image, of becoming part of and dissolving into the mainstream American middle class.

In his article "The Jewish Writer in America," Eugene Goodheart argues that the second generation seems to complete their parents' immigration by finally becoming part of American mainstream society. I would agree with this idea, however, Goodheart also argues that in doing so, the second generation does *not* get rid of its Jewish heritage.[34] However, I would argue that to the contrary, this is not true for the second generation – who have indeed cast away much of their heritage – but instead for the third generation. This is the key difference between the second and the third generation of Jewish American writers: the complete and comfortable assimilation into American society *while* also being comfortable with – and even yearning for – their Jewish heritage. Bellow and his peers might be using Yiddish terms[35] while describing their Jewish homes in contrast to the gentile outside world. But at the same time they dread these surroundings, the world of their parents, and try to leave their homes as soon as possible.

---

32 Although Roth is eighteen years younger than Bellow and born to American-born parents, these three have often been characterized as the trinity of Jewish-American classics.

33 Bellow, Saul. *The Adventures of Augie March*. Trowbridge: Redwood Burn Limited, 1985. 7.

34 See: Goodheart, Eugene. "The Jewish Writer in America." *The Sewanee Review*. 116, 1 (2008): 93-107. 16 June 2015. 95-96.

35 Ruth R. Wisse points out that even though Saul Bellow was familiar with Yiddish and came from an Orthodox home, none of his protagonists are accustomed with this world. See: Wisse, Ruth R. "Writing Beyond Alienation. Saul Bellow, Cynthia Ozick, and Philip Roth." *The Modern Canon. A Journey through Language and Culture*. New York: The Free Press, 2000. 299.

It was Ruth R. Wisse who picked up Irving Howe's dictum about the end of Jewish-American literature in the middle of the 1970s and stated:

> The combined effect of literary saturation and a diluted Jewish culture has prompted some critics to prophesy the end of the Jewish movement in American writing. American Jewish literature, they say, derives its strength from the peculiar tension of the Jew who is native to two cultures while fully at home in neither; hence, the more fully the Jew becomes integrated into the larger culture, the less the tension and the fewer the creative energies generated by it. Jews, of course, will continue to write, but they will have lost the cutting edge of their hyphenated identity.[36]

This statement should have been the death blow for Jewish-American writers, especially for those who were not even born yet and about whom I am going to talk in this thesis. Although many Jewish-American writers have turned to non-Jewish themes in their novels since the 1970s, this by no means proves Howe's prediction on which Wisse elaborates here.[37] In 1999, Susanne Klingenstein responded to Wisse's article in some sort of sequel.[38] She tried to prove Howe and Wisse wrong by pointing to six major topics within contemporary Jewish-American literature that keep the story going and – in Wisse's terms, keep the hyphen from fading. The *shtetl* and the Holocaust are among these six themes, along with stories about Israel and about orthodox and Hasidic communities. But also two rather new fields of interest seem to be part of Klingenstein's literary sextet:

> Russian immigrants and gay Americans are new themes in Jewish fiction, whereas the victims and survivors of the Holocaust have long been one of its stables.[39]

---

36 Ruth R. Wisse, "American Jewish Writing, Act II." *Commentary* 61.6 (June 1976): 40.

37 And indeed, only a decade later, both Wisse's support of Howe's theory and the authors she had praised in her 1976 article were almost forgotten. See: Klingenstein, Susanne. "Jewish American Fiction, Act III: Eccentric Sources of Inspiration." *Studies in American Jewish Literature* 18 (1999): 83.

38 See: Klingenstein, Susanne. "Jewish American Fiction, Act III: Eccentric Sources of Inspiration." *Studies in American Jewish Literature* 18 (1999): 83-91.

39 Ibid. 84.

In the following we will see that the shtetl and the Holocaust are still major topics among authors of the third generation of Jewish-American writers, as can be found in Jonathan Safran Foer's and Dara Horn's novels. But also Hasidic communities are depicted in contemporary literature, for example in Shalom Auslander's autofictional memoirs. And unsurprisingly, we will see how immigrants from the former Soviet Union deal with the transition into a new society when looking at Ellen Litman and other authors who immigrated to North America not too long ago.

3 The Past of *Shtetl* and Family

> If we children did not remember these stories no one would.
>
> KADISH RACHEL. "THE DAVKA METHOD" 283.

As I have discussed in the first chapter, immigration was a crucial historical turning point for a young American Jewry: the departure from the old continent and the recommencement in the New World. It is significant as historical context, accordingly, that a large fraction of Jewish-American families arrived in America during the early 20th century. Of course not all young Jewish-American authors are grandsons and granddaughters of immigrants, not all share the same origin, family histories and life experiences. Nevertheless, it should be pointed out again, that at this time there exists in total numbers a huge fraction of young American Jews whose family background is to some extent similar. At the same time, I have found a chronologically and also thematically identifiable group of young Jewish writers, born roughly in the seventies and eighties of the 20th century. This group consciously turns to questions about their own heritage and about their own Jewishness in their texts.

As I have stated in the introduction, for this group of young Jewish-American writers, the topography of heritage seems to play a crucial role with regard to the question of what makes them Jewish, or in more general terms what their distinctive personal identity is. The abandoned and often lost spaces of Europe thereby become both a source for constructing the Jewishness in the family, and a site for projecting nostalgic desire. The topographies are being explored as a home to the immediate ancestors and get transformed – even if only as relics – to serve as a centerpiece of their own identity.

Accordingly, in this chapter I want to argue that for the narratives of a distinguishable group of American Jews, especially of the younger generation, who are missing any personal memories, dealing with the European past through fiction, story-telling and journeys, is an important matter. Especially the typical habitat of the *shtetl* often appears in their texts.[1] The fact that these young authors keep writing about a bygone form of life, which they have never themselves known, about a distant place, which they have never themselves been, is strongly reminiscent of the concept of 'postmemory,' as developed by Marianne Hirsch. Hirsch describes the longing for an unknown past as postmemory:

> Postmemory describes the relationship that the generation after those who witnessed cultural or collective trauma bears to the experiences of those who came before, experiences that they "remember" only by means of the stories, images, and behaviors among which they grew up. But these experiences were transmitted to them so deeply and affectively as to seem to constitute memories in their own right. [...] To grow up with such overwhelming inherited memories, to be dominated by narratives that preceded one's birth or one's consciousness, is to risk having one's own stories and experiences displaced, even evacuated, by those of the previous generation. [...] These events happened in the past, but their effects continue into the present. This is, I believe, the experience of postmemory and the process of its generation.[2]

As seen in this quote, Hirsch's concept of postmemory has been developed in a particular context, namely in order to characterize how families deal with the trauma of the Holocaust. Nevertheless, I would argue that in a broader sense the concept of postmemory can be applied in characterizing the typical literature of third generation Jewish-American writers, also if their families arrived in the US before the Shoah. They also "remember only by means of the stories, images, and behaviors among which they

---

1 See also: Windsperger, Marianne. "Narrative der Nacherinnerung. Spuren Galziens in der amerikanischen Gegenwartsliteratur." *Chilufim* 12. (2012): 97.
2 Hirsch, Marianne. "The Generation of Postmemory." *Poetics Today* 29.1 (Spring 2008): 106-107.

grew up."[3] In a similar way Jan Assmann generalizes Hirsch's theory by stating that a completely desolated human being does not possess any memory, since this is accrued only by socialization.[4] Therefore, in a sociological sense, all memory is postmemory, because no single private or collective memory can come into being strictly on its own and without any social context. Rather, all memories occur in a certain social context, and everybody who remembers does so in a certain social context, usually within the confines of the family. Similarly, Maurice Halbwachs confirms that every family has its secrets and shared memories, which are only accessible to the members of the particular family.[5] With respect to my overall argument, I would therefore conclude that within the third generation of Jewish-American authors, there seems to linger a kind of postmemory of *shtetl* life and of the European past, that may have skipped one generation's interest, but is nevertheless the expression of a particular streak of memory running within the family as social entity.

In the following we will see that especially with the help of objects such as pictures or books, the concept of postmemory comes into effect:

Such testimonial objects, lost and again found, structure plots of return: they can embody memory and thus trigger affect shared across generations. But as heavily symbolic and over-determined sites of contestation, they can also mediate the political, economic, and juridical claims of dispossession and recovery that often motivate return stories.[6]

Although such testimonial objects as Hirsch refers to are specific and unique in each family, in their entirety they seem to constitute a universal mechanism for memory. But also the motif of the *shtetl* is a good example

---

3 Ibid. 106-107.
4 See: Assmann, Jan. *Das kulturelle Gedächtnis. Schrift, Erinnerung und politische Identität in frühen Hochkulturen.* München: Verlag C.H. Beck, 2005. 35.
5 See: Halbwachs, Maurice. *Das Gedächtnis und seine sozialen Bedingungen.* Frankfurt am Main: Suhrkamp, 1985. 209.
6 Hirsch, Marianne. "Objects of Return." *The Generation of Postmemory. Writing and Visual Culture after the Holocaust.* New York: Columbia University Press, 2012. 206.

of how boundaries and differences become indistinct and how similarities emerge. As almost none of the actual former *shtetls* exist anymore, the *shtetl* becomes more of an imagined commonplace with quite universal traits. Not only in literature, but also in a great number of movies or plays, very typical depictions of the *shtetl* have been staged. In the American imagination, the *shtetl* is an archetype of former Jewish life and of one's own heritage. Also in the novels I will discuss here, a stereotypical Jewish way of life of the past is fictionally recreated, often in direct contrast and as an alternative draft to the modern urban life in the contemporary American city.

In order to address this issue of the grand identity quest of the current group of younger Jewish authors, I have already elaborated in the first chapter on the theory of immigration and generations as developed by Marcus Lee Hansen. Hansen's argument has been taken up and elaborated by the American historian Thomas J. Archdeacon:

The third generation, either because society is more tolerant or because the grandchildren of the immigrants come to recognize the high price paid in surrendering one's culture, embraces what the second thought it had to scorn.[7]

Archdeacon confirms Hansen's basic thesis, according to which only the third generation after immigration turns back to the cultural assets of their immigrant grandparents, while the second generation had turned away and consciously tried to distance itself from the event. However, Archdeacon also evokes the idea that in the course of the immigration process and the cultural dynamic thereafter, a loss has occurred. According to Archdeacon, the second generation has paid a high prize for their assimilation – the surrendering of their own cultural origin.

The third generation tries to reduce this damage by turning back to their family history. Writers of this generation therefore often become the chroniclers of events, which they have never experienced themselves. They are now trying to learn as much as possible about their ancestors who

---

7   Archdeacon, Thomas J. "Hansen's Hypothesis as a Model of Immigrant Assimilation." *American Immigrants and their Generation. Studies and Commentaries on the Hansen Thesis after Fifty Years.* Eds. Kivisto, Peter, and Dag Blanck. Urbana: University of Illinois Press, 1990. 50.

started the American branch of the family. This third generation of American Jews does not know the conflicts of identity and the difficulties of assimilation that encouraged the second generation to make a complete break. They are as American as any of their neighbors. For young American Jews, life's struggle is no longer about arriving and being accepted in society, but rather about the (re)discovery of their own Jewish identity and family[8] history. Of course the process of this new exploration can take different directions. However, it has become obvious to me that during the recovery-quest of their Jewish identity, some authors of the third generation encounter their families' former habitats in Europe. This following chapter will therefore focus on two such novels.

3.1 JONATHAN SAFRAN FOER – EVERYTHING IS ILLUMINATED

Probably one of the most popular and highest acclaimed[9] contemporary novels of a third generation Jewish-American author is Jonathan Safran Foer's *Everything is Illuminated* (2002).[10]

---

8   Interestingly, obsession with family has often been perceived as a typically Jewish trait, and family has often been described as more important for Jews than, e.g., for WASPs (see: Cohen, Steven M. and Arnold M. Eisen. "All in the Family." *The Jew within. Self, Family, and Community in America.* Bloomington: Indiana University Press, 2000. 43-44). Accordingly, Irving Howe has stated in 1977 that "in American Jewish fiction, the family becomes an overwhelming, indeed, obsessive presence: it is container of narrative, theater of character, agent of significance." Obviously this has not changed. (Howe, Irving. Introduction. *Jewish-American Stories.* New York: A Mentor Book, 1977. 8).

9   By both critics and fellow authors. It was awarded with the National Jewish Book Award, the Guardian First Book Award and the PEN/Robert W. Bingham Prize.

10 Since the novel has been discussed extensively in past years, I will restrict my analysis of the novel to those aspects relevant for my argument and deliberately leave out other motives and themes of this rich novel which are not essential for the sake of my thesis.

In this novel, a young Jewish-American man from New York, sharing the name of the author, Jonathan Safran Foer, travels to the Ukraine, because it bothers him that he does not know anything about his family history.[11] He hires a tour guide, called Alexander 'Alex' Perchov, who is of the same age (mid-twenties) and has specialized in offering heritage tours to foreign visitors. Along with them travels Alex Perchov's grandfather, who is supposed to help them find the former *shtetl* Trachimbrod and also a woman called Augustine, who apparently saved Jonathan's grandfather from the Nazis. Such 'heritage tours' as offered by Alex Perchov here, are clearly not purely fictional but quite close to real travel trends.[12]

The protagonist Jonathan Safran Foer poses as one of the two types of travel writers, as characterized by Heather Henderson in her essay *The Travel Writer and the Text: "My Giant Goes with Me Wherever I Go"* as he tries to fill in the blanks, the "white spaces" of his families' past by travelling.[13] Also Marianne Hirsch points to this specific kind of narrative that is based on a return to Europe:

[…] the narrative of return, in which a Holocaust survivor, accompanied by an adult child, returns to his or her former home in Eastern Europe, or in which children of

---

11 In fact, the author Jonathan Safran Foer himself has traveled to the Ukraine to find out more about the woman who had saved his grandfather during the Holocaust. "An idiotic trip, he says. He had done no research; he found no one." See: Wadler, Joyce. "Seeking Grandfather's Savior, and Life's Purpose." *The New York Times*, April 24, 2002.

12 In 2003, The New York Times wrote that each year more than 100,000 Americans and Israelis travelled to Eastern Europe to visit former concentration camps or ghettos to commemorate their lost relatives and see the places of atrocities with their own eyes. See: Green, Peter S. "Jewish Museum in Poland: More Than a Memorial." *The New York Times*, January 9, 2003.

13 See: Henderson, Heather. "The Travel Writer and the Text: 'My Giant Goes with Me Wherever I Go.'" Ed. Kowalewski, Michael. *Temperamental Journeys: Essays on the Modern Literature of Travel*. Athens: The University of Georgia Press, 1992. 230.

survivors return to find their parents' former homes, to "walk where they once walked."[14]

The only difference in the case of Foer's trip to the Ukraine is that he is the grandson of survivors who is not accompanied by anybody, but has to take his trip to the past alone and hire local people for help. During his journey with Alex and his grandfather, Foer realizes that his own family history is intertwined with the history of the Perchov family. Therefore, the constellation evoked by Marianne Hirsch holds true to some extent here, not for Jonathan himself, but for the Perchovs: due to Foer's journey, Alex Perchov is inevitably dragged into the past of his own grandfather. However, the young man has to realize soon that there is nothing left of the former *shtetl* Trachimbrod. It was literally razed to the ground. Nevertheless, Foer manages to become the chronicler of Trachimbrod, to tell its story as it must or might have occurred. Therefore, the novel oscillates between the present tense and reality of 1997, when Jonathan has returned to New York and an imagined *shtetl* life of the past, which starts in 1791 and takes the reader all the way to the year 1943. By reimagining the lost *shtetl*, he creates a utopian version of his ancestor's former home. As protagonist of the Ukraine trip, Foer has already travelled back to New York, but from there he keeps reconstructing the world of Trachimbrod. This reconstruction of Trachimbrod, however, must be largely fictional, as becomes obvious to the reader quite soon, because such an abundance of details are told that could not possibly have been accessed by the traveler Foer[15] during his trip. The following quote from the novel shows this imaginative richness quite impressively:

---

14 Hirsch, Marianne. "Objects of Return." *The Generation of Postmemory. Writing and Visual Culture after the Holocaust.* New York, 2012. 205.

15 I am referring to the protagonist Foer here. However, in the case of this novel, there seem to be significant overlaps between author, narrator and protagonist. Upon his return, the protagonist of the Ukraine-trip becomes the narrator of the fictional history of Trachimbrod. At the same time, he shares the name of the author, who has himself travelled to the Ukraine and then written the novel. While at times it can be confusing about whom I am referring to then – Foer as author or Foer as protagonist – I will not continue to make a distinction at all. As I have argued in the first chapter, the content of the story is more important

THE WELL-REGARDED RABBI paid half a baker's dozen of eggs and a handful of blueberries for the following announcement to be printed in Shimon T's weekly newsletter: that an irascible magistrate in Lvov had demanded a name for the nameless shtetl, [...] A VOTE! The Well-Regarded Rabbi proclaimed. [...] The next morning a polling box was placed outside the Upright Synagogue, [...].[16]

This quote shows with how much detail the returned travel writer Foer chronicles the *shtetl* life of Trachimbrod. It is not only described here how the little village was given its name, but also the protagonists, who make the *shtetl* unique are presented *en detail* and in a very endearing way. As readers we sense that the account of this episode must to a large extent be the product of the narrator's imagination, therefore fiction. The excerpt is part of an episode in which it is described how Trachimbrod actually came to its name. It is quite allegorical that before this scene, Foer imagined the *shtetl* to be nameless, because the *shtetl* seems to be a universal and ubiquitous place not requiring any names.

Accordingly, *Everything is Illuminated* is a novel about a young Jewish man from New York who travels back to Europe in order to rediscover his family's specific place of origin. Upon his return, however, he ends up writing the story of an entire *shtetl*, which is paradoxically both unique and universal at the same time. In this constellation, Foer seems to qualify as a typical 'travel writer,' somebody to whom travelling is not enough and who thus creates a fictional history. Debbie Lisle points out that such authors might be

[...] dissatisfied at being too late to see the 'real' thing, travel writers quickly invent a previous time of cultural authenticity for their destination. In other words, they locate it even further back on the evolutionary historical queue. [...] They can

---

than the questions who exactly is telling it or to what extent it is autobiographical or fictional. I will consider Everything is Illuminated as a piece of autofiction and the history of Trachimbrod as being told by the protagonist/author/narrator-voice of Jonathan Safran Foer.

16 Foer, Jonathan Safran. *Everything is Illuminated*. New York: Houghton Mifflin Company, 2002. 50.

certainly create a temporal utopia that remains untouched by the forces of modernity and globalization.¹⁷

Clearly, Lisle understands the moods and contents of such fictions to stand in contrast to our present and modern life. Also Heather Henderson uses the term 'travel writer' and argues that "the pleasure of imagining scenes from the past on the spot where they took place is often greater than the pleasure of witnessing scenes of today."¹⁸ Again, a richly imagined past is described as a more pleasurable setting than the feeble present. And in yet stronger terms, despite talking about Rebecca Goldstein, Susanne Klingenstein makes a similar point that can equally be applied to Foer's *Everything is Illuminated*:

> The nostalgic shtetl [accentuation by Klingenstein] novels often leave their readers unsatisfied because they create fantasies about a world that is cut off from the future. [...] yet the pressure to "return" to that fertile Eastern European matrix of Jewish culture is so great in an American [matrix of Jewish culture] perceived as barren that even a writer as resourceful as Rebecca Goldstein, [...] allowed her "Jewish dreams [to take her] backward in time, into a past in which the texture of Jewishness was more richly felt."¹⁹

Klingenstein evokes an entire "fertile Eastern European matrix of Jewish culture" as a common dwelling space for a writer's imagination in contrast to a seemingly "barren" Jewish America. All three of these researchers constitute, therefore, the existence of a trend in literature rather to reinvent a past *shtetl* life in search of Jewish culture than to examine the present.

---

17 Lisle, Debbie. "Looking Back: Utopia, Nostalgia and the Myth of Historical Progress." *The Global Politics of Contemporary Travel Writing*. Cambridge: Cambridge University Press 2006. 216.

18 Henderson, Heather. "The Travel Writer and the Text: 'My Giant Goes with Me Wherever I Go.'" Ed. Kowalewski, Michael. *Temperamental Journeys: Essays on the Modern Literature of Travel*. Athens: The University of Georgia Press, 1992. 232.

19 Klingenstein, Susanne. "Jewish American Fiction, Act III: Eccentric Sources of Inspiration." *Studies in American Jewish Literature* 18 (1999): 86-87. Quote within quote: Goldstein, Rebecca. "Against Logic." Tikkun 12.6 (1997): 42.

Klingenstein also evokes the notion that these *shtetl* fantasies are not only pleasant but also unsettling for the reader, because all these stories inevitably lead to the point where they can no longer be continued. The *shtetl* is forever stuck in the past, cataclysmically discontinued, and this is also true of Trachimbrod. Nevertheless, Foer, like other travel writers, follows the impulse to imaginatively revive the *shtetl* up from its extinction, and this is done in a somewhat nostalgic and dreamlike fashion.

The novel contains an episode with the very detailed description of an accident of a horse carriage in the year 1791. While the carriage is lost to the river Brod, the townspeople find a baby among the scattered remains of the load of the carriage. This baby turns out to be Foer's ancestor, more precisely his great-great-great-great-great-grandmother, who is eventually given the name Brod herself. This fabulous and fairy-tale-like story of an ancestral child, miraculously saved from the river is not only slightly reminiscent of the story of Moses, but also exemplary for the way Foer aestheticizes the life and events of the *shtetl*. He uses fantastic and mystic elements in his tales of Trachimbrod, which stand in strong contrast not only to the urban milieu of New York – the protagonist's actual living environment but also to his disillusioning travel experiences in the present day Ukraine.

Another example is the explanation of how the *shtetl* was divided into a "Jewish Quarter" and a "Human Three-Quarter."[20] The synagogue was built right on the division line. However, this division line was constantly shifting, depending on how many people lived in the respective quarters:

[…] usually no more than a hair in this or that direction, save for that exceptional hour in 1764, immediately following the Pogrom of Beaten Chests, when the shtetl was completely secular.[21]

While this shifting line – a hair to this or that direction – is meant to be a rendition of the *shtetl's* odd and funny ways, the name "Pogrom of Beaten Chests" sounds absurd in a way that could almost be understood as belittlement of the true horrors of these pogroms. Nevertheless, we learn

---

20 Foer, Jonathan Safran. *Everything is Illuminated*. London: Hamish Hamilton, 2002. 21.
21 Ibid. 21.

that in response to the ever shifting division line, the synagogue had to be repositioned appropriately each time by lifting and moving it. Only in 1783 were wheels attached to the building, "making the shtetl's ever-changing negotiation of Jewishness and Humanness less of a schlep."[22] Obviously, this episode is an example of how life in the *shtetl* is rendered not only as funny and obscure, but as downright fantastic and unreal.

At the same time, we recognize a typical trait that seems to be common among depictions of the *shtetl*, namely a tendency to idealize, sugarcoat and glorify. Elie Wiesel has once tried to provide an explanation for why the idealized depiction of the *shtetl* seems to be so important to Jewish writers. He argues that the *shtetl*

[...] became the illustration of our kingdom, [...] Jerusalem away from Jerusalem. [...] The shtetl can be found only in song, only in memory, only in words, in words alone. That is why the teller of its tale does whatever he can to present it in its most glorious aspect.[23]

Wiesel's argument seems to be that after its downfall, the world of the *shtetl* has to some extent become the New Jerusalem of the diaspora, the lost place away from Jerusalem. Thereby he elevates the remembrance of *shtetl* life almost to a semi-religious endeavor. Indeed, also in Foer's tales of Trachimbrod, *shtetl* life is "presented in its most glorious aspects" as Wiesel has observed. In Foer's *Everything is Illuminated*, this glorification can not only be found in the above mentioned episodes but also in the following: After the accident at the river, the *shtetl* community gathers, featuring such charming characters as "the good gefiltefishminger Blitz Blitz R,"[24] one "disgraced usurer Yankel D,"[25] not to mention the "unemployed Sloucher Lumpl W,"[26] to decide what to do next, as they

---

22 Ibid. 21.

23 Wiesel, Elie. "The Holocaust as Literary Inspiration." *Dimensions of the Holocaust. Lectures at Northwestern University.* Eds. Wiesel, Elie et al. Evanston: Northwestern University Press, 1996. 8-9.

24 Foer, Jonathan Safran. *Everything is Illuminated.* London: Hamish Hamilton, 2002. 8.

25 Ibid. 8.

26 Ibid. 21.

usually do: "A month before there had been the question of whether it might send a better message to the children to plug, finally, the bagel's hole."[27]

As can be observed in these scenes, Foer's fictional account of Trachimbrod is a quite typical example for *shtetl* life to be depicted as somewhat simple, naïve, funny and harmless. Thus the *shtetl* becomes aestheticized as a Jewish pastoral. Both literature and film have contributed to the creation of this pastoral.[28] The term *shtetl* alone seems to evoke images of simple and poor but happy people dancing barefoot to fiddle music while geese and goats stomp about. Clearly, Foer's tale of Trachimbrod joins this kind of discourse to some extent.

While the imaginative reconstruction of Trachimbrod interfuses the whole novel, the second plot line keeps evolving around Jonathan's recovery trip with the Perchovs', which – as I have hinted at before – turns out to be rather disillusioning. The deeper he and his travel companions dig into their shared history, the clearer it becomes that the former *shtetl* is not recoverable. What is left, however, are the up until now repressed memories of Alex's grandfather, which keep returning throughout the novel.

During his trip, the young hero Jonathan also has to put up with various annoyances such as his companions' anti-Semitism, discomforts such as finding a vegetarian meal, and minor cultural/linguistic misunderstandings. The omnipresent anti-Semitism of the two Ukrainian men is obvious, because they refer to the protagonist as "the Jew" constantly. While dining in a restaurant the waitress also exposes her naïve prejudices: "'Oh,' she said. 'I have never seen a Jew before. Can I see his horns?'"[29]

---

27 See: Ibid. 12.

28 Probably the most famous cinematic and iconic representation of shtetl life is Norman Jewison's musical *Fiddler on the Roof* (1971) which was an adaptation of the homonymous Broadway musical (1964), which again was based on Sholem Aleichem's Tevye the Dairyman, (Yiddish: טביה דער מילכיקער/ *Tevye der milkhiker*) which was first published in 1894. Although highly acclaimed by both critics and audiences, it can also be seen as kitsch depiction of a lost world.

29 Foer, Jonathan Safran. *Everything is Illuminated*. London: Hamish Hamilton, 2002. 107.

Jonathan shows Alex an old photograph picturing his grandfather Safran who was saved from the Nazis somewhere outside of Trachimbrod, while his wife and infant child were killed. He wants to visit the town where his grandfather once lived and also hopes to find the woman who saved him. "'I want to see Trachimbrod,' the hero said. 'To see what it's like, how my grandfather grew up, where I would be now if it weren't for the war.'"[30] Alex, on the other hand, seems to be completely unaware of any Jewish culture left in the Ukraine. When Foer tells him that he would like to talk to people who might have lived in the *shtetl*, Alex responds with bafflement, revealing that he does not even know what a *shtetl* is. However, soon Alex and his grandfather begin to feel their own kind of discomfort with this journey down memory lane. When the three men stay at a hotel for the night, it is Jonathan who can sleep soundly, while the grandfather and grandson Perchov toss and turn sleeplessly, both agonizing about what the grandfather has done during the war.[31]

Eventually, the three men find an old woman who tells them the story of Foer's grandfather and of the *shtetl* Trachimbrod, of which there is nothing left except for some random items that she has kept stored in boxes in her house. Among these items there are some documents that seem to tell the *shtetl's* history and she hands these records over to Jonathan. The old woman takes them to the site where the *shtetl* Trachimbrod used to be and tells them what had happened; how the Nazis made them all line up in the middle of the village, how they burnt the synagogue, unrolled the Torah, and made everyone spit on it or else their whole family would be killed. She goes on to tell them how her own father refused to disgrace the Torah, so her mother and sister were killed.

While the old woman is telling these stories, Foer starts to collect dirt from the ground in a plastic bag in order to bring it home to his grandmother. Travelling is his way of uncovering the past, and the empty Ukrainian soil becomes a sort of vessel for Foer to preserve the past and bring it back home to America. This is especially curious, because he wants to bring this relic back to his grandmother who has lived with his grandfather and could have known all the stories herself, possibly indeed knows them. Alex asks Jonathan to tell him more about his grandmother,

---

30 Ibid. 59.
31 See: Ibid. 74.

the second wife of Safran, and he tells him how she sometimes screamed out Yiddish words, but he was always too afraid to ask what they meant.

"[…] I knew I wasn't supposed to ask, so I didn't." "Perhaps she desired for you to ask." "No." "Perhaps she needed you to ask, because if you didn't ask, she could not tell you." "No." "Perhaps she was shouting, Ask me! Ask me what I'm shouting!"[32]

Although Alex Perchov is portrayed as a quite naïve and simple-minded young man throughout the novel, this seems to be a very strong and true observation. To all the authors, who so obsessively turn to their family histories in order to be able to tell their own life story, it is immensely important to find out more about their past. However, at the origin of all this curiosity and digging and searching and traveling, there seems to lie a silence that came before, a silence in the family, an omission and shortfall to have the family history conveyed and passed on through its natural and most direct way, namely as oral history through the talk between generations. Instinctively, therefore, Alex Perchov seems to have found the sore spot of Foer's whole endeavor, namely that he has failed to ask his own grandmother about her memories. It seems that quite often these memories were too traumatic and too deeply buried under a thick layer of silence within the family so the grandchildren did not dare to direct their curiosity towards their own remembering relatives. Possibly, Foer's story is quite reverberant of many other families in which the second generation did not care and the third generation did not dare to ask their questions.

However, Alex soon finds out, that within his own family, there has been a silence and omission as well: The old woman had also told the three travelers the story of a man called Herschel and his best friend Eli, and how Eli had betrayed Herschel, since otherwise he would have been shot by the Nazis himself. After their encounter with the old woman, Alex' grandfather finally tells them about his own past and admits that he once lived in a town right next to Trachimbrod, called Kolki. It turns out that when the Nazis came to this town and demanded to know who was Jewish, Alex's grandfather had stood next to his best friend Herschel and had indeed betrayed him, because he wanted to save the lives of his own family.

---

32 Ibid. 159.

Jonathan Safran Foer's novel Everything is Illuminated is an extension to Elie Wiesel's quote "If the Greeks invented tragedy, the Romans the epistle, and the Renaissance the sonnet, our generation invented a new literature, that of testimony."[33] But since not much is left of the shtetl and the history of Foer's family past, he himself becomes the bearer of the testimony and recreates an imagined and embellished past from scratch. One half of the novel provides a fictional history and reinvention of the shtetl Trachimbrod – allegedly based on the documents that Foer retrieved from his Ukraine trip. While this aestheticized history of the shtetl dwells in nostalgia for the lost Jewish life form of Eastern Europe, the second plotline of the novel gets nowhere close to nostalgia. This second plot line eventually leads to the sad and shocking truth about the events of 1943, when the story of Trachimbrod and many similar places was brutally ended forever.

3.3 DARA HORN – THE WORLD TO COME

Dara Horn's novel *The World to Come* also deals with the past in order to define the present and future for its protagonists. While her previous novel *In the Image* (2002), in a similar way as Jonathan Safran Foer's *Everything is Illuminated*, chose a (destroyed) location as a link between time and people, *The World to Come* focusses on a certain object instead. In this novel, everything begins with an art theft: Ben Ziskind steals a certain Marc Chagall painting from a museum in New York. This painting is a sketch called *Study for 'Over Vitebsk.'*[34]

For the last seven years, 30-year-old Ben Ziskind from New York has been a quiz question writer for a TV show called "American Genius." He has gone through a recent divorce from his wife, and both of his parents are dead, his mother Rosalie Ziskind having died only a few months ago. His twin sister Sara convinces him to go to a singles' cocktail hour at the

---

33 Wiesel, Elie. "The Holocaust as Literary Inspiration." *Dimensions of the Holocaust. Lectures at Northwestern University.* Eds. Wiesel, Elie et al. Evanston: Northwestern University Press, 1996. 9.

34 Incidentally, I chose this novel because this very painting decorated the Call for Papers of a conference which I attended in Budapest in February 2013.

Museum of Hebraic Art, which has a special exhibition called "Marc Chagall's Russian Years." At the museum Ben spots a certain Chagall painting dated to the year 1914: a painting of a street named *Study for 'Over Vitebsk.'* Ben realizes that this exact painting once hung over the piano in his parents' living room. He and his sister believe that this painting was once stolen or conned from their family and they have not seen or heard from it in years. So when Ben finds it in the museum, he cannot suppress the urge and desire to have it back and almost involuntarily, he steals it:

Ben stared more closely at the painting. It had been over fifteen years since he had last seen it. There was no way it was the same one. Artists often paint the same picture over and over again, he told himself. [...] But then he noticed, in the painting's lower right-hand corner, a tiny glossy area that gleamed white under the gallery lights – the same place where Sara, at the age of seven, had once tried to coat the painting with clear nail polish until their parents caught her. And the Ben's entire body started shaking with rage. He read the label again, still stunned. *On loan*, it read, from a Russian museum. He stretched his arms toward the painting without even noticing that he was doing so, reaching for it, ready to grip the bottom of the frame like the rung of a ladder.[35]

And so it happens that Ben Ziskind takes the painting with him, miraculously without hindrance.

As it turns out, the painting had become part of the family property, because Ben's grandfather Boris Kulbak once knew Marc Chagall in person. After a pogrom devastated his hometown Zhitomir in Russia, Boris Kulbak came to live in a Jewish boys' colony near Moscow.[36]

---

35 See: Horn, Dara. *The World to Come*. London: Hamish Hamilton, 2006. 10-11.
36 At first, the boy can only recall one single memory from his past life in the *shtetl*, which he describes as a beautiful spring day on which he witnesses a group of older boys beating away on a horse with a broken leg. While the boys take delight in battering the horse to death, Boris watches from afar with a morbid fascination. See: Horn, Dara. *The World to Come*. London: Hamish Hamilton, 2006. 12. Coincidentally also Nicole Krauss mentions a similar scene in her novel *The History of Love*, where a young man witnesses the beating of a

Living in the orphanage, Boris tells the other boys that he did not have any siblings, although this is not exactly true. He remembers that he used to have a baby brother who died at a young age. However, when the Zhitomir, where he lived with his family, was raided during the pogrom, his mother was pregnant again. His mother's pregnant belly was slashed open and the baby was tossed out of the window. His father being already dead, Boris was simply left by himself to die. When he was finally found, he was taken to a Jewish boys' colony in Malakhovka. The boys attend classes in math, literature and art. This is where Boris meets *Comrade* Chagall, who teaches an art class in the orphanage. Boris is fascinated by his teacher, who has a completely new approach to art. When Chagall gives the boys the task to paint something that they have seen and experienced themselves, Boris starts to paint a womb, the womb of his mother. Suddenly he starts remembering things from his past, also a story his mother used to tell him when he was little. She explained to him that babies, also go to school before they are born, but not to a school like Boris was familiar with. It is a school with angelic teachers who teach the babies the Torah and all the secrets of the universe. But just before the babies are born, an angel puts its finger on the spot between mouth and nose and says "Shh – don't tell." And like this, the babies forget everything that they have learned.[37] This image of the womb in which the unborn child is taught the secrets of the world by angels, only to forget them again before birth is a motif of great importance to return various times throughout the novel. It is a parable from the Talmud,[38] about which Yosef Hayim Yerushalmi has written in *Zakhor – Jewish History and Jewish Memory*:

---

dog by two men and eventually uses this image in his own novel. See: Krauss, Nicole. *The History of Love*. London: Penguin Books, 2005. 78.

37 See: Horn, Dara. *The World to Come*. London: Hamish Hamilton, 2006. 22.

38 See: *Babylonischer Talmud,* Vol. XII, Nidda III, vii, Fol. 30b. Trans. Goldschmidt, Lazarus. Frankfurt am Main: Jüdischer Verlag im Suhrkamp Verlag, 1996. 441. "Sobald er in den Weltenraum gekommen ist, kommt ein Engel, klapst [sic] ihn auf den Mund, und macht ihn die ganze Tora wieder vergessen, [...]". I would like to thank Sarah Werren for her tireless help with finding this passage.

And so I shall make a provisional distinction between memory (mneme) and recollection (anamnesis). Memory, for our purpose, will st hat which is essentially unbroken, continuous. Anamnesis will serve to describe the recollection of that which has been forgotten. [...] [A]ll true knowledge is anamnesis, all true learning an effort to recall what has been forgotten.[39]

This concept of memory seems to fit well with my argument about third generation authors like Foer and Horn who try to retrieve some information from the past in order to find out more about themselves. Everything they undertake seems to oscillate between *mneme* and *anamnesis* then. In their broken families they lack the continuous and unbroken memory of *mneme*, because too much is lost or unspoken. This leaves them with perpetual striving for recollection, for literally *re*-collecting the pieces of the past. Their big struggle consists in finding knowledge about their families' past and transferring it from the amnesia of their parents' generation to a form of *an*-amnesia of their own. The words of Yerushalmi can be understood almost as a condensed motto or theme for these authors of the third generation to whom indeed "all true learning [is] an effort to recall what has been forgotten." Ilan Stavans notes that Yerushalmi refers to a memory which is inherited and unforgettable, which is more connected to the ancestors than to the remembering individual itself: "the individual does not remember personal scenes but foreign ones, and more than remember, he invents them."[40] In this reading, the process of writing fiction can almost be understood as a mystic form of transgenerational telepathy in which memories of the ancestors are retrieved in the imagination of present writers. Be this as it may, the process of *an*-amnesia and "recalling what has been forgotten" seems to be the core endeavor in the works of such authors as Jonathan Safran Foer and Dara Horn, in which either the retrieval or the invention of their families' histories and background stories become the foundations for the protagonists in creating a story for themselves.

---

39 Yerushalmi, Yosef Hayim. Zakhor. *Jewish History and Jewish Memory*. Seattle: University of Washington Press, 1996. 107-108.
40 Stavans, Ilan. *The Inveterate Dreamer. Essays and Conversations on Jewish Culture*. Lincoln: University of Nebraska Press, 2001. 274.

So when asked by Chagall to paint what he has really seen, the boy Boris Kulbak paints his last memory of the past, his mother's womb. When the teacher Chagall sees it, he is so amazed by Boris Kulbak's talent that he asks the boy if he could keep the painting. In a brave attempt at negotiating, Boris asks Chagall what he will give him in exchange and Chagall agrees to trade one of his own paintings. Together they go to Chagall's studio so that Boris can pick out a painting. While looking about the studio and Chagall's work, a man enters the room whom Chagall introduces as his upstairs neighbor, a Yiddish writer by the name of Pinkhas Kahanovitch, who is also called *Der Nister*,[41] and teaches at the boys' colony like Chagall. After looking at Boris' painting, *Der Nister* asks him for his name, "[his] Jewish name,"[42] and the boy, at first confused, since "no one called him that in over a year,"[43] answers: "Benjamin." When he also tells the men his full name, "Benjamin son of Jacob," *Der Nister* answers: "Benjamin and Jacob. Nafsho keshura benafsho. You know what that means?" Boris feels uncomfortable and shakes his head, having forgotten what he knew of Hebrew.

"It's from Genesis, about Jacob and his son Benjamin," Der Nister explained. "Nafsho keshura benafsho – 'His soul was bound to his.' That's how it is with a father and son. What happens to him, happens to you." Boris froze.[44]

Obviously Boris is scared by this dooming prediction, because his father has died an early and violent death. As it turns out later in the novel, Boris Kulbak, Benjamin son of Jacob will suffer a similar fate. Notwithstanding the shock he puts into the boy with his threatening prediction, *Der Nister* continues by reading them a story he has just finished writing. The story is about a bridge created by God at the end of the week of creation, spanning from the lowest abyss of the world all the way to the door of the heavenly shrine. Later, Boris starts wandering through the studio in order to pick out a painting by Chagall to trade for his own. Eventually, he chooses a very special painting, because it reminds him of his childhood in the Zhitomir.

---

41 Also known as Der Nistor: Yiddish: דער נסתּר; the Hidden One.
42 Horn, Dara. *The World to Come*. London: Hamish Hamilton, 2006. 30.
43 Ibid. 30.
44 Ibid. 30.

Boris looked, and was surprised to find a series of miniatures of the larger paintings on the walls [...]. But most of them were too bright, the colors too imaginary to be real. And then his eyes stopped on a tiny dark painting, darker than all the others, a deep brooding street that looked very much like the street where he used to live, with a man who looked very much like Boris' own father hovering in the air over the town. This, he thought, was what he had once seen. "This one," he whispered.[45]

But before Boris leaves the studio, *Der Nister* crams the papers containing the story he had just read to them into the frame of the painting, a method which was not uncommon at that time for Jewish poets in order to protect their art from prosecution and destruction. "Don't stretch the canvas like that," Chagall complains, but *Der Nister* amusedly calms him down:

Don't worry, I'm sure our apprentice artist will take even better care of a pregnant painting. [...] I trust you will be an excellent curator of two works of art.[46]

Through this proclamation, the poet creates yet another link between the painting and Boris' memory of his former home in Zhitomir. The boy had chosen the picture because it reminded him of his home and of his dead father. However, the whole exchange had been initiated only because of his intuitive drawing of the very last memory about his home and family, namely the cut up womb of his mother. He had traded a painting of his mother's womb against a *shtetl* painting from Chagall that was now itself pregnant with a story about a bridge to the heavens. Thus it is obvious why the painting becomes of such great anamnestic importance to the Kulbak/Ziskind family.

When Ben's twin sister Sara finds out that Ben stole the painting from the museum, she is shocked and scared that Ben might go to jail. But Ben defends his action. He wants to return the painting to family property at all costs. "I'm sick, sick, sick of having things taken from me. Don't you get it? Our family is finished, Sara. This is the one thing we have left."[47] The painting becomes the manifestation of the European origin and family history. It is an integral part of the family, one last relic of the past.

---

45 Ibid. 40.
46 Ibid. 41.
47 Ibid. 51.

Therefore, the painting stands for the whole narrative of a family and incorporates the memories of its origin in the Pale of Settlement. It does not take long, accordingly, until Sara is also convinced that they should keep the painting.

In the novel, there follows the episode during which the Ziskind family lost the Chagall painting in the first place. Ben and Sara are still very young and their father has just died, leaving their mother Rosalie in financial difficulties. They need to sell the painti... in order to keep their New Jersey home and to afford college later. One day, Rosalie, accompanied by her daughter Sara, goes to New York in order to meet the Russian buyer, because she remembers that there were papers stuck in the frame that she would like to keep. She hopes that the buyer, whose name is Sergei Popov, would not mind giving them back to her.

On their way to retrieve the papers from the painting, again the Talmudic parable about the unborn child being taught and educated by angels in its mother's womb is evoked. When Sara asks her mother if she believes in reincarnation, Rosalie negates this, but instead offers her own way of thinking about life and death:

I believe that when people die, they go to the same place as all people who haven't yet been born. That's why it's called the world to come, because that's where they make the new souls st hat future. And the reward when good people die [...] st hat they get to help make the people in their families who haven't been born yet.[48]

In this episode it becomes clearer then who the angels in the "world to come" really are, namely the dead relatives and ancestors of the unborn child. What they teach the unborn, accordingly, is not only the wisdom of the Torah, but also the family's ancestral history. The child therefore learns all the forefathers' memories, only to forget them upon birth, and possibly to retrieve them during lifetime – like the hidden stories mother and daughter are now about to be retrieve from the canvas frame of the painting.

When they finally meet the buyer, Sara's mother seems to recognize the man and tells Sara in Yiddish that she should pretend she wants to leave right away. The girl is confused why her mother would speak in Yiddish to

---

48 Ibid. 149.

her. But it is too late for them to leave anyway, because Sergei Popov has already recognized Rosalie as Boris Kulbak's daughter, formerly Raisya Kulbak, now Rosalie Ziskind. As it turns out, Sergei Popov once knew Boris Kulbak and his daughter Raisya when she was five years old and they lived in the same apartment building back in Moscow.[49]

After Boris and his daughter return from a friendly visit at the Popovs' apartment, Boris gets a bad feeling and premonition, and hides the Chagall painting behind his daughter's books. Soon thereafter and without any reason he is being assigned to a lesser job. After another visit, Boris again gets an impulse, this time to check his important documents where he hides them under the mattress – their identity papers, mentioning that their nationality is Jewish and also secret clippings from American newspapers. One night Boris tells his daughter about the painting that Chagall gave to him, and adds that it is safely put away. During the same night, Popov enters their apartment with three other men to arrest Boris. "The charge is treason, for your role in the Zionist conspiracy to bring down the Soviet state."[50] Boris realizes that Popov is in possession of all the papers they had hidden under the mattress. When the men are about to take Boris with them, Raisya appears:

What do you say to a child you will never see again? That there really is an abyss? That it is easy to fall into it? […] That the world is nothing more than a very narrow bridge, and the most important thing is not to be afraid? Boris could think of nothing; his imagination failed him. He looked at Raisya and said only what he saw. "Baby" he whispered. And walked out the door. […] And when the time arrives, a year and a half later, for everything to end (because things do end, in the end), you still think nothing – not your wife, not your daughter, not even your mother or father – except perhaps of a baby you once saw flying through the air, or of the secrets that that baby had not yet forgotten, […].[51]

---

49 While the Kulbak family had to share their apartment, the Popovs had a big apartment for themselves full of paintings, which, as Popov claims are all reproductions. Ibid. 326.
50 Ibid. 340.
51 Ibid. 342.

In this scene father and child see each other for the last time, and again the image of Boris' unborn sibling, still bearing all the yet unforgotten ancestral memories and cut from his mother's womb, is evoked and linked to his own daughter standing in front of him. Boris says nothing but "Baby," as if to ask his daughter to keep this memory with her, just as the painting.

The novel also tells us about Ben's and Sara's father Daniel Ziskind, about his childhood and youth. His family moves to the suburbs of Newark in 1956 when he is twelve years old. During this time, he and Rosalie (Raisya Kulbak), who is now nine years old, meet for the first time. Together they read Yiddish stories by J. L. Peretz, Sholem Aleichem and also by *Der Nister*. After reading a story together that is called *The Dead Town*, Rosalie tears out these pages from the book to save them in her "library." She hides the pages behind the Chagall painting that is hanging in her house:

"Let's keep 'The Dead Town' with the dead town," she said. She took the painting down off the wall [...]. Then she took the pages and slid them between the wood and the canvas. On the opposite side of the backing, Daniel noticed a piece of yellowed paper peeking out from behind the wooden canvas frame. It seemed she had done this before. "What's that, another story?" he asked her. [...] "When you marry me," she whispered, "I'll tell you everything."[52]

As we find out here, curiously, Rosalie calls the painting "The Dead Town," and now that her future husband has picked a favorite Yiddish story that is itself called "The Dead Town," she decides to hide it in the canvas frame along with the original stories of *Der Nister*. Again, the intricate connection between the Chagall painting and the lost Jewish world of Eastern Europe – literally 'the dead town' of Rosalie's father Kulbak – is enforced here.

Accordingly, the novel evolves around the Chagall painting and tells the Kulbak/Ziskind family history. Eventually, Ben and Sara succeed in keeping the stolen painting and the stories that were tucked behind its frame. It has become clear, that in *The World to Come*, an entire family history is condensed and centered on one object, namely the Chagall

---

52 Ibid. 197.

painting *Study for 'Over Vitebsk.'* Acquired from Marc Chagall by Ben's grandfather Boris Kulbak who saw the memory of his own father and his own childhood home in the *shtetl* embodied in this painting, it had been kept and valued by Ben's mother Rosalie for as long as possible. The painting became lost to the family, taken by the same man who also took the life of Boris Kulbak. However, Ben and Sara Ziskind, grandson and granddaughter to Boris Kulbak, eventually return the painting and its 'appendices' where they belong: to their family. At the same time the painting is doubly linked to the image of the mothers' womb. First, because it was Kulbak's own painting of his mother's womb, his very last and most traumatic memory of her, that initiated the exchange with Chagall in the first place. And second, because over the decades the painting itself has become something like a pregnant womb, in the literal sense of housing and hiding the Yiddish stories of *Der Nister,* but also in the figurative sense of housing the ancestral memories of this family that need to be passed on to yet unborn future generations. In this latter sense, the womb metaphor is intricately linked to the Talmudic parable of the space that in Dara Horn's novel is called *The World to Come*, where the dead relatives and forefathers teach the unborn child about all their memories. Once the child is born, everything is forgotten. What remains, however, in the case of this family, is the painting, as a reminder and a venture point for the work of recollecting, the work of anamnesis.

3.4 CHAPTER CONCLUSION

In this chapter I have illustrated that novels, such as Jonathan Safran Foer's *Everything is Illuminated* or Dara Horn's *The World to Come*, attempt to (re)discover and (re)collect the memory of a family's European past.

The topography of the family background as a place of origin seems to play a crucial role in how the protagonist of Jonathan Safran Foer's novel *Everything is Illuminated* defines himself. He travels to the lost *shtetl* of Trachimbrod both literally and imaginatively. While the actual trip to the Ukraine yields no results but the disheartening fact that there is nothing left of Trachimbrod, the young protagonist turns into a travel writer of fiction upon his return and simply reimagines the history of his ancestors and of the *shtetl* Trachimbrod. To what extent these stories are based on the documents he brought back from his trip is neither distinguishable nor important. What counts is that the *shtetl* is resurrected in his writing.

Unlike in *Everything is Illuminated*, Dara Horn's *The World to Come* is neither an account of travel nor a fictional resurrection of the *shtetl*. Instead, the novel strictly deals with the little pieces that are really left to the family, namely the Chagall painting and the Yiddish stories, which thereby become highly condensed relics that symbolize everything that once existed and everything that was lost to the Ziskind family. The strong focus on this one and only relic symbolizing the family's past, makes it understandable why Ben and Sara Ziskind fight with such fervor to keep the painting.

What these novels have in common is their impressive representation of how young Jewish-American writers embark on fictional rediscoveries of their Jewish heritage while moving in the creative conflict zone between the urban here and now and the European past. Even if there are other trends and currents among the younger generation of Jewish-American authors and even if the presented novels differ in many aspects, it is obvious that a certain sub trend is defined by a group of Jewish-American writers: reference to a shared European past. These novels have in common the dedicated involvement with a Jewish heritage, which is found in the (fictional) reconstruction of a family history around the relics or places of former habitation in Europe.

The imaginative return to Europe corresponds very typically to the cultural dynamics of the third generation. The second generation was still more involved with the process of assimilation, whereas the fully arrived third generation is more at leisure to explore again the European past. The paradox of this constellation is however, that the third generation is much further removed from the family's European memories. Nevertheless, Europe frequently reoccurs to be a cultural projection in Jewish American literature, even in the writings of very young authors who never experienced life in Eastern Europe first hand and often do not even know the 'real' stories of their grandparents or more distant ancestors. This leaves them with a necessity to fictionalize.

As I have hinted at before, fictional representations of the *shtetl* by authors too young to have first-hand knowledge about *shtetl* life, have been criticized as nostalgia and overly glorifying aestheticization. This nostalgia can especially be observed when fictional recreations of *shtetl* life turn into some kind of utopian image of a better and simpler Jewish life in the past, omitting the hardships and the insecurity that were part of life in the Pale of Settlement. But what exactly is nostalgia? Svetlana Boym provides a fitting definition of the term:

Nostalgia (from nostos – return home, and algia – longing) is a longing for a home that no longer exists or has never existed. Nostalgia is a sentiment of loss and displacement, but it is also a romance with one's own fantasy.[53]

Boym argues that a longing for something or some place that no longer exists, is the essence of nostalgia. However, she also links this sentiment of loss with a romance – between the one who longs and the object he/she longs for – that continues in one's fantasy. If the first generation of immigrants could still rely on their own memories for engaging in this kind of romance, later generations will have to resort to their imagination. As I have tried to show in the example of Foer's *Everything is Illuminated*, such contemporary reimaginations of the *shtetl* can take the shape of something unreal, mystic, and – in a narrower sense of the word fantasy – fantastic. In this heightened form of nostalgia, accordingly, the *shtetl* gets depicted as the kind of magical place that has in truth never in this way existed. A strongly aestheticized icon of longing is therefore created.

Irving Howe – born in 1920 to Jewish immigrants in New York – who had predicted the end of Jewish-American literature in 1977, was not very enthusiastic about this upcoming trend of nostalgia that he saw arising already in the late 1980s:

What at times leaves me a little irritated is the upsurge of nostalgia I detect among a good many young people for the immigrant world to which I was already a latecomer and of which they barely know. They aren't nostalgic for anything they themselves experienced, with either joy or anguish; they're nostalgic for the nostalgia of other people. [...] For I don't want the immigrant-Jewish milieu – it's my life, you understand – to become "material" for chic museum display and cozy Yiddish musicals.[54]

---

53 Boym, Svetlana. "Introduction. Taboo on Nostalgia?" *The Future of Nostalgia*. New York: Basic Books, 2001. xiii.
54 Howe, Irving. "Immigrant Chic." *New York Magazine*, 12 May 1986. 76.

Irving Howe serves as a typical representative of the previous generation that is critical of the curiosity and creative freedom of this new generation concerning the past life of immigrants. In his opinion artistic representations, such as stereotypical images of the *shtetl* or life in the Yiddish ghetto of the Lower East Side, created by persons who never experienced this way of life personally, are merely a nostalgia for the 'real' nostalgia of others. However, for younger generations of American Jews, who lack any personal memories, an exploration of the European past through fiction, story-telling, journeys and metaphors plays an important role. Because in the case of many families, little information was passed on – largely due to the second generation's zeal for amnesia and assimilation, it is no wonder that young Jewish-American writers begin to deal with their own family history through fictional stories which often start in a *shtetl* in Eastern Europe. This was also recognized by the jurors of the Edward Lewis Wallant Prize, Mark Shechner, Thane Rosenbaum and Victoria Aarons. They identify a significant change in dealing with Jewish identity in contemporary Jewish-American literature:

At no time before have Jewish writers turned so uniformly to history for their fictions. […] it's not just that some of the new Jewish writers are themselves from elsewhere, but that the American born writers are now better traveled. This is the very opposite of shtetl writing; no longer insulated and suffocating, gone are the tenements and even the suburban ambitions.[55]

So the judges of the literary prize notice that journeys and a positive rediscovery play a major role for young authors, in contrast to the sad stories of the actual immigrants who knew life in the *shtetl* with all its hardship. This rediscovery also stands in contrast – as the jurors point out – to the conformist suburban ambitions and exaggerated desire for assimilation of the second generation. Accordingly, the jurors take a positive view on the fictional appropriation of the past by the current generation of young authors.

However, Irving Howe was not alone in criticizing the nostalgia trend, and there are others who disagree with this new way of writing about an unknown past, as indulged by many young Jewish-American writers. Steve

---

55 Schechner, Mark et al. The New Jewish Literature. *Zeek*, 15 May 2014.

Stern, who actually delivered a good example of *shtetl* literature himself in his before mentioned novel *The Frozen Rabbi* (2010), takes a similar critical view on contemporary Jewish-American fiction which tries to recapture *shtetl* life:

> I'm not an unqualified booster of recent Jewish American writing. There's a strain that disturbs me, as represented in the works of writers like Nicole Krauss, Jonathan Safran Foer, Michael Chabon, and others – immensely virtuosic writers who nevertheless play fast and loose with Jewish sources in what amounts to a Yiddishkeit lite. They know just enough of the traditional lore and literature to infuse their narratives with the flavor of "the turbulent saga" without taking responsibility for a confrontation with its essence. This is to my mind a kind of theme park mentality, wherein the Jewish past is presented in language and settings that evoke a sepia sentimentality, that defang a ferocious experience until it's safe for nostalgia.[56]

Stern seems to criticize less the fact *that* the younger generation of authors returns in their narratives to the Jewish past, but rather *how* they do it. He perceives of a "theme park mentality" and "sepia sentimentality," that has to do – according to Stern's opinion – with the young authors being insufficiently informed about Jewish history and tradition. He insinuates that authors like Foer, Chabon and Krauss create a kind of "Yiddishkeit lite" by picking some cherries from the little they know. While I agree that in the literature of the younger generation, Yiddish terms are casually dropped here and there, I find it difficult, on the other hand to accuse them of cherry-picking and of being uninformed. Stern accuses these writers of not taking the responsibility of confronting the "essence" of the Jewish saga, however, he neglects defining what this "essence" is. Nevertheless, Stern and others have criticized that current re-imaginations have sometimes overly aestheticized life in the *shtetl* and left out much of the suffering and hardships that were part of this chapter in Jewish history.

Whether this is the case or not, in support of my overall argument of a new generation of Jewish-American writing, it has mainly been important to point out that there *is* such a trend of re-imagining the European past.

---

56 Parker Royal, Derek. "Tugging at Jewish Weeds: An Interview with Steve Stern." *MELUS* 32.1. (2007): 158.

Whether in nostalgic, sentimental   istic or realistic manners, young
authors like Jonathan Safran Foer   Dara Horn choose to revisit the
places and items of recent Jewish h   ind thus deliberately engage with
their Jewish heritage.

4 New Beginnings

> "Call us	nch of seachers. Call us post-
> Holocau	s. Call us Generation J"
> SCHIFFM	SA. GENERATION J. 11.

As I have tried to show in the previous chapter, a group of young Jewish-American writers tends to work with images of the past to create a sense of Jewish identity in their writings. The *shtetl* as a point of origin seems to be predestined for such intentions. But clearly there is also another group of young authors whose writing stands in contrast to the endeavors of exploring the past and family history as shown by the previous group. I would like to call this group 'detaching,' 'searching' or 'self-shaping.' In the texts of Shalom Auslander, Allegra Goodman, Lisa Schiffman or Gideon Lewis-Kraus, to name only a few, we get to know about a new world of American Judaism, which is significantly detached from the generation of their parents and grandparents. The protagonists of these authors, young Jewish men and women, try to define their own identities by themselves, try to create something new and want to determine on their own terms what is and what is not part of their character and life story. Significantly, their paths often lead them not back to, but away from their families, sometimes causing not only conflict but even a complete break from the family.

The characters I would like to present in this chapter are certainly not the first to break away from their families in order to shape their own lives. Much the opposite, one could call this breaking-away a common *leitmotif* if not the most central theme in the literature of the previous generation of Jewish-American authors. Saul Bellow and even more so Philip Roth – one could call them the Jewish-American classics – made the detachment from the family an important subject matter in their work. Like the current generation of young authors, they also used the genre of the *Bildungsroman*, the coming of age story to tell the tales of their heroes' individuation. However, their stories had a different context, namely the struggle for assimilation in a yet foreign society. But unlike these predecessors and heavy weights of Jewish-American literature, the contemporary approach to questions of identity, to finding one's own way and understanding of being a Jew in America is not ultimately connected to the issue of assimilation in the American society. Plainly said, it is easy, clear and natural for the new generation to be American – *Jewish-American*. If anything in this identity label needs closer scrutiny and specification to them, it is the hyphen 'Jewish,' not the underlying state of being an American.

Much the opposite, one could even say that nowadays it has become unclear to many what the distinction of being Jewish-American even is, what might actually be the difference from non-Jews. Lisa Schiffman, one of the authors I would like to introduce in this chapter, wrote about this phenomenon in her book *Generation J* which was published in 1999:

For better or for worse, secular Jews have learned to hide these differences [to Gentile Americans]. Cultural Historian Irving Howe, in his epic book World of Our Fathers, predicted that this would be the case. He said that by the mid-twentieth century, Jewish life would enter an entirely new and unpredictable phase. By then, he said, the offspring of Eastern European Jewish immigrants would have achieved what he saw as the goal of secular Jews: to seem "normal" in American culture. I think we're there.[1]

I believe that Lisa Schiffman makes a very important point here which is well reflected in the writings of her generation. Nowadays young Jewish-Americans ask themselves *what* it means to be *Jewish* rather than *how* to be *American*. Because being a Jewish-American is so 'normal,' the new generation of authors needs to search and define what distinguishes them from non-Jewish-Americans. The search for an answer can often be found in classic coming of age stories which can take very different trajectories and lead to a multifaceted spectrum of outcomes. The return to family and

---

[1] Schiffman, Lisa. *Generation J.* New York: Harper San Francisco, 1999.

history as described in the previous chapter has been nothing but one possible path out of a bouquet of others. Morris Dickstein makes a similar argument as Schiffman and gives a good overview of other possible literary trajectories for redefining the Jewish self:

Jewish life in America has become far more assimilated, but younger Jewish writers have both taken advantage of this and sharply criticized it. They have turned to Israel, to feminism, to the Holocaust, to ea... Jewish history and to their own varied spiritual itineraries, ranging from neo... odoxy and mysticism to Eastern religion, as a way of redefining their r... n to both Jewish tradition and contemporary culture. If they have lost the ol... onnection to Europe, to Yiddish or to immigrant life, they have begun to substitute their own distinctive Jewish and American experiences.[2]

Dickstein agrees that assimilation is no longer an issue for current Jewish writers; rather the opposite has begun, namely the critique of an exaggerated assimilation. However, he enlists a number of themes and motifs that have occurred in recent literature. I understand his argument also in the sense that younger writers, while substituting the former canon of Jewish-American themes – the immigrant milieu, the Lower East Side, the strive for assimilation in the suburbs of New Jersey – with their own experiences, will inevitably have to embrace contemporary culture, the cultural environment they grew up in, if not as a substitute then at least as an addition to Jewish tradition. I would even go one step further and argue that much of the Jewish tradition has itself become part of contemporary popular culture. Not only have the Jewish immigrants of the last century – over the course of two or three generations – fully assimilated into American society, but also American culture has assimilated to its Jewish infusion. Many typical icons of Jewish tradition – certain meals, Yiddish words, or customs – have become commonplace in contemporary and popular American culture.

This leaves us with the question again of how to define oneself as Jewish in a secular environment, if being Jewish-American has become simply normal, sometimes almost to the extent of invisibility. In her article

---

2   Dickstein, Morris. "The Complex Fate of the Jewish-American Writer." *The Nation*. 4 October 2001. 27 September 2012. 16.

"Identity Matters: Contemporary Jewish American Writing," Tresa Grauer gives this question yet another twist by arguing, that Jewish-American writers today are fully aware of who they are and rather deal with the question of how to represent themselves:

> [...] while Jewish American writers may once have asked the question, "Who – or what – is a contemporary American Jew?", they are now asking instead, "How do we, as contemporary American Jews, represent ourselves?"[3]

In this quite radical reading, current Jewish-American literature is less about being Jewish and more about what this looks like. This means that being Jewish might have become more of a trait that can either be stressed or not, a condition that is so natural that it makes a difference only if the individual chooses to represent it as such. In *Generation J*, Lisa Schiffman draws a similar picture about the young American Jews of her generation, in which being Jewish is not an inevitable state of birth anymore, but rather an activity, an option for self that can be played out at leisure:

> It occurred to me that most of us were third-Generation American Jews. We had at least two grandparents who came, accent intact, from somewhere else. We had parents who had either followed a Judaism by rote or rejected the religion altogether. [...] We were a generation of Jews grew up with television, with Barbie, with rhinoplasty as a way of life. Assimilation wasn't something we strove for; it was the condition into which we were born. We could talk without using our hands. When we used the word schlepp, it sounded American. Being Jewish was an activity: Today I'll be Jewish. Tomorrow I'll play tennis. [...] To us, anything was possible.[4]

Schiffman thus confirms that it is completely natural for her generation to be assimilated into American culture and society. It requires no effort to be American, it is their birthright. In addition, however, being Jewish seems to be an option which is available – if wanted – like an exciting accessory.

---

3   Grauer, Tresa. "Identity Matters: Contemporary Jewish American Writing." *The Cambridge Companion to Jewish American Literature*. Eds. Kramer, Michael P. and Hana Wirth-Nesher. Cambridge: Cambridge University Press, 2003. 272.
4   Schiffman, Lisa. *Generation J*. New York: Harper San Francisco, 1999. 4.

In this chapter I will deal with the works of such authors who are taking new paths in exploring what being Jewish-Americans means to them. Lisa Schiffman's very loose and relativistic definition of being Jewish seems to be one end of the spectrum and I will therefore discuss her book *Generation J* in greater detail later in this chapter. While authors like Schiffman tell stories of detachment from tradition within a secular Jewish milieu, there are also authors with very different experiences, telling very different stories. I am thinking of authors from religious and orthodox backgrounds. There are stories of breaking free from orthodoxy but also stories of conversion from secularism to religious Judaism. Also these stories and literary approaches expand the spectrum of problems of this current generation of Jewish writers in the US. I will therefore start this chapter with the example of Shalom Auslander, who tells about such a breakout story from a religious environment and family.

4.1 SHALOM AUSLANDER – FORESKIN'S LAMENT

Before delving into the actual plot of Shalom Aulander's *Foreskin's Lament: A Memoir* from 2007, I would like to point out again that the title of this self-proclaimed memoir is obviously a reference to Philip Roth's famous novel *Portnoy's Complaint* from 1969. What has been a 'complaint' in 1969 is now a 'lament,' and like Roth, Auslander forgoes the use of an article despite replacing the name of a person with an object (one would have expected the title to be 'A Foreskin's Lament'). Also both novels tell the story of a young Jewish man, coming of age in America, struggling with sexuality and the rules of a Jewish home that seem to be irreconcilable with the growing boy's ambition for a detached and secular life. Tova Ross sees yet another similarity:

Much in the same way that Philip Roth's Portnoy's Complaint became a defining monologue for so many Jewish American males, many of the writers interviewed for this story [her article] cited Auslander's memoir as particular inspiration to them, both personally and professionally, as they grappled with defining their post-frum narratives.[5]

In other words, like Roth's classic novel, Auslander's seeming homage has become a point of reference and key literary and personal milestone for many other authors. By giving his novel this title, Auslander sets the stage and raises the readers' expectations for a book full of both frustrating situations and comic relief, family conflicts and sexual explicitness. Auslander even escalates wittily by calling his book the lament of a 'foreskin,' instead of just – he seems to imply – some other 'shmuck's complaint.' As I have discussed in the first chapter of this thesis, this kind of reference to the title of another book, is an example of intertextuality that is deliberately crafted and tagged by the author. If we read Auslander according to Kristeva, we will therefore read it as a *double*, with Roth reverberating in our reading. Clearly, Auslander bows to one of the key texts of the previous generation of Jewish authors, and thereby turns his own memoir into some kind of reply to *Portnoy's Complaint*. However, this gesture can also be interpreted in the psychoanalytic sense of Harold Bloom, as I have equally outlined in the first chapter, namely as an oedipal gesture of both anxiety and rebellion in the new author's striving for poetic independence. By evoking the Godfather of Jewish-American literature already in his title and thereby openly admitting to his influence, one could say Auslander renders a preemptive blow against any accusations of repetition. At the same time, he seems to make the claim of providing a corrective, a better and updated version of the story. This aggressive claim is reflected in Auslander's bold and lurid title, in the radical exchange of the protagonist's name (Portnoy) with foreskin on the title page.

The subtitle of Auslander's novel is "A Memoir" thus suggesting an autobiographical piece. In my opinion, however, the novel should be considered *autofiction*. As outlined earlier in the first chapter of this thesis, the term 'autofiction' has been introduced by the French critic and author Serge Doubrovsky in order to account for the fact that in many autobiographies the extent of fiction – and vice versa in many fictions, the extent of autobiography – is unclear. As I have tried to argue, the extent of

---

5   Ross, Tova. "How Ex-Frum Memoirs became New York Publishing's Hottest New Trend." *Tablet Magazine*, 7.1.2014. 9 January 2014.

fiction or autobiographic truthfulness quintessentially does not matter, and neither does who exactly is speaking to us, author or fictional narrator. What really matters for the sake of my overall argument is the content of the story.

In Foreskin's Lament, Auslander describes his childhood and youth, living in an orthodox family and community in Monsey, New York. Nevertheless, he also tells us about his attempts to break free from it. Growing up with a choleric father and a home full of religious rules, the little boy likes to test his parents' authority early on. In school, Auslander is told that until the age of 13, all of a boy's sins are credited to their fathers. This seems to be the perfect excuse for the young boy to misbehave:

> That night, just before bed, I ate a drumstick, washed it down with some milk, touched myself, and flicked the bed-room light on and off. – Break those lights and I'll break your hands! my father shouted. It was going to be a busy week.[6]

The tense relationship with his father seems to be rooted also in his father's own insecurity and shortcomings. While most of the other boys' fathers are rabbis or doctors, Auslander's father is a craftsman. The boy himself admires his father's craft, but at the same time he senses early on that most other people have little respect for manual labor of the kind that his father does:

> I felt bad for my father. I wondered what it would feel like to be great at something nobody thought was all that great. To be good with your hands in a world that juged people by their heads. To be a creator in a world that kneeled before quibblers, beggars, and handshakers.[7]

When Auslander is a little boy, he enjoys building furniture and other things together with his father, but the older his father gets, the more enraged he becomes. In a society where men are destined to become rabbis

---

6 Auslander, Shalom. *Foreskin's Lament. A Memoir*. London: Picador, 2009. 15. Interestingly, almost one hundred years before, Mary Antin wrote a very similar passage about testing God by violating the Shabbat. See: Antin, Mary. *The Promised Land*. Boston: The Riverside Press Cambridge, 1912. 99-100.

7 Auslander, Shalom. *Foreskin's Lament. A Memoir*. London: Picador, 2009. 59.

or scholars, Auslander's father feels debased and gives vent to his aggressions within his family. When the father is asked by the rabbi to build a bigger ark for a new Torah, it turns out to be a difficult undertaking because of his temper. A friend hears Auslander's father cursing while he is building the ark and is confused about the whole situation. He confronts Auslander about his father:

How come your father has so many tools? Ephraim asked. – He builds things, I said. – Why? – Because he likes to. – Why? – I don't know, I said. – It's cool. – No, it isn't. – Yes, it is. – My father says anything that takes away time from serving God is wrong, said Ephraim. – He's building a holy ark, you stupid idiot. That shut him up for a while, [...].[8]

Auslander's mother's family seems to consist mainly of rabbis, one even being a rabbi *and* a doctor. Clearly, this is not an ideal constellation for his father's self-confidence. Even after the new ark is unveiled in the synagogue, neighbors and friends congratulate Auslander's mother for her famous family rather than for her talented husband. The surroundings of his upbringing are therefore an orthodox family, living in an orthodox community, and an increasingly choleric father who is ashamed of his own work of craftsmanship and takes out his anger on the family. It might not be overly surprising that the boy will eventually start rebelling against the rules and confines set within this family and community. It seems that although he never openly breaks with the community, the father also has underlying issues with the orthodox way of life that values nothing higher than serving God.

An early form of breaking out of his tight traditional and religious household are Auslander's secret expeditions into the world of *traif* food. During the course of his childhood and youth, Auslander continuously eats unkosher food, starting with the infamous *Slim Jim* – a special and highly unkosher Hot Dog he buys at the Snack Shack at the town pool for the first time when he is nine years old. Lured in by the smell of something unknown, "something sweet and sharp, foul and fantastic all at the same time,"[9] Auslander decides to ignore his religious upbringing and indulge in

---

8   Ibid. 54.
9   Ibid. 78.

this forbidden treat. While at the beginning he has difficulties with his conscience, over the course of the summer he tries various versions of the "stick of meat."[10] He even becomes a regular at the Snack Shack, so when he and his sister stand in line one day to order a Coke, it almost gets him into a precarious situation, as the vendor assumes he comes to order his regular, a *Slim Jim*: "Jimmy? Asked the Snack Shack man. – Who's Jimmy? She asked. – How should I know? I said."[11]

Since his mother refuses to buy unkosher candy for her son, Auslander also begins to steal sweets and other forbidden treats. Almost like a drug addict, the young boy hides his urge for unkosher food, telling himself: "I can stop at any time."[12] However, he cannot stop and keeps eating unkosher, although he never loses the feeling of sin and shame. Because of his strict upbringing, he is gripped by self-doubt and anxiety, waiting for God's wrath to come over him:

I was sick. I was diseased. I was a criminal. I was a Sodomite, an Amorite, a Hittite, a Sinite, a Givite. I was Cain. I was Esau. I was Lot's wife. I wondered what was God taking so long to punish me, to throw me under a bus with a pocketful of Slim Jims, to give me a heart attack mid-Moon Pie, and when I thought that He was – when I felt a stabbing pain in my chest (heart attack) or a sharp pang in my head (brain aneurysm) – I ran to the bathroom and forced my fingers down my throat, trying to regurgitate the sins I had already swallowed, heaving and retching and hoping that God this evening was feeling All-Forgiving, or at least Partially Forgiving, or maybe just Somewhat Exculpatory.[13]

This quote shows already at this early age a compulsive thinking, driven by guilt and fear that will remain with Auslander for the rest of his life, even after completely breaking with orthodoxy, namely the expectation that at any moment God will punish him for his sins. He cannot resist the temptation of eating unkosher food, but at the same time he feels that what he keeps doing is wrong.

---

10   Ibid. 80.
11   Ibid. 85.
12   Ibid. 86.
13   Ibid. 86.

Before entering fifth grade, his parents transfer him from the ultra-orthodox yeshiva to a regular orthodox school. The boy is surprised to see that there are teachers without beards, wearing regular black suits. The students wear tiny and colorful yarmulkes, unlike the big black velvet yarmulkes they used to wear in his former school. But the biggest difference is that there are girls at his new school – a completely new experience for the young boy.

[…] half the girls came into the boys' classroom, and when they did, the room smelled like a meadow, like a thousand meadows, like a thousand meadows covered in a fine, soothing mist of Aqua Net hair spray, and I inhaled deeply as they walked by […].[14]

These are the first moments that Auslander spends with girls and he tries to be as close to them as possible, touching their hair and inhaling their scent. Around this same time, sexual feelings awaken in him for the first time, when he finds a porn magazine in the woods and discovers therein what he could do to his mother's panty hose. He fills the legs up with dirty laundry to form them like women's legs. While sitting intimidated next to his construction, only the arrival of his father prevents 'worse.' Like the novel's title, this episode is also reminiscent again of Philip Roth's *Portnoy's Complaint* in which the sexual awakening of the young hero plays an important role and takes similarly awkward shapes. However, Auslander keeps finding porn hidden under a certain stone in the woods, which he calls the "Stone of Pornography," and he believes that God put them there for him to find:

It was the hand of God and I knew it – if He could speak to Moses from a bush that was on fire but was never consumed, was it too much to imagine that He could speak to me from a pile of pornography that was never exhausted?[15]

While Auslander keeps receiving the heavenly gift of porn, he is equipped with less success in real life and realizes that the girls in his school do not pay much attention to him. Unfortunately, his first love Deena is not

---

14 Ibid. 90.
15 Ibid. 95.

interested in him, but she tells him that s[...]s a friend, Lisa, who likes him. Again, Auslander takes what God s[...] to hand to him: "Lisa was Deena's best friend. She had black hair a[...]ark rings around her eyes. Good one, God."¹⁶ It is this sarcastic und[...] in a private dialogue with God – which is in fact only a monologue [...]t continues throughout the entire novel. Paradoxically, the more the [...] distances himself from the strict rules of his community, the more he [...]s this talk to God, because he remains scared that He will eventually t[...] venge. As the young boy violates the *Shabbat* for the first time and d[...] to the mall in a taxi, he is scared that his family will be punished for hi[s...]

Maybe God had already punished me and I didn[...]. Maybe He had killed my family. Maybe he burned down the house while I [...] alking here. Hadn't I heard sirens earlier? Did killers break in after I had left[...] re they in my house right now? Maybe they were tying my family up at this very moment, guns pressed to the side of their heads, and maybe God was waiting to see what I would do — if I left right now, He would make the kidnappers leave.¹⁷

Again, we get to witness the boy's tormented and compulsory way of thinking, infused by guilt and fear. In his mind he constantly imagines the worst of all possible scenarios, all the potential catastrophes which God could get back at him with. Strikingly, these horrible thoughts are not of the naïve or simple kind, such that God would harm him directly and immediately. Rather, the boy develops a complex neurosis, expecting God's wrath to be looming behind every corner. Auslander begins to live life under the impression of constant threat, especially for the lives of his loved ones, because by taking their lives – he is convinced – God would inflict the most suffering on him.

Nevertheless, the older he gets, the more uncomfortable he feels in the strict confines of his community. In his junior year of high school, in 1987, he discovers rap music, which becomes yet another outlet for his rebellion. Although he does not understand what the rappers talk about, he feels connected to their music and to their anger.

---

16 Ibid. 109.
17 Ibid. 131.

Rap was a perfect fit; I was at least as angry as the rappers [...]. I didn't always know what they were saying, but I sure liked the way they were saying it. [...] Damn straight. Something wasn't right. I felt, again, like a stranger in a strange land, except the strange land I was in was my own [...]. I felt like the horse on the Polo logo, unsure whether the man on my back with the menacing mallet was God, or family, or community, or all three, but knowing that if I could just throw the son of a bitch, I could run away forever. My attitude toward the world I had come from and the attitude toward the God that I had come from were the same: I was tired, finally, of trying to find favor in someone or Something else's eyes, particularly when that someone or Something seemed to be assholes and/or an Asshole. Our philosophy teacher told us of a man who claimed that God was dead; if only, Friedrich. He was alive, and He was a Prick.[18]

In this dense quote there are two important aspects to be considered. The first is that he does not blame his family or his community for the narrowness of the world he grew up in. He also does not hold them responsible for imposing so many limits onto him with all their expectations. They are not the great 'Something,' the eternal Polo rider, the 'Asshole' and 'Prick' who did all this to him. Rather, Auslander blames God himself for his unhappy life. It should have become clear by now that Auslander's mindset is first and foremost that of a believer. He believes in God, whether he wants to or not, and the more he tries to break away from a religious life, the more his belief expresses itself both in his anger at God and his fear of God.

The second aspect to mention about the above quote is the notion of feeling like "a stranger in a strange land." Auslander feels strange in America although, as he says, this strange land is his own. This is a very curious statement, because it seems to contradict directly the argument that I have made so far, about Jews feeling native and naturalized in America nowadays. However, Shalom Auslander's experience is different. Because of growing up in a strictly religious community, he feels like a stranger to the surrounding world outside of this community. The word he chooses is 'stranger,' not foreigner or alien. Therefore, I would argue, his experience is both similar to and different from the experiences of earlier generations of Jews. While the immigrants really felt as foreigners in a new land, the

---

18 Ibid. 163-164.

experience of the second generation is to some extent comparable with Auslander's situation. They grew up, born in America, but socialized in household and families whom they themselves soon began to perceive as different from their neighbors and friends. Henceforth, the second generation grew up in a constant struggle between the two conflicting spheres of family and public, tradition and assimilation. This situation is quite comparable to Auslander's who also suffers from increasing difficulties to keep these two spheres in harmony. Therefore, the memoirs of Auslander are a good example in showing, that despite belonging to the same generation of young Jewish-Americans, born and raised in the 70s and 80s of the last century, the individual experiences and attitudes of these authors can differ very much, and accordingly also the stories they tell.

Inevitably in his teenage years, Auslander's mother finds out about his trespasses when she discovers a hamburger wrapping in his car: "- Are you ... non-kosher?"[19] It is the ultimate sin for the adolescent boy. Although he wants to confess everything, he knows his family would not understand his hunger for the strange and forbidden world beyond the closed community life. As usual, when he has done something bad, he expects his mother to be devastated and to relate his sins to the horrors his ancestors had to endure during the war, so that he could live: "She would go Holocaust. Do you know how many Jews died at the hands of Nazis so you can keep kosher?"[20] The suffering of the Holocaust seems to be the ultimate thought-determining cliché in Auslander's family, especially for his mother, whether it is about keeping kosher or other things affecting their lives. But also later in his life, when Auslander is contemplating whether to circumcise his son or not, he remembers the story a rabbi once told him, about an old woman circumcising a baby boy in a concentration camp just before her certain death: "You have given us a child, she cried aloud to God, - and we return to you a Jew,"[21] the story goes, and obviously it has left a mark on Auslander.

Nevertheless, his daily routine of shoplifting, eating unkosher and smoking weed, makes him so careless that one day finally he gets caught carrying shoplifted clothes worth more than $ 500 and a bag of weed. After

---

19 Ibid. 168.
20 Ibid. 169.
21 Ibid. 149.

being convicted, Auslander gets sentenced to do community work in the Good Samaritan Hospital. At this time, he becomes so frustrated with his own life that he decides to go to Israel for a while, to the satisfaction of his worried mother who had suggested the same before.

His parents decide to put him in a yeshiva for troubled teenagers. Soon after his arrival in the holy land, he realizes that everything is quite similar as his life back in the US: "I spent my first few months in the Holy Land of my forefathers getting drunk and trying to find a pot connection."[22] It seems, accordingly, as if Auslander would continue causing trouble for himself. However, after his first year in Jerusalem, he turns back to God and to orthodoxy, because he realizes that this is the only way to be accepted by his surroundings – and to impress a girl he likes. He begins to keep kosher again, quits his job at a bar in Jerusalem and even moves up to an advanced Talmud class.

> I was tired of fighting Him. I wasn't getting anywhere and I didn't want to go home. I wrapped myself in the warm security blanket of absolute belief, and it felt good. It felt safe. [...] Over the next few months and into the following year, I became the most extraordinary devout Jew for the most extraordinary of reasons: I was loved. My rabbis welcomed me into their families. [...] In exchange, all I had to do was wear a yarmulke, and a black hat, and phylacteries, and tzitzis; grow a beard and long peyis; cut my hair short; study Talmud, the Torah, the Prophets, and the Book of Psalms, keep the Sabbath, and keep kosher, and keep from cursing; and stop reading English books, and stop speaking to my old friends, and stop talking to girls; and promise to move to Jerusalem. It seemed like a good deal at the time.[23]

But as fast as this return has come, is also goes again. After a series of incidents, Auslander starts to question his belief again. One day he walks by a store and sees himself in the window: "I didn't recognize myself anymore."[24] Although his rabbis try to convince him of staying, he has made up his mind, and decides to travel back to the US, where he starts living in a tiny basement apartment in Queens, New York.

---

22 Ibid. 211.
23 Ibid. 226.
24 Ibid. 229.

After a while Auslander meets his future wife. There are many further moments of hesitation, but Auslander and his wife eventually end up living a secular life. The conflict between orthodox and secular life seems to be unsolvable, so that Auslander breaks completely with his tradition and his parental home. But even though he does not follow the religious rules anymore, he still remains a deeply pious man. When he and his wife find out that they are going to be parents, Auslander starts to quarrel with himself:

My relationship with God had been an endless cycle not of the celebrated "faith followed by doubt," but of appeasement followed by revolt; placation followed by indifference; please, please, please, followed by fuck it, fuck You, fuck off. I do not keep Sabbath or pray three times a day or wait six hours between eating meat and milk. The people who raised me will say that I am not religious. They are mistaken. What I am not is observant. But I am painfully, cripplingly, incurably, miserably religious, […]. I believe in God. It´s been a real problem for me.[25]

As I have stated before and as it had shown already during his childhood and adolescence, Auslander indeed remains deeply religious. He himself offers a good distinction; he says he is a believer and a religious man but not *observant*. In particular, feelings of guilt and the fear of God's revenge remain a constant presence in Auslander's life that cannot be switched off despite all rational attempts of coping. He particularly fears for the life of his unborn child:

The kid doesn't have a chance. It's a trick. I know this God; I know how He works. The baby will be miscarried, or die during childbirth, or my wife will die during childbirth, or they'll both die during childbirth, or neither of them will die and I'll think I'm in the clear, and then on the drive home from the hospital, we'll collide head-on with a drunk driver and they'll both die later, my wife and child, in the emergency room just down the hall from the room where only minutes ago we stood so happy and alive and full of promise. […] The teachers from my youth are gone, the parents old and mostly estranged. The man they told me about, though – he's still around. I can't shake him. I read Spinoza. I read Nietzsche. I read National

---

25 Ibid. 71-72.

Lampoon. Nothing helps. I live with Him every day, and behold, He is still angry, still vengeful, still – eternally – pissed off.[26]

As on the day in his childhood, when he broke the Sabbath for the first time in his life, Auslander expects the worst of things to happen. Again, he is afraid that God will punish him by hurting his loved ones. When he and his wife find out that they are going to have a boy, this news makes him fall into a deep crisis about whether or not to circumcise the boy. Of course he receives plenty of advice from his friends, either pro- or anti-circumcision. After a while, he *himself* feels like a foreskin: "Cut off from my past, uncertain of my future, bloodied, beaten, tossed away."[27]

Eventually their child gets circumcised, not on the intended eighth day by a *mohel*, but on the day after his birth by a doctor in the hospital. When Auslander's mother finds out, she is devastated. Although his parents come to visit, Auslander realizes that this will probably be the last time he will ever see them. With his wife he moves away from New York, to live outside of Woodstock, the ultimate symbolic place of liberal and freedom-loving America.

The memoirs of Shalom Auslander are both an amusing and disturbing account of a Jewish boy coming of age in contemporary America. He tells quite a different story than many authors from a secular background might, and also contradicts to some extent the general arguments I have made about current Jewish-American literature. Unlike many of his peers, Auslander tells a story that shares many features that were common to the literature of the second generation – like Philip Roth. Due to the special conditions of his upbringing, he also tells awkward tales of managing the estrangement and unbridgeable conflict between the world at home and the world outside. In the end, we find Auslander living a good life with his family, a life that looks normal and secular from the outside. As readers of his memoirs, however, we have gained access to the twistedness and the turmoil of his mind, in which he continues living in constant fear of God, in whom he continues believing and with whom he continues having his imaginary dialogue.

---

26 Ibid. 3.
27 Ibid. 153.

If by the title's allusion, Auslander has deliberately set the stage for a comparison with Roth's Portnoy, in the end, one can indeed interpret his memoir as a reply that is both a sequel and a corrective. Auslander's experiences are anachronistic and different from most of his peers, because they tell the old story of assimilating by turning one's back to the family, its rules and surroundings. In this regard, indeed this is the good old story of Portnoy. However, Auslander's story is the story of a minority among American Jews, a small group of strict observers of orthodoxy. This sets his experience aside, both from his peers *and* from Roth. Finally, I would argue that Auslander's version of the classic breakout story is one that ends on a different and very special note, namely because he keeps believing in God and keeps living a tormented life due to this unshakable belief. Auslander thus takes the old story into a different direction and provides a corrective to Roth, because his account is really rather a 'lament,' as opposed to Portnoy's 'complaint.'

Shalom Auslander's memoirs are certainly not the only account of young religious Jews trying to break free from their pious homes and surroundings. There are also various books about women who have broken away and liberated themselves from an orthodox environment. However, unlike Auslander's snappy and funny memoirs, these books tend to describe the suppression of women within the orthodox community in a brutal way which leaves almost no room for humor and absurdity. To set a female example and account with a similar experience next to Auslander's, I will next introduce the memoirs of Deborah Feldman.

4.2 Deborah Feldman – Unorthodox

Deborah Feldman's memoir *Unorthodox: The Scandalous Rejection of My Hasidic Roots* (2012)[28] deals with a similar topic as Shalom Auslander's *Foreskin's Lament*, namely the physical and psychological escape of a young person – in this case a woman – from the Hasidic Satmar commu-

---

28 Feldman, Deborah. *Unorthodox: The Scandalous Rejection of My Hasidic Roots.* New York: Simon & Schuster, 2012.

nity.[29] Feldman describes her life as being patronized by her family, especially by her aunt, who eventually decides that she should find a husband when she is seventeen years old. Her mother has left the strict world of the Satmar community herself, when Feldman was a child, so the girl grew up with her grandparents, because the father could not take care of her due to a mental illness. She grows up being ashamed of her father, because of his behavior and appearance, and secretly dreams about imaginary parents who would get her braces for her crooked teeth. Basically Feldman fantasizes about living life like a typical WASP girl, playing tennis and having a girly bedroom overlooking the suburban lawn.[30] Like I have stressed in my reading of Auslander, such fantasies are rather reminiscent of the second generation's aspirations for assimilation. One could say that Feldman fantasizes about turning into the typical *shiksa* here, the character that has notoriously inhabited the stories of the second generation during the previous decades of Jewish-American literature.

One childhood memory of Feldman is about going ice-skating in the park with her cousin who attends a regular high school and is allowed to travel by herself. When they sit down for lunch – kosher tuna sandwiches on rye – a girl comes up to Feldman and offers her candy. To make sure that the candy is kosher, Feldman asks whether the girl is Jewish, and she replies: "I even go to Hebrew school and everything. I know the aleph-bet."[31] When Feldman sees that the candy is made by Hershey's, she quickly concludes that *Hersh* is the Yiddish word for deer, *ey* must be a diminutive form of it, so it has to be kosher indeed. But before she can devour it, her cousin tells her that it is in fact not kosher, since it is missing the *cholov Yisroel* stamp. Feldman is confused about how the girl can be

---

29 In a note to the book, Feldman describes the Satmar community as a Hasidic sect, originating from a city on the border of Hungary and Romania named Satu Mare (in Yiddish Satmar). During the Holocaust, the rabbi of Satu Mare was saved by Rudolf Kasztner and later immigrated to America. To commemorate their hometown, the rabbi and his followers named their religious movement after it. See: Feldman, Deborah. A Note from the Author *Unorthodox: The Scandalous Rejection of My Hasidic Roots*. New York: Simon & Schuster, 2012.
30 See: Ibid. 101.
31 Ibid. 15.

Jewish and still eat something that is not kosher. Like in Auslander's memoirs, this first encounter with unkosher food is a moment of importance in Feldman's memoirs. Although Feldman does not seem to develop the same fetish for unkosher food as Auslander, this first encounter is nevertheless interesting, because it is one of the very few points of contact with the secular or gentile outside world. It becomes obvious that this outside world is still something mysterious and strange to her, and this first encounter is one of innocent ignorance and naivety.

Feldman describes how she grew up in an unloving family, where nobody hugged, kissed or even said compliments to each other. A cold environment, where children get scolded and family members are watched "closely, ever ready to point out someone's spiritual or physical failing."[32] Upon the advice of her aunt Chaya and for unclear reasons, Feldman is sent to see a psychiatrist, but when she realizes that everything she tells the physician is being passed on to her aunt, she refuses to talk. Feldman questions her own behavior and thinking and wonders why she cannot be like all other pious girls at her age. She constantly has forbidden thoughts and wishes, wants to do things which are clearly not allowed in the rigid world of the Satmar community.

So while she feels mistreated by her aunt and grandparents, she has better memories of the times when her mother was still there. One memory is about her mother reading to her from a children book, something that Feldman misses and wishes to experience again. In general, she is very fond of books, but in her grandparents' household there are only prayer books. Secretly she goes to the public library in order to read secular books which are forbidden in her community, since reading English books "leaves [her] soul vulnerable, a welcome mat put out for the devil."[33] The young girl cannot understand the strict rules of her grandparents, telling her only to speak in Yiddish, the language of her ancestors. Instead, she confesses to the readers that she does not even think in Yiddish anymore, even questions the alleged holiness of her mother tongue:

---

32 Ibid. 18.
33 Ibid. 26.

Zeidy [her grandfather] says the English language acts like a slow poison to the soul. If I speak and read it too much, my soul will become tarnished to the point where it is no longer responsive to divine stimulation. Zeidy always insists I speak Yiddish, the language of my ancestors that God approves of. However, Yiddish is nothing but a hodgepodge of German, Polish, Russian, Hebrew and other random dialects. Many of them were once considered as secular as English. How is it that Yiddish is suddenly the language of purity and righteousness? Zeidy doesn't know it, but I don't even think in Yiddish anymore.[34]

Obviously the girl feels more connected to the English language than to Yiddish, and she has arrived at a point of doubting the rules and explanations of her grandfather. While Feldman feels uncomfortable with Yiddish, at the same time she feels strangely familiar with all the prohibited English literature she is secretly consuming:

Sometimes it feels like the authors of these books understand me, that they wrote these stories with me in mind. How else to explain the similarities between me and the characters in Roald Dahl's tales: unfortunate, precocious children despised and neglected by their shallow families and peers?[35]

When she reads *Pride and Prejudice,* she compares her life with the life of the Bennet sisters. Like them, she has to hope for a wealthy husband (either money- or character-wise) to marry her and provide her with a better life. She especially compares herself to Elisabeth Bennet, the witty heroine of the novel, who is too proud and independent to simply marry the first man with the right background and fortune. Although these comparisons are to some extent nothing but the childish fantasies of a young girl, the secret acquaintance – through literature – with such strong and independent female characters as Elisabeth Bennet, leave their mark on Feldman. Indeed, very much of Feldman's slow and continuous thought process of distancing herself from the community, seems to be sparked by books. Since her grandfather forbids her to read not only English but even Hebrew books – "they are for men only, he says; girls belong in the kitchen"[36] –

---

34 Ibid. 89.
35 Ibid. 20.
36 Ibid. 26.

Feldman hides a volume of the Talmud with English translations under her bed, so that she can learn more about what is denied to her. Retrospectively, she realizes that this must have been the moment when she lost her innocence and started to develop her own critical mind:

> One day I will look back and understand that just there was a moment in my life when I realized where my power lay, there was also a specific moment when I stopped believing in authority just for its own and started coming to my own conclusions about the world I lived in.[37]

Interestingly, in Feldman's memoirs, the young girl tries to escape the narrow world of her community by reading both worldly and holy books. It is in books, accordingly, that Feldman finds an alternative world and a secret way of rebelling against her community, which Shalom Auslander in his memoirs had achieved rather by consuming unkosher food and porn.

An important aspect of the Satmar community is living a pious life with strict rules about clothing and behavior. Interestingly, although the whole world of the Satmar community is built upon the pillars of abstinence, modesty, and religious faith, the religious elite is described as being wealthy – "rabbis are chauffeured in black Cadillacs and have private ritual baths built into their opulent homes"[38] – and extremely hierarchic in terms of familial connections to the rabbi:

> Mrs. Friedman is Satmar royalty; her maiden name is Teitelbaum and she is a second cousin of the rabbi himself. Rebbish, they call the lucky ones who can claim some connection with rabbinical ancestry.[39]

Obviously, everybody who can claim a relation to the Teitelbaum bloodline is looked up to as royalty. Accordingly, these hierarchies by birth are an important question to consider when it comes to finding a suitable husband or wife. Afraid that in this context she herself will have nothing to offer, Feldman again summarizes the community's sentiment with regard to family and descent: "If you have no roots, you have no legacy. All our

---

37 Ibid. 29.
38 Ibid. 87.
39 Ibid. 90.

worth is defined by the worth of our ancestors."[40] Although in a very different context, strikingly it seems to be this exact same credo that is powering the stories of such authors as Jonathan Safran Foer and Dara Horn. Their stories may take place in a completely secular environment that has little to do with the Hassidic world, but nevertheless, one gets the impression that at the core of Foer's and Horn's literary endeavors, there lies the same assumption, namely that the identity of a person – the term 'identity' here in exchange for the term 'worth' – depends on their ancestors and that a person is defined by the roots of the family.

While the young girl yearns for more freedom and possibilities, she senses that the restrictions of the Satmars and the deliberate separation from the surrounding outside world of New York City has to do a lot with clothing and looks. Not only do women have to shave their heads but they also have to dress in a certain way to cover certain body parts such as their collarbones, wrists and knees. Also men have to dress according to a pious code, to be recognized as servants of God. "'Assimilation,' my teacher always says, 'was the reason for the Holocaust. We try to blend in, and God punishes us for betraying him.'"[41] This religious contortion virtually blames secular Jews for having caused the Holocaust themselves, bringing God's punishment upon all Jews because they had assimilated. Like before, in Auslander's *Foreskin's Lament*, in moments like these, it seems as if the evocation of the Holocaust is misused to awaken feelings of guilt and shame in young people. Similar to the Holocaust-obsession that Auslander reported about – "Do you know how many Jews died at the hands of Nazis so you can keep kosher?"[42] – Feldman experiences pressure being put on her, for example when her grandmother constantly reminds her that "[she] survived only so that you could be born."[43] The declaration "We too are part of the legacy of loss"[44] becomes a constant reminder of this distinctive position in life.

---

40 Ibid. 95.
41 Ibid. 35.
42 Auslander, Shalom. *Foreskin's Lament. A Memoir*. London: Picador, 2009. 169.
43 Feldman, Deborah. *Unorthodox: The Scandalous Rejection of My Hasidic Roots*. New York: Simon & Schuster, 2012. 43.
44 Ibid. 43.

It is clear that women in the religious community are not allowed to speak their mind and act on their own. Every move outside the allegedly safe surrounding of the tight knit world seems like a betrayal of their religious belief, and attempts by women to speak their mind are not appreciated:

An empty vessel clangs the loudest. That's the adage I hear continuously, from Chaya, from the teachers at school, from the Yiddish textbooks. The louder a woman, the more likely she is to be spiritually bereft, [...].[45]

In the course of the book, the inferior standing of women in the ultra-orthodox community is often described. Women have to serve their husbands, bear children, but not engage in anything else, least of all with religious texts. It is also not the place for a woman to talk about herself. Feldman wonders how her grandmother, who survived the concentration camp Bergen-Belsen and lost all of her relatives during the Holocaust, can live without talking about her previous life in Europe. Silently she serves her family and never speaks about what happened to her in the past. In this aspect we might find yet another similarity to such authors as Foer and Horn, whose stories are largely infused by the search for a family history which has failed to be orally conveyed in the first place.

The most troublesome and dreadful experiences of Deborah Feldman's early teenage years seem to have happened exactly because she is a woman. When she is thirteen years old, her cousin Moshe comes to stay with her and her grandparents for a while. Although she knows that men and women are forbidden to be alone together, and although her grandfather scolds the cousin for even talking to her, she spends time alone with Moshe. Between prank calls and roasting marshmallows on the stove, there is a moment between them, which is not familiar to the young girl.

The air in the room changes. [...] I scrape the last of the marshmallow off the metal skewer with my teeth. Moshe watches me lick my lips and shakes his head in wonder.[46]

---

45 Ibid. 21.
46 Ibid. 65.

This strange atmosphere that Feldman in her innocent way cannot yet comprehend, turns into violence a few days later when Moshe tries to rape the young girl in the basement of their grandparents' house. When Feldman tries to tell her grandfather about it, she cannot find any words to describe what happened, because of her inexperience and plain ignorance of what the boy was actually doing to her. Eventually, she opens up to her aunt, and the cousin is sent off to Israel – unpunished – to get married there. Equally shocking as the attempted rape in this episode seems to be the lack of sexual education allowing the girl even to comprehend what is happening to her.

Talking about sexuality and the female body, accordingly, seems to be a taboo that had so far never been broken in Feldman's life. When she gets her first period, she is not aware of what this means and also the way her grandmother deals with the situation is less than comforting to the young girl.[47] At the same time, this episode reinforces the earlier impression that the female body is never properly talked about, quite to the disadvantage of the young girl. Despite being kept ignorant and intellectually undernourished, Feldman develops a strong and independent mind even at this young age. She decides that she does not want to a live life like her grandmother's:

I never want to be a rabbi's wife. Not if it means being like my bubbe and always having to submit to my husband's will. I am hungry for power, but not to lord over others, only to own myself.[48]

Regardless of her own wishes, a few years later, a traditional wedding is arranged for Feldman. Soon the preparations for a proper *shidduch* – a matchmaking process – are under way.[49] Although Feldman is familiar with

---

47 Although her grandmother provides her with sanitary articles, she also tells her granddaughter to hide them: "Such things don't need to be talked about, [...]. It doesn't do anyone any good." Ibid. 72.
48 Ibid. 87.
49 Feldman and her aunt and uncle meet up with the mother and sister of her possible husband-to-be. This meeting clearly serves the one and only purpose of looking at the girl and determining whether she is decent looking and suitable for the boy. On the other hand, also the possible husband must make his

this whole procedure, she feels like an animal being presented at a show. After the families approve, a meeting between Feldman and Eli, the future husband, is arranged. Of course the rest of the families are also in attendance and wait in the room next door. While talking to each other for the first time, Feldman feels sympathy for the young man, who tells her that he would like to travel to Europe. For a moment she even believes that after all, marriage might be her "plane ticket to freedom," a way to break free from the isolated walls of her religious home.[50]

Soon after the engagement, Feldman has to attend bridal classes where she is expected to learn everything about marriage and about her duties as a wife. She now hears about the term *niddah* for the first time, about being 'kicked aside,' being impure and forbidden during the days of her menstruation. Like many times before, Feldman is shocked and appalled by the things she is taught and what they imply about her community:

Every time I exit the [...] building where my *kallah* teacher lives, I am compelled to divide the women on the street into two categories – the ones who know all this, and the ones who don't. I am in the middle, beginning to learn about the pulse that really beats through this world I live in, but still in the dark about many things. I can't help but stare accusingly at the pious married women pushing double strollers down Lee Avenue. "Is this okay with you?" I want to ask. "Agreeing that you are dirty because you are a woman?" I feel betrayed by all the women in my life."[51]

Accordingly, Feldman feels insulted as a woman by the concept of *niddah* and cannot comprehend how all the other women of the religious community can accept such rules. Although she is not even finished with her lessons yet, she feels disappointed by the beliefs and rules at the core of her community. It is explained to her that this concept of *niddah* keeps a Jewish marriage alive:

---

    appearance before the Feldman family. Only if both parties approve of what they see, a chaperoned meeting between the two young people is arranged.
50 Feldman, Deborah. *Unorthodox: The Scandalous Rejection of My Hasidic Roots*. New York: Simon & Schuster, 2012. 131.
51 Ibid. 141.

It never gets boring. (Does she mean to say it never gets boring for the man? I shouldn't ask that question.) Men only want what they can't have, she explains to me. They need the consistent pattern of denial and release. I don't know if I like thinking of myself that way, as an object made available and the unavailable for a man to enjoy.[52]

Obviously, Feldman's mind is critical and independent enough to recognize and criticize the patriarchal and misogynist structures underlying the marriage she is about to enter. However, she does not yet have the strength to act accordingly and to break away from her family and community. At the *kallah* lesson, she voices her unease but decides to remain silent – once again – after being confronted, being too afraid that everyone will know about her raising a fuss. Feldman also has to go to the *mikvah*, but this has to be done under the cover of darkness, as in general, female hygiene is a topic which is not to be spoken about. In another class, girls like Feldman learn how to behave as wives, meaning how to seek compromise, which she quickly exposes as women's obligation to give in. In her last marriage class, Feldman learns about the 'holy' bond of husband and wife. It is quite obvious that these are topics which are never openly discussed in the religious community, and only this late in her life Feldman inspects herself to get to know her own body. It is alarming and saddening that in an age where the female body is celebrated as a stronghold, women are told to be proud of their bodies and feel empowered by their femininity, this girl lives in a world where sexuality and intimacy are something to be ashamed of and not to be talked about.

A week later, Feldman gets married. The description of the wedding night sounds anything but relaxed and intimate, because both partners are completely unaware of what they are doing.[53] On the next morning, her aunt comes by to shave off Feldman's hair according to Satmar rules. Soon thereafter the new mother-in-law arrives to ask very bluntly how the wedding night was and also tells Feldman that she already knows that "it

---

52 Ibid. 140.
53 As a sex therapist later tells her, it is probably the repressive way of dealing with sexuality and intimacy that causes Feldman to have vaginal cramps preventing the newlywed couple from having intercourse. See: Ibid. 168, 184.

wasn't finished."[54] Feldman is shocked to hear that her husband has already gone around talking about the night, and it becomes obvious that there is no privacy even in marriage. Accordingly, Feldman is terrified that soon the entire community might know about their problems: "[...] having people point and whisper about me, about the girl that couldn't do it. Oh, the horror. I will never live this down."[55]

A few days later, Feldman's husband explains to her his own 'performance difficulties' by confessing that in the Yeshiva the boys were sexually pleasing each other, since masturbating was strictly prohibited and that hence he is used to being aroused only by the sight of a man. "I don't even know if I should be attracted to you. I didn't even have an idea of what a girl looked like before I saw you."[56] Naturally, Eli would never consider himself homosexual, and his confession does not ease Feldman's own feeling of guilt. The couple goes to see various doctors and therapists, but they still fail to consummate their marriage. After a while, Eli refuses to come home and stays with his family, who suggests that he should get a divorce, because his wife seems to be unable to have sexual intercourse. Again, the couple's intimate problems are publicly discussed and attributed solely to Feldman as a woman. Finally, the two are reconciled and to everybody's delight, Feldman gets pregnant. Before the baby is born, the couple decides to move upstate to Airmont, NY, a town next to Monsey, which we already know from Shalom Auslander's *Foreskin's Lament*.

After her son is born, Feldman starts to think about leaving her husband. She finally comes to the point of realizing that she does not fit into the Hasidic community with all her religious doubts and secular dreams. She stops going to the *mikvah* and instead takes up reading (forbidden) women magazines in parking lots. The longer she lives her life as a wife and mother in the small town, the more she doubts it:

---

54 Ibid. 170.
55 Ibid. 171. In this moment of shame, Feldman blames only herself for not being able to consummate the marriage. Even though her husband also played a role in the failed attempt, she sees herself as the only one who is responsible for the situation.
56 Ibid. 172.

I can't bear the thought of living an entire lifetime on this planet and not getting to do all the things I dream of doing, simply because they are not allowed. [...] I don't think I can be happy unless I'm truly independent.[57]

When she rents a documentary about gay orthodox Jews whose sexual orientation and religious beliefs were incompatible, she finds out that her own mother once left their community because she was gay. Feldman starts to look for colleges in order to earn a real degree for a real job, but does not yet tell her husband about it. However, she does tell her mother, with whom she got back in contact, when she is admitted to college and enrolls in creative writing and literature. Her professor tells her about Yiddish poetry and seems to know a lot about orthodox culture, which leaves Feldman surprised, because she has always experienced her world to be so secluded from the outside world and would have expected this outside world in turn also to be ignorant about her community.

On a day out in Manhattan with a class mate and after eating *treif* food, Feldman suddenly declares: "I don't want to be a Hasid anymore."[58] But deep inside she hesitates, since this is the only life she ever knew. She is also worried about her young son, who is about to start his religious education. Feldman is torn between the religious and familiar world of the Hasidic community and the freedom and joy she feels in the secular world of her college. She decides to start an anonymous blog where she writes about her daily struggle as a woman in a religious world and is amazed by the positive feedback she receives. Bit by bit, Feldman starts to dissolve her old life, selling her jewelry to get some money, and renting a car to move her belongings. She moves away from her old community and changes her phone number. Her son learns English and Feldman is happy to see him grow up as a 'normal' American child. Although she is relieved to have left her old life behind, she still has positive thoughts about it: "I have freed myself from my past, but I have not let go of it. I cherish the moments and experiences that formed me. I have lived the story."[59]

This story, the life story of Deborah Feldman, is quite a different story after all, not only from other writers of her age with a secular background,

---

57 Ibid. 229.
58 Ibid. 232.
59 Ibid. 247.

but also from Shalom Auslander's memoirs. The perspective of a female dropout on the orthodox community turns out to be yet more shocking in many regards. While the tone of Feldman's narrative is one of seriousness and at times bitterness, Auslander's account was rather fueled by a sinister and sarcastic, yet comedic tone. Towards the end, however, she finds the strength to look back at her past with a certain closure that allows her to embrace her former life simply as part of her life story. She will live free of her family and free of the Satmar community, but she will remember them as the origin of her story and future life. Auslander's memoirs, on the other hand, end on a somewhat darker note of cognitive dissonance, as he seems unable to shed his feelings of fear and guilt for doing what he nevertheless knows is right.

Curiously, Feldman's story – like Auslander's – seems to escape to some extent the logic of Hansen's three-generations-theory. Unlike most of their peers, these two young Jewish American authors have not comfortably been born to be part of American mainstream society by birth, but had to fight their way into this society as young adults. However, these stories of orthodox life – stories of breakout, as much as stories of return, as I will show in the next subchapter – are part of the contemporary Jewish-American mix. According to my own definition of a new generation of Jewish-American writing, based mainly on authors' similar experiences during upbringing and resulting in similar interests and issues, I must admit some concessions here. Certainly, the stories of Feldman and Auslander are different from most of their peers, as was their upbringing. However, Mannheim's theory of a generation – on which my definition of a new generation of writers is based – allows for such discrepancies, which can be understood as separate generational units. Breakout stories from orthodoxy certainly form a minor sub-stratum in the generation of young contemporary American Jews. These stories tell a very specific early life experience that differs in many aspects from the experiences of others. Yet, these stories take place within the larger setting of an open American society at the turn of the 21st century that allows for individual life choices taking multiple paths. Like other authors' stories, after all, the stories of Feldman and Auslander deal with their generation's major question of how to be Jewish in America today. Even if they are part of a small and very particular sub-stratum within their larger generation, these breakout stories from orthodoxy thus add to the mix and can be understood both as product of their time and co-contributor to contemporary Jewish culture. Although different from the fictional explorations of family and past, theirs are nevertheless new stories of searching and finding one's own way of being Jewish in contemporary America.

4.3 ALLEGRA GOODMAN – THE FAMILY MARKOWITZ

Having presented two stories of escape from the world of ultra-orthodox Jewish life in America, one by a man and one by woman, I think it is necessary to point out that such transformations are not mono-directional. I have presented two out of many accounts of religious Jews 'making over' to the secular side. However, it is possible that there are equally as many stories of the opposite: formerly secular and disaffected Jews turning to a religious and orthodox life. This classic return to religion, *baalei teshuva*, is described, for example, in Wendy Shalit's *A Return to Modesty: Discovering the Lost Virtue* (1999) or in Carol Orsborn's *Return from Exile: One Woman's Journey Back to Judaism* (1998). As early as 1989, such literary encounters with orthodoxy have been noticed and discussed as a new trend by Thomas Friedman,[60] as described by Tresa Grauer in her own study of contemporary Jewish-American writing:

An early herald of what has come to be seen as a major literary trend: a new era of Jewish American writing that looks seriously at issues of theology, religious observance, and traditional Jewish texts.[61]

Accordingly, the deliberate return to matters of religion and to the traditional texts of Judaism is yet another possible theme within the wide spectrum of current Jewish-American writing. In an attempt at sorting through and organizing this wide spectrum, Susanne Klingenstein has

---

60 See: Friedman, Thomas: "Back to Orthodoxy: The New Ethic and Ethnics in American Jewish Literature." *Contemporary Jewry* 10.1. (1989).
61 Grauer, Tresa. "Identity Matters: Contemporary Jewish American Writing." *The Cambridge Companion to Jewish American Literature*. Eds. Kramer, Michael P. and Hana Wirth-Nesher. Cambridge: Cambridge University Press, 2003. 274.

suggested six overarching and frequently recurring topics in contemporary Jewish-American literature:

Six marginal worlds have most frequently served as sources of creative inspiration and Jewish authenticity: the shtetl, [accentuating] Klingenstein] Israel, Orthodox and Hasidic communities, Holocaust survivors, and immigrants.⁶²

While my own argument with regard to Israel would be that the old world seems to be equally, if not even more present in contemporary Jewish fiction, I agree with the rest of Klingenstein's list. The three major themes of *shtetl*, immigrant life, and the Holocaust are understood to be parts of the broader trend of looking back at the past and at family histories, as I have discussed in the third chapter. I will not deal with homosexuality as a major theme explicitly, although it does resonate not only in Deborah Feldman's account but also in Gideon Lewis-Kraus' *A Sense of Direction* which I will discuss at the end of this chapter. However, in recognizing orthodox and Hasidic communities as a major theme, I have so far only spoken about departures from this "marginal world," in the terms of Klingenstein, and would therefore like to provide – at least briefly – an example of literature that deals with a departure from the secular world, a story of return to the orthodox.

In her collection of entangled short stories called *The Family Markowitz* (1996), Allegra Goodman touches upon the topic of somebody reconnecting with religion, somebody from the young third generation of American Jews. Goodman's book about the lives of a Jewish American family has been depicted "as a microcosm of community, the place of generational continuity and rift."⁶³ I am especially interested in the rift that is caused between the youngest (third) generation, and the parent generation, because of religion.

---

62 Klingenstein, Susanne. "Jewish American Fiction, Act III: Eccentric Sources of Inspiration." *Studies in American Jewish Literature* 18 (1999): 83.
63 Aarons, Victoria. "The Orthodoxy Unbound, or Moses in Suburbia: Allegra Goodman's The Family Markowitz." *What Happened to Abraham? Reinventing the Covenant in American Jewish Fiction*. Newark: University of Delaware Press, 2005. 107.

In one of the short stories called "The Four Questions," Goodman writes about how the family Markowitz comes together for Passover. Sarah and Ed Markowitz, the parents, are expecting their adult children Miriam, Ben, Avi, and Yehudit for the *Seder* diner. This celebration is to be held at the old ranch house of Sarah's parents on Long Island. Over the past couple of years one of their daughters, Miriam, a twenty-three-year-old medical student at Harvard, has become more and more observant. She has even started bringing her own dishes and cutlery to her grandparents' home, because they do not themselves keep kosher. Before she arrives, Sarah and her mother Estelle talk about Miriam and who might have influenced her to become more religious. The grandmother suspects Miriam's fiancé Jonathan to be the 'bad' influence causing her to change; "it wasn't from anyone in this family."[64] Although this would be a simple and convenient explanation, Miriam's mother Sarah has to admit that her change started even before she met Jonathan. When Miriam arrives and her father rushes out in order to welcome his daughter and pay for her taxi, the first thing Miriam notices is that he is still holding a piece of pastry in his hands, which is technically forbidden during Passover. He knows that his daughter disapproves of his behavior, herself probably having cleaned her apartment from all *hometz* during the last couple of days:

She has become very puritanical, his daughter, and it baffles him. They had raised the children in a liberal, rational, joyous way – raised them to enjoy the Jewish tradition, and Ed can't understand why Miriam would choose austerity and obscure ritualism. She is only twenty-three [...]. How can a young girl be attracted to this kind of legalism. It disturbs him.[65]

Obviously, Miriam's father is bothered by her choice to follow the religious rules of Judaism more strictly. Having raised his children in a secular and "rational" way, he does not understand why she would now choose what he calls "ritualism" and "legalism." However, whatever her reasons, she has decided to leave the broad and liberal path onto which her parents have sent her, and chooses the seemingly narrower path of a life according to the

---

64 Goodman, Allegra. "The Four Questions." *The Family Markowitz*. New York: Farrar, Straus and Giroux, 1997. 185.
65 Ibid. 187-188.

rules. Victoria Aaron has interpreted Miriam's urge to find a safe haven within orthodoxy, as the return

[...] to an origin, to what she perceives to be, ironically, the protection of the covenant and the well-defined structures and strictures of Ancient Jewish Law.[66]

This reading assumes that it is probably exactly *because* of her very liberal upbringing – by her typically second generation parents, who symbolize an assimilated, secular, liberal, and intellectual American Jewry – that Miriam, in search for clearer guidance and more structure in life, has turned to the safety and dependability of orthodoxy. It seems that the young woman is overwhelmed by the endless possibilities and "seductions of American life"[67] and longs for more assurance and constancy in her faith. Or as Dara Horn puts it in a more amusing way:

When Jews came to this country, the way to piss off your parents was to eat pork and marry a shiksa, now the best way to piss off your parents is to go to Chabad [...], marry at 18, have 10 kids, and refuse to eat in their house because they're not kosher enough [...].[68]

If according to Hansen's sociological thesis every generation feels the need to break with the ways of the previous generation and to try their own new paths, ironically, for Miriam this means 'pissing her parents off' by becoming observant. And this indeed she does: When Miriam brings her plastic dishes into the kitchen, her grandmother Estelle tries to stop her, but Miriam reminds her that these dishes are for Passover. Estelle, piqued, replies: "This is the good china. [...] These are the Pesach dishes."[69]

---

66 Aarons, Victoria. "The Orthodoxy Unbound, or Moses in Suburbia: Allegra Goodman's The Family Markowitz." *What Happened to Abraham? Reinventing the Covenant in American Jewish Fiction.* Newark: University of Delaware Press, 2005. 104.
67 Ibid. 105.
68 Dara Horn quoted in Sax, David. "Rise of the New Yiddishists." *Vanity Fair* April 2009. 12 June 2015.
69 Goodman, Allegra. "The Four Questions." *The Family Markowitz.* New York: Farrar, Straus and Giroux, 1997. 188.

Curiously, Miriam surpasses even the Jewish ambitions of her own grandparents, possibly a certain deviance from the Hansen-scheme. Interestingly, Estelle is annoyed by her granddaughter's observance and seems to side with the liberal standpoint of her daughter Sarah. At the same time, however, she is worried about the seriousness of her other grandson Avi's relationship with his non-Jewish girlfriend Amy, thereby taking the typical role of the first generation mother/grandmother again who disapproves of intermarriage. To Estelle's regret, Amy is actually everything she could wish for: focused, helpful and considerate. If only her uncle was not a Methodist priest! As it seems, the poor grandmother is being 'pissed off' by both grandchildren at this Passover, one bringing home a *shiksa*, and the other turning orthodox.

When it is time to begin the *Seder*, Ed, the father, starts to read from the *Haggadah* and talks about the meaning of Passover. However, "he can't help noticing Miriam as he says this. It's obvious that she is ignoring him. She is sitting chanting to herself out of her orthodox Birnbaum *Haggadah*, and it offends him."[70] Miriam tells her father that he has skipped the most important parts of the *Seder* and accuses him of shortening the whole service from year to year. Ed, on the other hand, feels undermined by his own daughter in his traditional role as the head of the family who is leading them through the ceremony. It becomes obvious that the family's Jewishness is demonstrated by tradition rather than by actual religious observance. This is why the rest of the family is so confused and even offended by the fact that Miriam actually takes the religious aspects of her Judaism seriously and begins to follow the rules.

Clearly, out of the wide spectrum of possibilities in rediscovering their Jewishness that is available to the current generation of young Jews in America, the return to Judaism in a stricter sense, namely to the rules, to the written word, and to orthodox observance, is an important option that needs to be mentioned. The story of Miriam in Allegra Goodman's *The Family Markowitz* is an example showing us that such a return to religion is a trajectory that can be taken and that reverberates in the fictions of the young generation of authors.

---

70 Ibid. 193-194.

4.4 LISA SCHIFFMAN – GENERATION J

In *Generation J* (1999), the American anthropologist and writer Lisa Schiffman creates a completely different image from the three previous accounts. Unlike Auslander and Feldman, Lisa Schiffman grew up in a secular, if not completely atheist Jewish family. Her parents' relationship to religious Judaism is coined by indifference, disregard and even hostility. As a child, Schiffman once attends a Christian service with a friend, and later asks her parents why her own family never goes to any religious service. She is quickly rebuffed by her father who says that he himself "went as a kid and understood nothing." He goes on to explain his point of view which is a generalized rejection of everything religious: "Religions, all of them, are a hoax. They're a business. And religious leaders? They're the smartest businesspeople around."[71] So while Schiffman's father does not believe in any spiritual content and perceives of religion only as a shell that is run like a business, her mother chooses less hostile words but nevertheless agrees with her husband, that religious services and rituals are of no importance to her: "I don't go to synagogue. It's just not for me. The prayers, the sermons – they're not what makes me Jewish. I don't believe in them."[72] As it seems, Schiffman's parents are perfectly content this way and do not seem to feel the necessity to raise any further questions. Schiffman's mother says that it is not religion that makes her Jewish, however, she fails to provide her daughter with a sense of what else it might be instead that makes her Jewish. It is exactly this question, therefore, that Lisa Schiffman raises in her early adult years and which is the central theme of her book *Generation J*.

Schiffman was born and raised in Levitown, New York, probably the archetype of all post-war suburbs. In this neighborhood Jews were a minority, and as a child, Schiffman often feels a burning desire to be as 'normal' as her Christian friends:

If I could have ditched my religion, I would have. I was embarrassed to be a Jew. It made people notice me in a way that made me uncomfortable. I wanted to be like my friend Gina Gagliano. I wanted a house where Christmas lights hung outside all

---

71 Schiffman, Lisa. *Generation J*. New York: Harper San Francisco, 1999. 6.
72 Ibid. 6.

year, where the Virgin Mary was immortalized on dishware, where grace was something you and everyone around you at the dinner table said while holding hands.[73]

Accordingly, Schiffman reports that she felt uncomfortable for being noticed as Jewish and being distinguished as different in a surrounding that was predominantly Christian. Although she has never been raised to have any affiliation with her religion, she admits that she would easily have sacrificed it in order to blend in. However, because her family is not even religious, it cannot be due to their religion that they are noticed as different. Rather, what Schiffman experiences during her childhood is being called out and stamped as Jewish by a kind of ethno-cultural racism of others. At school she is sometimes ridiculed for being Jewish for no apparent reason, and also in the adult world, anti-Semitism could often be encountered: "Levitown, where expressions like *Jew'em* down and words like kike were heard as frequently as the roar of lawn mowers."[74] As a child, Schiffman would have done anything to become more like her Christian friend Gina Gagliano. Curiously, this ambition to blend in, that Schiffman shows at a young age, is quite reminiscent of the assimilation-aspirations of the previous generation of Jewish-Americans. However, she notices herself, that there is not even something she could shed in order to be more like the others. She may not be wearing a cross necklace and her family may not display any Christmas lights on their house, but other than such omissions she and her family do not seem to be any different than others, except for being looked at as Jewish and therefore being labelled different.

Only after graduating from college with a degree in anthropology and after marrying a gentile, Schiffman consciously and on her own terms, turns to the question of Judaism and being Jewish, the result of which is *Generation J*. In this autobiographical text, Schiffman recounts how she sets out on a quest for her Jewish identity. In the beginning, Schiffman attends a workshop in which she is asked to describe what it means to be Jewish from the perspective of each of her relatives. Her first instinct tells her to run for the door, but then she decides to stay and take part in the exercise, in order "to make sense of the question that American Jews kept

---

73 Ibid. 5.
74 Ibid. 5.

asking: What does it mean to be Jewish?"[75] A woman in the workshop is asked to reveal her results to the group and offers a possibly typical spectrum of Jewishness. Her grandparents, she explains, fled persecution in Europe, and therefore being Jewish meant unsafety and hardship for them. Another grandparent's point of view getting presented is: "I'm a Jew, and that means following the rules without question."[76] Also the component of reproduction and raising Jewish children is an answer the woman would expect one of her grandparents to give, thereby showing an awareness that ensuring the continuity of Judaism could be an important factor. However, she also tells the class about what her father would probably say, namely: "I'm an atheist Jew – formerly a Communist – and to me that means religion is meaningless."[77] When the woman is finished with her presentation, the workshop leader, an ethno therapist, asks her what her own point of view is. Her answer clearly shows the current indecisiveness and surplus of possibilities of living Judaism in the United States: "'I'm a Jew who is spiritual,' she says, 'and to me that means I haven't found my own way.'"[78] Although she admits to not having found her way of being Jewish yet – a fact that is also reflected in her attendance of the workshop in the first place – the woman claims to be a 'spiritual' Jew. She claims the term 'spiritual' for herself, accordingly, although unable to define what that means except if one takes the contorted definition of 'not having found one's way' as a proper definition of the term. Obviously, the woman does not notice the contradiction inherent to her point of view. Nevertheless, Schiffman picks up on the idea and on the term of 'wayfinding' from this woman's awkward self-description, and contemplates this to be like the process of mapping an identity:

My own Jewish identity was impossible to map. It defied the idea of precise boundaries, refused to have its coordinates pinned down and traced. Its borders shifted. There were variations and anomalies in the landscape. I knew this. Still, I

---

75 Ibid. 2.
76 Ibid. 3.
77 Ibid. 3.
78 Ibid. 3.

imagined trying to map my own path. Was there a path for an ambivalent Jew? I wanted to create one.[79]

So while the term 'wayfinding' has lead Schiffman to this metaphor of cartography, she admits that her own path is equally unclear, her own way equally unfound as that of the 'spiritual' woman. She calls herself an 'ambivalent' Jew which can only be interpreted as somebody who has not found a single definition (yet) but who loosely swings between various definitions.

Schiffman then continues to tell the reader about her own first steps in finding out more about Judaism. Living in Manhattan and having just earned her degree in social anthropology, she decides to put some of the methods she has learned to work and starts a documentary film project on the Lubavitchers of Crown Heights:

I wanted to film Jewish life rather than take part in it. I'd just gotten my degree in social anthropology. This meant that I was a trained outsider, a watcher; someone who knew how to question, film, take notes on other tribes. Now the tribe I planned to observe was my own.[80]

Once she starts shooting, Schiffman is surprised at what she finds, namely a world that is so utterly different from her own, that indeed she rather seems to be watching a foreign tribe than her own:

It was village life, a shtetl. That first day, our lens caught sight of the accoutrements of devout Jewish life: images of flickering candles, fingers touching mezuzah, [...] a forearm wrapped in teffilin.[81]

Schiffman decides to dig deeper and is welcomed to attend the Shabbat with one family. When she sits at the table with them, she suddenly notices that "these people [...] seemed to have something that [she] didn't." Schiffman admits that "they seemed whole. They knew who they were.

---

79 Ibid. 4.
80 Ibid. 6.
81 Ibid. 7.

However extreme, they inhabited their religion."[82] Although she deliberately chooses not to live a religious life, nevertheless, Schiffman seems to envy the orthodox family for their apparent confidence in themselves. Noticing that not only religion but also this sense of clarity is lacking in her life, she decides to return to Crown Heights in order to film inside the synagogue on Eastern Parkway, the Lubavitch world headquarters. Sitting upstairs in the section for women, again she senses a chasm between herself and the others. A strange feeling of separation and estrangement overcomes her:

> I felt like there was an invisible wall between me and the women surrounding me. [...] Around me were opaque walls bounding the synagogue, separating those inside from the unkosher world outside. Walls, I thought – they separate Jews from the rest of the world and separate Jews from each other. Suddenly, in the midst of so many other Jews, I felt alone. I didn't belong. Not at this temple or at any other. Not, perhaps anywhere in this religion. I had no one with whom to be Jewish. [...] My family was uncomfortable with organized religion – even their own. And me? I hadn't a clue what it meant to be a Jew. I was lost, a Jew without a path.[83]

It is interesting how Schiffman notices the same virtual wall, the same separation and barrier between the orthodox and the secular world as Shalom Auslander and Deborah Feldman. While theirs had been a gaze from the inside out, now we get to know the counterpart, Schiffman's gaze from the outside in. Both parties are unsatisfied with their own world at the time of contact and look at the other world beyond these virtual walls as a place of wonder and mystery, and a place where people seem to live simpler and possibly better lives. Nevertheless, Schiffman notices that she does not belong there. She feels alone among all the religious people surrounding her, because she knows that she will never share their experience and religious belief. It hurts her to admit it to herself, but in this moment in the synagogue she notices two things, the first being that she will not find her answers in religion and the second that this leaves her completely lost and clueless.

---

82 Ibid. 7.
83 Ibid. 8.

Experiencing orthodox life has not helped Schiffman much in finding answers to her questions, and her search continues, leading her on a series of often funny and awkward experiences. There is a chapter about intermarriages and the predicament of finding a rabbi who would marry a Jewish woman to a non-Jewish husband. Next, there follows a chapter called the 'Zen of Being Jewish' that deals with Jewish Buddhism and a formerly secular Jew who – with the help of Buddhist meditation – found his calling to become an orthodox Jewish rabbi. Feldman also takes part in another workshop with ritual dances and chanting. She goes to a *mikvah* for the first time in her life, because she feels this "was something that reached the upper limit of that state of being I'd call *very Jewish*".[84] She drags her parents to a synagogue to attend a *Rosh Hashanah* service together. She attends a *Shabbat* service at a center for Jewish meditation, realizes she does not sing well, and finds a German voice therapist who should lead her to God – to the sound of God – through singing, only to find out that the woman is the daughter of a high ranking Nazi official. She tries cabalistic mysticism, reads the Torah, and has a Star of David painted using henna on her shoulder for the pagan wedding of a friend. In short, Schiffman seems to be – as she herself has announced – afloat. Schiffman also deals with the question of keeping kosher. Although usually she does not keep kosher, she feels uncomfortable with eating pork:

No, I'm not kosher. Well, yes, maybe I am. Kind of. It's an assimilated-Jewish thing. Pork freaks me out. Shrimp is fine. Lobster's fine. [...] But I know I'm not alone. Ask another Jew.[85]

At first, Schiffman thinks she should start an experiment about eating kosher for a while, but then decides to do exactly the opposite: to eat *un*kosher for a week, that is: pork fried rice, bacon strips, Pastrami with melted Swiss cheese, pork loins. Especially the latter – served on the fourth day of the experiment – she has to force down almost violently as her stomach tightens. "I kept going," she reports, "forking in piece after piece, chewing, nearly drowning in the taste and smell of that pig."[86] Even though

---

84 Ibid. 77.
85 Ibid. 129-130.
86 Ibid. 133.

Schiffman, like most of her Jewish frie[nds ha]s never followed the *kashrut*, the Jewish dietary requirements, she ob[viousl]y disdains pork. She does this experiment only to see if it changes a[nythin]g about her attitude towards *being Jewish*. And to her surprise, it real[ly do]es, because in the moment of forcing herself to eat the pork loins, she [realiz]es that paradoxically "eating pork made me feel Jewish."[87]

Early on her obscure path of finding [a J]ewish identity, after visiting the great Lubavitch synagogue, Schiffman [ ] realized that she "was lost, a Jew without a path." This dictum sets not [only] the tone for the chapters to come, but also serves as a decent [sum]mary in retrospect. Her autobiographic account *Generation J* tells [a]bout an individual's bizarre quest for a Jewish identity without a gu[ide] and without a goal. She herself summarizes this obscure journey i[n ter]ms that seem to grapple and ridicule its inanity:

Jews in search of a perfect clarity. We're turning a[wa]y from the religion into which we were born. We're turning to Wicca, to New Ageism, to Buddhism, to nothing. We're burning sage sticks at home and pounding drums in the forest. We're meeting with psychics, shrugging our shoulders at rabbis, listening to the music of twelfth-century nuns. Our chakras are opening, our kundalini is bursting. Our mouths open in the shape of questions.[88]

Although Schiffman does not arrive at a fixed answer to her questions or a solution to her identity problem, she nevertheless manages to drag out into the open the paradoxes of being Jewish without being religious in contemporary America. Towards the end, Schiffman learns to embrace what she has initially called being an "ambivalent Jew," because this means precisely that she has the freedom of going her own path, as convoluted as it may be:

Somehow, I've learned the thing that matters. In the years that have passed since I began my journey into Judaism, I've changed. I've become Jewish by choice as much as by birth.[89]

---

87 Ibid. 133.
88 Ibid. 11-12.
89 Ibid. 166.

She realizes, accordingly, that it was exactly this journey of searching that has defined her Judaism, simply because she chose to take it. For Schiffman, there will be no clear cut answer to the question what being Jewish means today, however, she gives in to this openness and embraces it: "Judaism was a trajectory, a continuum, an intuitive process punctuated by moments of cognition."[90] Accordingly, Schiffman's Jewishness is not something static, but rather fluid, turning into a form of identity process that is neither a fixed cultural nor religious entity.[91]

Being part of the third and post-assimilated generation of American Jews, Schiffman longs for an update of her Judaism or Jewishness, which can be connected to her generations' lifestyle and values. By trying to modernize Judaism, she also tries to evolve her own identity in a religious, cultural and spiritual way.[92] Clearly, Schiffman's book is a prime example for my argument of how the members of her generation long for their Jewish heritage, almost desperately trying to reconnect to it. Unlike Foer and Horn, Schiffman does not turn to the past. Also the family and religious return are of no help to her. Instead, she goes on her private trip of experimentation in order to find out about all the possible ways of 'being Jewish.' Schiffman's conclusion is that there is not the one and only way, but that the process of searching has brought her closer. This exact process of searching and looking and trying and wondering is – according to my argument – the essential and defining feature of her generation. Lisa Schiffman makes the battle call for her entire generation, the 'Generation J,' in what seems to be an ideal rephrasing of my overall argument:

---

90 Ibid. 157.
91 Again, I would like to refer to Sara R. Horowitz's quote as already mentioned in the introduction of this thesis, which confirms Schiffman's notion: "The best of contemporary Jewish American fiction seeks to complicate a foreshortened and simplified discussion about Jewish identity and Jewishness in our time. In looking at America's Jewish question, they opt to explore the in-betweenness, the shifting borders, rather than to resolve them by engraving the borderlines." Horowitz, Sara R. "Mediating Judaism: Mind, Body, Spirit, and Contemporary North American Jewish Fiction." *AJS Review* 30.2 (Nov. 2006): 253.
92 See: Schiffman, Lisa. *Generation J.* New York: Harper San Francisco, 1999. 75.

I'm not alone. I'm part of a generation of fragmented Jews. We're in a kind of limbo. We're suspended between young adulthood and middle age, between Judaism and atheism, between a desire to believe in religion and a personal history of skepticism. Call us a bunch of searchers. Call us post-Holocaust Jews. Call us Generation J.[93]

There is nothing to be added.

4.5 GIDEON LEWIS-KRAUS – A SENSE OF DIRECTION

In Gideon Lewis-Kraus' *A Sense of Direction* (2012), the author starts on a journey that is mentioned in the subhead of the book: "Pilgrimage for the Restless and the Hopeful." Lewis-Kraus belongs to a generation of young professionals, who are highly educated, full of potential and opportunities, and yet they cannot decide what to do with their lives. Lewis-Kraus calls these the

[...] problems of indecision, boredom, and the suspicion that more interesting things were happening in more fashionable places to more attractive people.[94]

With little financial worries and possible stopovers in Saigon, New York, Kiev or Rome, this generation really lives on the theme of globalization. Accordingly, a friend of the author has moved to Tallinn because he hopes to find new productivity and focus there as a writer. This is the opposite of what Gideon Lewis-Kraus hopes for: "I'd moved to Berlin precisely for its lack of constraint, hoping that its sense of vast possibility would help me figure out what I wanted."[95] Lewis-Kraus who lives in Berlin as an American expatriate and feels that he has plenty of time to spare, decides to go and visit his friend in Tallinn. However, upon his return four days later, strangely, he does not remember a single thing about this trip and checks his little black notebook to find clues about the past days he apparently spent in a blur. The only entry he finds is a short note: "Camino de Santiago

---

93 Ibid. 11.
94 Lewis-Kraus, Gideon. *A Sense of Direction*. London: Penguin Books, 2012. 4.
95 Ibid. 4.

– sense of purpose – June 10."[96] As it turns out, he has agreed to go on a pilgrimage in Santiago de Compostela with his friend Tom.

After living with his brother in San Francisco for a year, Lewis-Kraus had decided to move to Berlin:

> Everyone I encountered in Berlin seemed to have the freedom – economically and culturally – to do exactly what he or she pleased. [...] The other reason was that, perhaps because of that freedom, Berlin felt like the center of something surprising and important, and I couldn't help thinking it would be a good place for an aspiring writer. The rumors of a new Lost Generation were a terrible cliché, but it was hard to resist them.[97]

Unlike his brother, he did not have a real job in San Francisco and with the help of a Fulbright scholarship, relocating to Berlin is no difficulty at all to him. On the one hand Lewis-Kraus hears Berlin's calling as the new place to be, the new world capital of party and leisure. On the other hand, he tells himself that as a writer he will creatively profit from this relocation. And indeed, after his trip to Talinn, he develops an idea which becomes the origin of his book: "I wanted to write about what it meant that secular people were taking up these religious pilgrimages in large numbers."[98] The remainder of his book indeed tells us the story of how Lewis-Kraus himself sets out to undertake a number of such pilgrimages in order to write about this experience.

Nevertheless, both the book and his journey begin with his time in Berlin, the city which seems to consist mainly of American students, artists and other seekers, finally wanting to escape the world of productivity and in order to live in Berlin as the new world capital of creativity and personal freedom. In Berlin, as Lewis-Kraus finds out, nobody seems to have a job, nobody seems to wake up before noon and nobody seems to talk about real estate or the latest restaurants, as people in New York or San Francisco usually do. Also the rents are low and he can easily afford sitting in cafés

---

96 Ibid. 5.
97 Ibid. 14-15.
98 Cox, Christopher. "A Sense of Direction: Six Questions for Gideon Lewis-Kraus." *Harper's Magazine*. 21 June 2012. 15 June 2015.

all day smoking cigarettes. Accordingly, he and his artsy friends hang out in cafés or the latest art galleries during the daytime and plunge into the famous Berlin night life after midnight. There seems to be no better deal for young people from New York, Los Angeles or San Francisco with a degree from a liberal arts college. The question comes to mind however, what everybody's purpose in Berlin might be, what all these international and mostly Americans citizens were actually trying to achieve except for party and leisure. Lewis-Kraus admits that in truth quite often not much else – if anything at all – was achieved by living in Berlin. However, he notices that in Berlin, the mere fact of being Jewish seemed to give people a sense of purpose:

As far as doing nothing was concerned, if you couldn't be an artist, you could at least be Jewish; in a way all the Americans in Berlin were honorary Jews. (Many of them were actual Jews.) In the first quarter of the twentieth century the saying used to go that "every Berliner comes from Breslau," from the shtetls of the Pale of Settlement. They also said that "the Jew comes from the East and has no time." He was an avatar of restless commercial modernity. These days the Jew comes from the West and has more time than he knows what to do with. He is an avatar of restless noncommercial modernity.[99]

Staging himself as "an avatar of restless noncommercial modernity," Lewis-Kraus coquets with being an American Jew in Berlin, with being unproductive and having plenty of time. The mere fact of being Jewish seems to serve as a sufficient life purpose in Berlin, although it never seems to have been an issue of importance before. Only when he comes to Berlin does Gideon Lewis-Kraus realize that he has to deal with this part of his identity. The reason is that it is only in Berlin where he feels noticed as a Jew for the first time. His Jewishness is highlighted by the awkwardness in the way that German people respond to Jews. He feels as if there are some unexpressed feelings and issues between Germans and American Jews, "as though they needed to say something to one another, but never quite knew what."[100] When his mother comes to visit, they go to see the Holocaust

---

99 Lewis-Kraus, Gideon. A Sense of Direction. London: Penguin Books, 2012. 25.
100 Ibid. 25.

Memorial and other 'Jewish' sites in Berlin. His mother, who is a rabbi and psychoanalyst, believes that it is important to keep the conversation between the two parties going, a "way towards healing [the wounds] through talk."[101] But Lewis-Kraus is not so sure about this. He has the dim feeling that the people he talks to, especially Germans above a certain age, seek some kind of absolution from him, "some sign that everything had finally become okay."[102] While he himself mostly *does* feel like everything had become okay, he cannot and will not speak for the actual victims of the Holocaust: "The people who could offer real forgiveness were dead, or they were dying."[103] Therefore he refuses to ease the conscience of young Germans with gestures of absolution, because he does not feel entitled.

It is because of such conversations with Germans during which the topic of the Holocaust always seems to be directly or indirectly present, that Lewis-Kraus feels like a Jew in Berlin. "The ubiquity of such conversational templates," he concludes, "made it impossible to forget that I was Jewish."[104] This curious constellation clearly shows the dilemma of the third generation or any generation of Jews born after the atrocities of the Holocaust. No matter what their personal link to the Shoah may be, and no matter in what kind of terms they may think of themselves as Jewish, in a setting like Berlin they get defined as Jewish and as descendants of survivors by the gaze of onlookers. The overreaching awareness of others forces Lewis-Kraus into a position of heteronomy in which he does not feel comfortable, because in these moments it is not his own choice to talk about the Holocaust and to think of himself as Jewish. In fact, thinking of himself as Jewish is not something he was used to before coming to Berlin:

In the States it was something I'd never thought much about, which had always struck my friends as strange. They assumed that I, as the son of two rabbis, would have a strong religious commitment. But my parents had been savvy enough to know that if they made a big deal out of observance, we'd certainly end up defecting; [...] they left it up to us, which meant we'd ended up mostly like normal,

---

101   Ibid. 25-26.
102   Ibid. 26.
103   Ibid. 26-27.
104   Ibid. 26.

suburban, disaffected cultural Jews. Our Jewishness meant Woody Allen and latkes, like anybody else's.[105]

Despite both parents being rabbis, Lewis-Kraus seems to summarize his upbringing as similar to Lisa Schiffman's. They share the childhood in the suburbs and although his parents may not be as secular as Schiffman's parents, he himself turns out even more disaffected from religion than she. Lewis-Kraus uses the term 'cultural Jew' in describing himself, as opposed to being a religious Jew. No specific definition of this term is offered except for a vague hint at typical culinary customs (latkes) and cultural prototypes (Woody Allen). However, it becomes clear that Lewis-Kraus has never felt the need to give more thought to his Jewish identity before, because it seemed normal. Only in Berlin is he made to feel special and is forced to deal with his Jewishness, and soon he realizes that this must not only be to his annoyance but can also be to his advantage:

But in Berlin this ambivalent patrimony was foisted upon you. It was immediately clear that Jews had a certain purchase in Berlin. [...] Being a Jew in New York is a mark of some considerable banality, but being a Jew in Berlin makes you special. You have the Holocaust in your pocket, the run of a city you rightly deserve.[106]

Gideon Lewis-Kraus realizes that the Holocaust gives American Jews some sort of free ride in Berlin. It only "furthered the idea that you were in Berlin to do just as you pleased." Whether this means to sleep around with German girls, "even if she had a boyfriend,"[107] being contemptuous towards Germans, or ignoring the local culture, being Jewish gives him enough of an excuse to do anything in Berlin. Lewis-Kraus continues to explain that another possibility – chosen by many American Jews in Berlin – is to make the Germans feel good about themselves by playacting as cultural ambassadors who congratulate them on their accomplishments of overcoming Nazism. However, he has noticed that by complimenting Germans for their achievements in working through their past, American

---

105 Ibid. 26.
106 Ibid. 26.
107 Ibid. 27.

Jews were actually seeking a way of complimenting themselves for overcoming the tension of their own Jewish-American identity:

> [It] – counterintuitively – meant congratulating themselves for having overcome their own fraught Jewish-American identity. It was a gesture of forgiveness that had everything to do with the forgiver and little to do with the forgiven. It was forgiveness as power, as arrogance.[108]

Lewis-Kraus admits that due to the looming presence of the Holocaust and the special relation between Germans and American Jews in Berlin, the latter seem to have a moral advantage that can also be used for power and arrogance. Lewis-Kraus himself decides that he likes those Jews best that talk little about the Holocaust. However, these seem to be a minority, according to his observations:

> But a healthy relationship to the Holocaust wasn't the norm. Melodrama was easier, more cheaply satisfying, and it was one way to explain to yourself what you were doing in Germany: just existing there was an act of defiance and strength.[109]

Although he would like to remain on the sober side of the whole issue, Lewis-Kraus has noticed that there is something to gain from taking a more sentimental perspective. It helps in justifying his own presence in Berlin as a writer who has not found his own topic yet. He admits that "as uncomfortable as it made me, it was often easiest just to give in to the sense of Holocaust-related entitlement."[110] At a party, he meets a German girl who tells him that she has just earned a degree in Anti-Semitism Studies. He seems to know already what he is about to do, but to be sure, he asks his friend Max for advice, who confirms: "The only way we – Germans and Jews alike – will heal these old wounds," his friend tells him, "[…] is if we take seriously our duty, difficult as it may often be, to take women like that

---

108 Ibid. 27.
109 Ibid. 26. Lewis-Kraus goes so far as listening to Paul Celan's *Todesfuge* on his iPod while walking around in Berlin. See: Ibid. 27.
110 Ibid. 27.

home."¹¹¹ It is on this rather funny note that Lewis-Kraus' subchapter on being a Jewish-American in Berlin ends.

Eventually, Lewis-Kraus gets bored by the never ending series of gallery and club opening events in Berlin and comes to realize that the sweet idleness of his days there are beginning to paralyze him. Therefore, he decides to join his friend Tom on a walk along the famous pilgrim route of Santiago de Compostela. During this journey on the Camino he keeps his apartment in Berlin, but quickly understands that he cannot return to the daily routine of smoking cigarettes in cafés and staying out late. During the Camino trip he has also made up his mind to write a book about such pilgrimages and about how it felt to experience these walks as a secular person. Thus he decides to try other famous routes. He returns to his hometown in New Jersey to be with his mother for *Rosh Hashanah* and *Yom Kippur*, which is something he has not done in a long time. Even though he is not a religious man and states not to care about the High Holidays as such, he knows it makes his mother happy and confesses that "after so many years, I had, despite myself grown attached to this listless annual synagogue attendance."¹¹² Accordingly, having returned from his trip to Berlin and Santiago de Compostela, back at home Lewis-Kraus does not seem to feel any different towards Judaism than before. As the next journey he chooses to wander the 1200 km long Shikoku pilgrimage with its 88 sacred places on the Japanese island of Shikoku. While in Japan, thousands of miles away from his family, he tells them that he misses them on the night of the Passover *Seder*, although he has not been celebrating Passover with his relatives for years.

For some reason missing the *Seder* makes me feel actually lonely, not bored-lonely or rejected-lonely but just sad to be by myself. And Passover, for some reason, maybe because of my attachment to the family Seder, maybe because of those dead Egyptians, has always made me more remorseful than Yom Kippur does.¹¹³

Obviously, because of the inclusion of the whole family into the procedures of the Passover *Seder*, Lewis-Kraus shares more memories of this holiday

---

111 Ibid. 28.
112 Ibid. 146.
113 Ibid. 235.

and clearly connects it to his childhood and upbringing in a Jewish family. Despite being very detached from Judaism, he feels remorseful on this Passover night out alone on the mountains of the Shikoku trail and is reminded of both his family and the *Haggadah*. Indeed, when this pilgrimage is over, he decides to return to San Francisco to meet with his family.

For his last pilgrimage Lewis-Kraus has chosen Uman, a little village in the Ukraine, where every year a festival takes place during which forty thousand Hasidic Jews join each other in celebrating Rosh Hashanah at the grave of the famous Rabbi Nachmann of Breslov, an important historical figure in Hasidism. Lewis-Kraus has the idea of asking his father to join him in an attempt to fix their complicated relationship. This is also meant as a symbolic gesture of forgiving the father for leaving their family after coming out as gay when Gideon and his brother were younger. Because he himself feels insecure about this trip, he tries to convince his younger brother Micah to join them. Finally, Lewis-Kraus succeeds in persuading both his brother and their estranged father to join him on this last journey to the Rosh Hashana celebrations of Uman which are also called "Jewish Woodstock" or "Jewish Burning Man"[114] by some of the participants. It is on the way to Uman that Lewis-Kraus is confronted with his Jewish identity again, because of the way others interact with him:

Though I was in the only *treyf* row in the whole plane, and needless to say was wearing neither *payos* nor even a yarmulke, the flight attendants gave me a kosher meal. It was a little horrifying that, despite my jeans and uncovered head, I was recognizable to an Aeroflot flight attendant as just another Jew; I felt like Woody Allen in the scene with Grammy Hall.[115]

Again, Lewis-Kraus is looked at as Jewish by a foreign person, without wearing any recognizable attributes that would indicate his religious affiliation. Only from the context of the flight and his looks, the flight attendant deduces he must be Jewish and serves him a kosher meal. Probably because he is not used to sticking out in this way, it makes him uncomfortable. Nevertheless, arriving in the solitude of Uman and

---

114   Ibid. 275.
115   Ibid. 271.

surrounded by thousands of orthodox Je... ideon Lewis-Kraus quickly realizes that this is obviously not his worl... act, he, his brother and their father all feel quite misplaced and unco... ble around all the religious men. They seem to come from a differe... orld, one that Lewis-Kraus thought existed only in fiction:

I had not realized until I got to Uman that all ...e people are actually named Shlomo and Moishe and Shmuel and all the oth... ls of Chelm I'd thought Isaac Bashevis Singer invented for comedic effect.[116]

This quote shows quite impressively how di... nt the two worlds are, that Lewis-Kraus as a secular American Jew ... pposed to the orthodox Brooklynites inhabit. He is so unfamiliar w... heir anachronistic way of living that he really thought such names ... hlomo and Shmuel were created as jokes by writers such as Singer who wrote the classical *shtetl* stories upon which the American imagination of this *topos* was built. While Lewis-Kraus cannot take all the Hasids quite seriously, he and his co-travelers do not want to be identified with them, even hate being perceived as part of this congregation.[117] On the other hand, the Hasids seem to avoid Lewis-Kraus and his family. During a meal at a food tent nobody wants to come and sit with the three men, who are obviously the only ones wearing civilian clothes. Despite both parents being rabbis, the brothers also seem to stand out as particularly uneducated about Judaism, which makes them feel even more misplaced. When they are asked if they know what the *tashlikh*[118] means, the two young men seem to have no clue:

Micah looked at me, as if I'd prepared for this. We shook our heads. We're both terrible Jews, especially considering our pedigree. We never know anything about anything [...].[119]

---

116 Ibid. 275.
117 See: Ibid. 282.
118 A religious custom during Rosh Hashana, where pockets are emptied of breadcrumbs and such in order to symbolically get rid of last years´ sins.
119 Lewis-Kraus, Gideon. *A Sense of Direction*. London: Penguin Books, 2012. 279.

There is also a scene when the three walk into a Ukrainian grocery store. At that moment a Hasidic man walks by, sees them, wags his finger and snarls "Not kosher!"[120] They enter the store anyway and buy some local salami with bread. Once back in the street, they are ashamed to eat their *treyf* lunch out in the open. Sitting on a park bench with their food, they feel "judged and ashamed together," although in their regular lives they never keep kosher.[121] As a consequence, they feel like outsiders both to the Hasidic community and to the Ukrainian people, and ironically this experience of being outlaws makes them feel closer to each other: "We felt huddled together and protective and close in a way that felt new."[122] They decide, therefore, to take the trip serious in their own way, and spend time with each other, as a family, and as a way of forgiving each other, just as it is intended between *Rosh Hashanah* and *Yom Kippur*.[123]

Gideon Lewis-Kraus understands his pilgrimages as approaches to grapple with his past, his present but also with his future:

I figured it rounded the whole thing out: the Christian one, a line to Santiago in exchange for a get-out-a-purgatory card, was all about the future; the Buddhist one, a circle around Shikoku, was all about the present; and a Jewish one, a dot in the middle of the Old World, would almost certainly be neurotically about the past. The first was finding a sense of direction. The second was about returning to where you started. The third would be about knowing where we stand.[124]

Lewis-Kraus admits that his pilgrimages have become more than a mere project for entertainment or research for his book, but rather turned into a journey to himself. On his previous pilgrimages on the Camino and on Shikoku he was "more interested in the form of the ritual than in the content." In the case of *Rosh Hashanah* in Uman, however, things are

---

120 See: Ibid. 287.
121 See: Ibid. 287.
122 See: Ibid. 287.
123 In the end, they succeed in having the talk that helps to resolve some of the problems that they have had in the past. And over the course of the festival, Lewis-Kraus and his brother also get to know some of the religious men, even making a few friends.
124 Ibid. 256-257.

different and he admits to "care nearly as much about the form as I did about the content."[125] This may have less to do with the religious dimension of the holiday than with family and the importance of apologizing and forgiving, which yet in turn *are* important aspects of the high holidays. Lewis-Kraus has correctly predicted that his last pilgrimage, the 'Jewish one' will notoriously be about the past, both for him personally and for the Hasids who travel to Uman in remembrance of the Rabbi Nachmann of Breslov. Towards the end of their stay in Uman, Lewis-Kraus and his brother attend the traditional *tashlikh* ceremony at the river. Their father does not attend, but neither Micah nor Gideon are mad, although both are disappointed. They realize that apologizing to him is even more satisfying than getting an apology from him. When they part ways, everyone returns to their own lives, and a few days later the brothers eventually receive a sincere apology from their father.

Although Lewis-Kraus' A *Sense of Direction* is not explicitly and exclusively about the question of what it means to be a Jewish-American today, it is a journey to the self *by* a young Jewish-American. He does not seem to look for the 'Jewish thing' with so much desperation as Schiffman, and in general he asks different questions. His book, which is literally the account of a journey, the travelogue of a pilgrimage that leads him to himself, does not in the first place set out to answer such questions as who he is and what his identity is. But as he travels, he nevertheless touches upon these questions, where he stands with regard to Judaism and mainly with regard to family. Also in the life of Gideon Lewis-Kraus, religion plays no major role. But unlike Schiffman he seems to be content and at peace with being a secular American Jew. He is surprised that being a Jewish-American can be a topic of interest at all, something he realizes and gets to know only due to the special status he enjoys in Berlin. Being Jewish seems to have more to do with his family and with being part of a broad culture of Jewish life in America. He calls himself a 'cultural Jew,' whose Jewishness, "like anybody else's" – as he assumes – has to do with "Woody Allen and latkes." Because he is not – like Lisa Schiffman – on the hunt for a better definition or categorization of this Jewishness, Lewis-Kraus leaves it in the open, what this 'cultural Jewishness' might be other

---

125 Ibid. 281.

than 'Woody Allen and latkes.' For him, everything seems to be just fine this way.[126]

4.6 CHAPTER CONCLUSION

On the basis of these five examples, Shalom Auslander's *Foreskin's Lament*, Deborah Feldman's *Unorthodox*, Allegra Goodman's *The Family Markowitz*, Lisa Schiffman's *Generation J*, and Gideon Lewis-Kraus' *A Sense of Direction*, I have shown how the search for one's Jewish identity in contemporary America can take very different trajectories. This shows that nowadays there are various Jewish life styles and approaches to Judaism available for a generation of American Jews who are eager to explore these possibilities and shine a light on themselves. For Shalom Auslander, being a young Jewish-American meant having to fight for a life outside the narrow world of his family and community. But as a result of this breakout, his orthodox past will nevertheless accompany – if not haunt – him forever. A constant struggle with God and the religious world that he has left behind have become the foundation of his new identity. Deborah Feldman tells a similar story, only from a female perspective. Much of her suffering in the orthodox world had to do with being a woman. Like Auslander, she has had the courage and resilience to escape that world and to make a living independently and on her own terms. Allegra Goodman's Miriam, on the other hand, chooses exactly the opposite direction by becoming more religious than her parents and grandparents. Yet on the other hand, there are characters like Lisa Schiffman and Gideon Lewis-Kraus who seem to define their Jewish identity as a variety of possibilities. At the beginning of this chapter I have quoted a passage from Schiffman's *Generation J* before that seems to capture this mentality quite aptly:

It occurred to me that most of us were third-Generation American Jews. [...] Assimilation wasn't something we strove for; it was the condition into which we were born. [...] Being Jewish was an activity: Today I'll be Jewish. Tomorrow I'll play tennis. [...] To us, anything was possible.[127]

---

126 See: Ibid. 26.
127 Schiffman, Lisa. *Generation J*. New York: Harper San Francisco, 1999. 4.

Schiffman confirms my argument once more that much of the curiosity for the question of Jewishness as displayed by the current generation of young Jewish-American authors has to do with the fact that most of them are third generation Americans. She confirms the cultural dynamic as suggested by Hansen and as I have argued throughout this thesis, namely that the grandchildren of immigrants try to revive something – in this case we can broadly call it Jewishness – which their parent generation had tried to cast away. Accordingly, Schiffman sets out on a seemingly endless escapade of variants in acting out her Jewishness. Many of her approaches appear as quite esoteric and New Age, however, her book makes a clear statement and is a case in point that her generation is on the search. The same is true for Gideon Lewis-Kraus who almost accidentally realizes that he is a Jew for the first time while living abroad in Berlin. Also his account is a typical example of how this generation sets out to explore their own position as Jewish-Americans with regard to religion, family, and history. Both, Lewis-Kraus' and Schiffman's books are examples of how these journeys and searches are a matter of their own free choice, self-initiated, self-directed and self-empowering quests within a contemporary and global culture that has practically no borders.

No matter where these authors started on their journeys, they share one common ground: whether they grew up within religious communities and eventually abandoned these concepts or whether they were brought up in a secular and liberal way and went on their journeys – both literally and figuratively speaking – to figure out their own Jewish identity, ultimately their Jewishness always stayed a part of their lives. As Deborah Feldman states at the end of her memoirs:

For a while I thought I could un-Jew myself. Then I realized that being Jewish is not in the ritual or the action. It is in one's history. I am proud of being Jewish, because I think that's where my indomitable spirit comes from, [...]. I am Jewish; I am invincible. I feel this more than I ever did, like I have come home into myself, and God is no longer a prescription for paradise but an ally in my heart.[128]

---

128 Feldman, Deborah. *Unorthodox: The Scandalous Rejection of My Hasidic Roots*. New York: Simon & Schuster, 2012. 251.

A clearer answer indeed cannot be found in any of these stories. As hard as the authors may try, in the end they seem to fail in finding a single and unequivocal definition of their Jewishness and eventually all give in to a vague sense of being Jewish for various reasons. This is what can be learned then from their stories, that for young Jews in contemporary America there seem to exist multiple and shifting possibilities in how to live out and perceive one's Jewishness, however, there seems to be no way to let go of being Jewish, or in the words of Feldman of "un-Jewing" oneself. While none of these books provide a single answer, they all share the basic fact that they are notoriously raising the question of what being Jewish means. This common curiosity ties these books and authors together and allows me to present them as a new and distinguishable generation of Jewish-American writing.

5 The New 'Russian-Jewish-American' Literature

> I was a Russian. [...]
> I was finally granted the identity I had been denied my whole life.
> VAPNYAR, LARA. "THE WRITER AS TOUR GUIDE." 103.

I have tried to divide current Jewish-American literature into three central streams which are quite oppositional approaches to the generation's search for their Jewish heritage and identity. In addition to the two groups of third generation authors I have discussed so far, in the following chapter I would like to introduce a third group of young Jewish writers, namely Jewish authors who immigrated to America in the 1970s and 80s from countries of the former Soviet Union.[1] It is important to stress that although they represent a new generation of immigrants, they also belong to the same

---

[1] I should note that lacking a better word I will call this group of new immigrant writers 'Russian-Jewish-Americans' throughout this chapter despite the fact that some of them have come from other countries of the former Soviet Union such as the Ukraine or the Baltics. I have chosen nevertheless to use this expression because the double hyphen highlights the complexity of their identity situation and the transitions they are going through. In the case of single authors, I will specify their actual home countries and discuss their specific stories. As a group, however, I will subsume them under the roof of the title 'Russian-Jewish-Americans' for simplification.

generation age-wise as American-born authors such as Jonathan Safran Foer, Shalom Auslander or Dara Horn.

These new émigrés include Gary Shteyngart, David Bezmozgis, and Ellen Litman, and I would argue that they can be seen as an alternative if not antithetical stream to the group of authors who are returning their focus on the *shtetl* and their families' Eastern European past. The *shtetl* as a mystical Eastern European place of origin does not exist for these new immigrants. They have recently migrated from Eastern Europe themselves, the real place, where there are no *shtetls* left. To them, neither the *shtetl* nor Eastern Europe as such can be a dwelling space of nostalgic imagination then. It also cannot serve as a topography of Jewishness, because basically nothing Jewish is left there. Their families have lived mostly assimilated and secular lives in the cities of the Soviet Union, often even hiding the fact that they were Jewish. In fact, what it means to be Jewish is not even a question they would have likely asked themselves before arriving in America, and much less a question they would have tried to answer by imaginatively returning to long gone historical versions of the exact countries that they have just left behind. As Adam Kirsch fittingly summarizes, for new immigrant authors such as David Bezmozgis,

[…] there is no 'back home' to visit or nostalgize over: that heartland was doubly destroyed, first by Soviet power and then by Nazi violence. Jewishness, if it is to live, must continue to live here [in America].[2]

Accordingly, the texts of these Russian-Jewish-American authors are less about fictional return journeys to the past and to the vanished nameless villages of their forefathers, but rather about their own and recent journeys from east to west, from socialism to capitalism, from one (eastern) metropolis to the (western) other. Unsurprisingly, most of their novels are set in the present of the late 20th century.

A question arises then, whether these authors really belong to the same generation as the Jewish-American natives of third or fourth generation, or whether they should rather be compared to the first generation of immigrants one century ago. As I will argue, they do belong with their

---

2   Kirsch, Adam. "David Bezmozgis' Brilliant Alt-History of an Adulterous Shransky Who Never Was." *Tablet Magazine* 17 September 2014.

contemporaries despite all differences. They are – in the sense of Mannheim's generation theory – a very particular stratum, nevertheless within the frame of one generation. While some of their experiences, topics and approaches are particular – as was the case with the imaginative *shtetl* returnees, religious converters or New Age experimenters respectively, others are rather universal and reminiscent of their peers of age, such as obsessively dealing with the question of what it means to be Jewish. This is the link, accordingly, that groups the young 'Russian-Jewish-American' writers with the larger contemporary generation of Jewish writing in America: whether they like to or not, they are faced with the same questions about what makes them Jewish and what their Jewish heritage is. After arriving in America, they get in touch with their native Jewish-American kin and get pulled into the game of the grand Jewish identity quest.

As to the question of how these new immigrants compare to their predecessors at the turn of the 20th century, this will remain an interesting question throughout parts of this chapter. In terms of Hansen's cultural theory of immigration, the experience of the late Russian arrivés should indeed resemble that of the earlier immigrants because they are both first generation arrivals. While there seem to be some similarities, a closer look reveals that the experiences, challenges and desires of the new immigrants differ in many ways from those of the early 20th century. Therefore, a comparison with these earlier 'first generation' authors and appreciation of significant differences will help to underpin my argument that these 'new immigrants' do indeed rather belong with their American born peers of the same age.

At the turn of the last century when those thousands of Eastern European Jewish immigrants arrived in poverty and misery on the Lower East Side of New York, they met an almost homogeneous Yiddish ghetto. Besides the Yiddish language, numerous life styles had remained intact there. Sheer survival, moneymaking by simple manual labor in textile factories and the acquisition of the American idiom and customs were of paramount importance for these immigrants. Morris Dickstein has made a curious remark about this milieu:

In any ethnic subculture, it's almost never the immigrant generation that writes the books. The immigrants don't have the language; their lives are focused on survival, on gaining a foothold in the new world and insuring an education for their children.[3]

But contrary to Dickstein's argument, the immigrants *did* write about their experiences, both today and back in the early 20th century. This latter immigrant milieu and their struggle for survival on New York's Lower East Side during the early decades of the 20th century is portrayed in numerous classic American novels, such as Henry Roth's *Call It Sleep*.

The immigrant Jew is typically portrayed in this literature as a transitional figure, a character who not only straddles "old" world and "new," but who resists the impulse to abandon previously conceived hopes for America with the realities found there.[4] As an example for the hardships of everyday life on the Lower East Side, the following episode from Henry Roth's classic immigrant novel *Call It Sleep* can be consulted: When David Schearl is sent to buy a newspaper for his father and loses some of the change, his father threatens to punish him for his alleged carelessness. David's mother tells the father that he has no heart, and he reacts furiously: "Woe me, to labor as I labor, for food for the two of you and a roof over your heads. To labor and to work overtime."[5] Obviously, David's father laments about how hard he has to work in order to earn a modest living for his family, and the poverty can be felt.

Unlike their predecessors, however, the new immigrants from Russia and other former Soviet states neither seem to arrive in utter poverty nor to be completely alienated by the culture they find.

In short, while earlier Jewish immigrant literature was largely written by the children of poverty, reflecting on their parents' hardscrabble and their own struggle to live on different terms, the new immigrant literature comes from the children of educated professionals; their own formation is as much North American as European, since

---

3   Dickstein, Morris. "The Complex Fate of the Jewish-American Writer." *The Nation*. 4 October 2001. 27 September 2012.
4   Aarons, Victoria. *A Measure of Memory. Storytelling and Identity in American Jewish Fiction*. Athens: The University of Georgia Press, 1996. 6
5   Roth, Henry. *Call It Sleep*. New York: The Noonday Press, 1995. 80.

they came here so young. The global reach of mass culture and the English language introduced them to America even before they arrived.⁶

As Morris Dickstein stresses, the new immigrants, in the age of globalization, seem to be better prepared, and not only that, some of their writers have arrived at an age, young enough to adapt easily and to become hybrids between the cultures of their origin and America. In addition to such economic and educational differences, Adam Rovner argues that there is a crucial difference between the new immigrants and their predecessors exactly with regard to the question of 'Jewish distinctiveness.' The previous immigrants had tried to get rid of this distinctiveness in the general process of acculturation. The new immigrants, on the other hand, seem to embrace it in an exactly opposing trend:

> As chroniclers of the world of their fathers, the narrators of recent Jewish American immigrant fiction seem more preoccupied with status than with simple existence. [...] Unintentionally, perhaps, Shteyngart and Bezmozgis parody previous narratives of Jewish immigration and assimilation. Today, the discovery of Russian Jewish immigrant "hopes and surviving pains" may really be an attempt to claim a vicarious Jewish distinctiveness that only underscores the successful acculturation of earlier generations of Jews into American mainstream. Contemporary American-Jewish-Russian writers offer readers a new immigrant chic, their multiply hyphenated identities nesting like *maroyshka* dolls.⁷

Accordingly, the new immigrants' experiences of arrival and assimilation seem to differ significantly from their predecessors', as I will continue to stress throughout this chapter.

In Gary Shteyngart's *The Russian Debutante's Handbook* (2002) it can be seen that for this latest generation of Jewish immigrants it is no longer

---

6   Dickstein, Morris. "Questions of Identity. The New World of the Immigrant Writer." *The Writer Uprooted. Contemporary Jewish Exile Literature.* Ed. Rosenfeld, Alvin H. Bloomington: Indiana University Press, 2008. 115/116.

7   Rovner, Adam. "So Easily Assimilated: The New Immigrant Chic." *AJS Review* 30.2 (2006): 317. Quote within quote: Howe, Irving. "Immigrant Chic." *New York Magazine*, 12 May 1986. 76. Print.

about the simple creation of a livelihood, but rather about acquiring a proper status in the land of unlimited opportunities:

The delivery of this Sony Trinitron is possibly the happiest moment of my life. Finally, in a real sense, I become a naturalized citizen of this country. I turn it on, and I never turn it off. For the next ten years, I will write almost nothing.[8]

The promise of America and the urge to achieve higher social status, accordingly, are manifest first and foremost in material things, in consumer goods. In Shteyngart's novel the Sony TV set becomes the quintessential embodiment of all of the protagonist's desires. Only the Sony Trinitron – a consumer good as iconic object – can provide him with the feeling of naturalization as an American citizen "in a real sense." So while Shteyngart's protagonist dreams of luxury goods, in contrast David Schearl in Henry Roth's *Call It Sleep* dreams about the food he hopes to get from his mother: "Milk-supper, maybe, when he came upstairs. [...] Sour cream with eggs. Sour cream with what else? Borscht... Strawberries... Radishes [...]."[9]

However, the achievement of such "naturalization" and higher social status, as hoped for by Shteyngart's protagonist, is of course not the only struggle of this new generation of immigrants. Like earlier immigrants they have to deal with problems of assimilation and complex questions about their own identity. As David Bezmozgis states:

There is the tension between the Old World and the New. Tensions rooted in traditions that are religious or cultural or both but that are in any guise different from those of the host community.[10]

---

8   Shteyngart, Gary. "The Mother Tongue Between Two Slices of Rye." *The Threepenny Review* (Spring 2004) 13 January 2014.
9   Roth, Henry. *Call It Sleep*. New York: The Noonday Press, 1995. 95. Admittedly, one can also ascribe these different cravings to the fact that David Schearl is still a little boy and Shteyngart's Vladimir Girshkin is a young adult.
10 Bezmozgis, David. "The End of American Jewish Literature, Again." *Tablet Magazine*. 17 September 2014. 22 September 2014.

Accordingly, the immigrants have to master tensions of cultural difference, not all of which they are even aware of at times. This complex situation forces the young authors to reflect on their own identity and state of cultural belonging. The author Lara Vapnyar, who emigrated from Russia to New York in 1994 provides a fitting point in case:

My first awareness of belonging to something like a Jewish community coincided with the mass Jewish emigration from the Soviet Union. [...] I hardly knew what to expect from my new life, but I believed that I was finally coming to the place where Jews were free of the self-hatred, inferiority complex, and shame that were characteristic of Russian Jews, where Jews were at peace with their identity, well-assimilated but also proud of their heritage, and had all the opportunities for success. [...] The ironic thing was that when I finally arrived in the United States, I saw that I couldn't be considered either Jewish or American. What exactly was it that was Jewish about me? [...] The Americans [...] defined me easily: I was a Russian. [...] I was finally granted the identity I had been denied my whole life.[11]

It becomes clear that Vapnyar's sense of identity must remain inextricably interwoven with the context of her origin, while a more self-construed sense of self – as could be found in the other two groups of young authors – seems to be further out of reach. As much as she might think about her Jewishness, the (unwanted) identity label – Russian! – remains imposed upon her by others. Adrian Wanner even stresses that Jewish immigrants coming from Russia became less Jewish once they arrived in the United States.[12]

Nevertheless, such reflections as Lara Vapnyar's show the tendency of the new immigrants from the former Soviet Union to develop a strong meta-awareness of their own transitory state. And exactly in this aspect, I would argue, they differ crucially from their predecessors of the early 20th century. Be it due to their higher levels of education, due to the lack of a homogenizing milieu such as the Lower East Side ghetto, or simply due to

---

11 Vapnyar, Lara. "The Writer as Tour Guide." *The Writer Uprooted. Contemporary Jewish Exile Literature.* Ed. Rosenfeld, Alvin H. Bloomington: Indiana University Press, 2008. 103.

12 Wanner, Adrian. "Russian Jews as American Writers: A New Paradigm for Jewish Multiculturalism?" *MELUS* 37.2. (Summer 2012): 169.

the broader confines of today's *zeitgeist*, socioeconomic possibilities and cultural sensibilities, for whatever reasons, the new immigrants proactively and articulately raise the question of their own identities – ethnic, national, cultural and religious – in a way that their struggling predecessors never had. And in this very aspect, in this grand searching for identity (Jewish, Jewish-American, American), finally, the new immigrant authors are more like their American born peers of age, who are quintessentially 'third generationers' in the sense of Hansen and therefore quite typically wrestling with questions of identity and hyphenation.

5.1 DAVID BEZMOZGIS – NATASHA AND OTHER STORIES

David Bezmozgis was born in Riga in 1973 and moved to Toronto with his parents in 1980. In his collection of seven short stories called *Natasha* (2004) that Bezmozgis himself calls a *bildungsroman*,[13] he writes about the experiences of a young protagonist called Mark Berman and his parents Bella and Roman. A number of Berman's experiences are probably based on Bezmozgis' own. I will refrain, however, from determining the extent to which *Natasha* is autobiographic, as discussed in the first chapter, because I consider all stories as autofiction in which the extent of fictionality or factuality quintessentially does not matter.

Early in *Natasha*, more precisely in the short story "Tapka," Mark Berman introduces his family:

My parents, Baltic aristocrats, took an apartment at 715 Finch [...] one respectable block away from the Russian swarm. We lived on the fifth floor, my cousin, aunt, and uncle directly below us on the fourth. Except for the Nahumovskys, a couple in their fifties, there were no other Russians in the building. For this privilege, my parents paid twenty extra dollars a month in rent.[14]

---

13 Bezmozgis, David. "The End of American Jewish Literature, Again." *Tablet Magazine*. 17 September 2014. 22 September 2014.

14 Bezmozgis, David. *Natasha And Other Stories*. London: Vintage, 2005. 3.

It is quite obvious that the family tries to distance themselves from fellow Russian immigrants in order to gain a higher status in the new world: "A fully detached house was the ultimate accomplishment."[15] On purpose they avoid comingling and being associated with other immigrants. In order to keep this distance of one single block, the family is willing to afford higher rents. Also the ultimate aim becomes quite clear from the start: a fully detached house, rather than a rented apartment. As stated above, from the start there is a desire for proper social status as reflected in material possessions, living conditions and real estate.

In the short story "Roman Berman, Massage Therapist," the reader finds out that after his lay-off from the Ministry of sport in Riga, Mark's father Roman Berman starts to work as a massage therapist in various sanatoria along the Baltic Sea. While he never needed any registration or permission for this work back in Latvia, he has to take a test in Canada, which turns out to be quite difficult due to his poor English. Nevertheless, he manages to pass the exam and is thus allowed to open a small massage studio in Toronto soon after the family's arrival. However, business is bad, even though the family hopes for the solidarity of their patients: "This was 1983, and as Russian Jews, recent immigrants, and political refugees, we were still a cause. We had good PR. We could trade on our history."[16]

When the clients fail to appear, Roman Berman decides to ask the local rabbi for help, because he knows that this had proved successful for other immigrants in trouble. In order to make the best possible impression, Roman is accompanied by his son Mark who is of course dressed up nicely. During their conversation, Roman bloats about the fact that his son is a well-behaved student at the Jewish school. Hence, in a rather embarrassing chat with the rabbi, Mark gets to demonstrate his nothing but rudimentary knowledge of Hebrew. He is then even forced to prove his singing skills by performing "Jerusalem of Gold." Unfortunately, the rabbi seems to be less impressed by these performances than hoped for and sends the couple home with the kind suggestion of running advertising for a massage studio.

This is not the only episode in which the Berman family – who are actually a completely secular family – tries to make an appearance by connecting to their Jewishness. Later in the short story "Roman Berman,

---

15 Ibid. 31.
16 Ibid. 21.

Massage Therapist," the Berman family is invited to a *Shabbat* dinner at the Kornblum's, a family of Canadian benefactors caring for Jewish immigrants from Russia. In order to impress the host, Bella Berman decides to bake an apple pie because this reminds her of her Jewish childhood back in Stalinist Latvia. This must be explained in more detail: As readers of the story we find out that during the time preceding the Stalin-era, Bella's grandmother used to light the Shabbat candles every Friday night and bake an apple pie. When Stalin came to power, there was only the pie for Shabbat, the candles were no longer lit. Eventually, there were neither candles nor a pie, but the missing dessert still symbolized something vaguely Jewish in the mind of Bella. This reminds me strongly of the parable about the Baal Shem Tov again, which I have cited at the beginning of this thesis. Clearly, the role of the story teller as taken by Rabbi Israel of Rizhyn in the parable, is now Mark Berman's in *Natasha*. He narrates the story of the apple pie, which has come to stand for everything else that is forgotten. The Berman family tries to revive their very own family tradition of Shabbat, and the apple pie is all they are left with. This story of the apple pie is also faintly reminiscent of the Chagall painting in Dara Horn's *The World to Come*, as discussed in chapter 3.2. Like the painting, the apple pie also becomes a token representing the family history and the family's forgotten Jewish heritage. In both cases, it is the grandson's task to tell the story of these items that embody the lost past.

However, in preparing for the occasion, Mark's parents try to make a show of their Jewishness by dressing their little son accordingly "[...] with a silver Star of David on a silver chain not under but over the shirt."[17] But the Bermans are not the only Russian Jewish immigrants who have been invited to the Kornblums. There is another immigrant family (from Ukraine) who also brought their little son. This other family 'succeeds' to tell the story about their life as *refuseniks*,[18] which plucks the Kornblum family's heartstrings. Unfortunately, the Bermans cannot offer any similar stories about endured suffering and violence against Jews, because after all they were no *refuseniks*. The embarrassing anticlimax of this Shabbat dinner follows towards the end of the story: When the Bermans get ready to

---

17 Ibid. 31.
18 This term refers to Jews in the Soviet empire who were denied the right to emigrate and then had to endure hardships.

leave, the hostess hands the apple pie – which she had baked especially for the occasion – back to Bella, because it is not kosher! Strikingly, the most Jewish gift Bella Berman knew to bring to their hosts, turned out to be not even faintly Jewish enough by the standards of the Kornblum family. The Bermans seem to have failed in displaying their Jewishness. This experience as told in Bezmozgis' *Natasha* seems to be quite typical. For most of the new immigrant Jewish writers who migrated to the United States/Canada as children or adolescents, Judaism barely existed anymore. Many of them did not have any remaining ties to the religious culture and traditions of their ancestors. Only through stories and orally conveyed memories of their grandparents did they remain connected to an otherwise forbidden and often forgotten world.[19] Indeed, the author Anya Ulinich confirms – as cited by Wanner – "that her exposure to the Jewish tradition was limited to the stories she heard from her 'wonderful grandparents.'"[20]

Another story called "An Animal to the Memory" deals with the emigration of the Bermans. Mark and his parents decide to immigrate to Canada. His grandparents, however, decide to go to Israel, Mark's grandfather being a strongly convinced Zionist. Before their departures the family has the same discussion about anti-Semitism in Canada over and over again:

Grandfather: There [Israel], I'll never have to hear dirty Jew. Father/Uncle: So instead you'll hear dirty Russian. Grandfather: Maybe. But where you're going you'll hear one and the other.[21]

After arriving in Canada, Mark has to confirm some of his grandfather's premonitions: In his private Jewish school he is called "dirty Russian"[22] several times, which he takes as an opportunity in trying to convince his

---

19 See: Dickstein, Morris. "Questions of Identity. The New World of the Immigrant Writer." *The Writer Uprooted. Contemporary Jewish Exile Literature.* Ed. Rosenfeld, Alvin H. Bloomington: Indiana University Press, 2008. 125.
20 Wanner, Adrian. "Russian Jews as American Writers: A New Paradigm for Jewish Multiculturalism?" *MELUS* 37.2. (Summer 2012): 164.
21 Bezmozgis, David. *Natasha And Other Stories.* London: Vintage, 2005. 68.
22 Ibid. 68.

parents to send him to a public school. But his mother cannot be persuaded because she is convinced that Mark should get everything he would have been denied back in Latvia – including a decent Jewish education: "As far as she was concerned, I wasn't leaving Hebrew school until I learned what it was to be a Jew."[23] Accordingly, for Mark the migration to Canada accomplishes the double paradox of fostering two identity attributes that would otherwise – if the family had stayed in Riga – played only minor roles: being Russian, and being Jewish. Mark keeps attending the private Jewish school then. Despite these efforts of deliberately strengthening the family's ties to Judaism (mainly through Mark's education), there are quite often awkward moments in which the Bermans do not seem to feel comfortable with their 'new Jewishness.' Such episodes as at the Kornblum's Shabbat dinner or during the Rabbi consultation exemplify the family's 'failures' in becoming more Jewish. Similarly, Mark feels that his school lunch does not properly fit:

Because of dietary laws, the school prohibited bringing meat for lunch. Other students brought peanut butter or tuna fish, but I – and most of the other Russians – would invariably arrive at school with smoked Hungarian salami, Polish bologna, roast turkey. Our mothers couldn't comprehend why anyone would choose to eat peanuts in a country that didn't know what it meant to have a shortage of smoked meat.[24]

In moments of alienation like these, the stories in David Bezmozgis' *Natasha* seem to retell the typical mishaps encountered by many immigrants, quite regardless of when and from where they arrived. However, the Berman's situation is complicated by the fact that they try to master not only the transition from Soviet to Western city life, but try in addition to reverse the family's estrangement from Judaism.

The stories in *Natasha* are classic coming of age stories, focusing on the young Mark Berman growing up in the new country. It becomes clear that

---

23 Ibid. 69.
24 Ibid. 70.

often the younger immigrants can adjust quickly and more easily, as Mark confirms:[25]

I was nine, and there were many things I did not tell them [...]. They were strangers in the country, and they recognized that the place was less strange to me, even though I was only a boy.[26]

While the boy finds it easier to enter the new society and become accustomed to its ways, he also develops an awareness for the difficulty this poses to his parents. The child senses that his family remains 'off' in various regards. Especially in bringing the question of Jewishness into the equation, the whole identity situation of the family becomes quite complicated and at times embarrassing. It is this complete mess of a family identity under re-construction, in development and in transition that the narrator Mark Berman shares with us in *Natasha*, however, without offering final resolve.

5.2 GARY SHTEYNGART – THE RUSSIAN DEBUTANTE'S HANDBOOK

Another author writing about the experiences of Russian Jewish immigrants in North America is Gary Shteyngart, aka Igor Shteyngart Semyonovich. Born in Leningrad in 1972, he immigrated to New York with his parents at the age of seven. In his debut novel *The Russian Debutante's Handbook* (2002), Shteyngart depicts the story of Vladimir Girshkin, a 25-year-old Russian-Jewish immigrant. Having grown up in New York and after his college graduation, Girshkin starts working for the Emma Lazarus Immigrant Absorption Society, an agency committed to the integration of immigrants. Taking some crooked turns, he soon makes acquaintance with the criminal underworld and finds himself back in the 'Wild East' for a short while. More specifically he ends up in the fictional city of Prava, the

---

25 Dickstein, Morris. "Questions of Identity. The New World of the Immigrant Writer." *The Writer Uprooted. Contemporary Jewish Exile Literature.* Ed. Rosenfeld, Alvin H. Bloomington: Indiana University Press, 2008. 116.
26 Bezmozgis, David. *Natasha And Other Stories.* London: Vintage, 2005. 24.

"Paris of the 90s" or the "SoHo of Eastern Europe."[27] The description of this imagined city refers to the typical ex-Soviet metropolis in Eastern Europe during the early 1990s time of gold digging, which brought together many shady characters hoping to earn a quick buck. Girshkin's father is a doctor who specializes in insurance fraud, and his mother an investment banker who is an overly ambitious character as can be seen during his childhood and adolescence:

Vladimir [...] suffered under his mother's accusative wails as B-plus report cards were ceremonially burned in the fireplace; as china was sent flying for chess-club prizes not won [...].[28]

His mother only accepts top performances and keeps pushing her son with her ambition. She wants to offer Vladimir the best possible conditions for a successful life and lets him attend a liberal arts college in the Midwest. However, in her eyes Vladimir is too effeminate and an underachiever. She even tries to cast out his 'Jewish pace:'

"I've been keeping an eye on you for years, but it just hit me today, your little Jew-walk. Come here, I'll teach you to walk like a normal person." [...] *You, too, could walk like a gentile.* You had to keep your chin in the air. The spine straight.[29]

Significantly, in *The Russian Debutante's Handbook*, it is Vladimir's own mother who stigmatizes him as a Jew due to his physical features, his movements and appearance. The implication is that he must lose the stereotypical feature of his "Jew-walk" and walk like a gentile in order to seem strong, to be fit for making it in America. Shteyngart seems to evoke a certain bodily image of his protagonist here. Similarly, in his later novel *Super Sad True Love Story*, Shteyngart characterizes his protagonist in a way closely reminiscent of anti-Semitic caricatures:

---

27 Shteyngart, Gary. *The Russian Debutante's Handbook*. London: Bloomsbury, 2004. 20.
28 Ibid. 14.
29 Ibid. 45/46.

A slight man with a gray, sunken battleship o   ace, curious wet eyes, a giant
gleaming forehead on which a dozen cavemen c   have painted something nice, a
sickle of a nose perched atop a tiny mouth, and   the back, a growing bald spot
whose shape perfectly replicates the great state of   [...].[30]

This stereotypical image of a Jewish app   nce, depicted as stocky,
(almost) bald and unathletic, is certainly not   w, we have all seen plenty
of it in the anti-Semitic propaganda of Natio   Socialism and sometimes
find it even today.[31] However, Shteyngart s   ms to evoke such images
deliberately in his novels by attributing them   his Jewish protagonists,
thereby rendering them physically distinct. Unlike the Berman family in
Bezmozgis' *Natasha*, the Girshkin family in Shteyngart's *Handbook* does
not try to become more Jewish again, but cru   ly hopes to achieve the
exact opposite: strive off everything Jewish, like a bad habit that puts itself
in the way of success and being a "normal person." Curiously, this ambition
to blend in, as displayed by Vladimir's mother who tries to teach him to be
a 'gentile' and therefore the proper way of walking, is quite reminiscent of
the typical dynamic of the second generation of immigrants.

In Shteyngart's novel it is accordingly the mother's character who
embodies the ambition of the newly arrived, the urge to have a better
standing in society. It turns out that while older literature about immigrants
mostly dealt with the sheer survival in the new and unknown country,
Shteyngart's novel is yet another case in point about how this more recent
immigrant literature chooses a different approach. The new immigrants are
highly sophisticated and want to provide their children with a maximum
higher education. Life in the new world should reach a new climax, high
social status is everything, and the families strive for the typical insignia of

---

30 Shteyngart, Gary. *Super Sad True Love Story*. New York: Random House, 2010. 4-5.

31 After the acquisition of WhatsApp by Facebook, the founder and CEO of the company Mark Zuckerberg was portrayed as a kraken with a big nose, thick lips, and curly hair, its tentacles grabbing for every possible private computer in an illustration of the national German newspaper Süddeutsche Zeitung on February 21, 2014. This was meant as a symbol for the company's far-reaching and monopolistic influence, however, it looked exactly like the hateful anti-Semitic propaganda drawings of the 1930s.

a good life in America. In comparison with the sorrowful stories about the earlier Russian immigrants on the Lower East Side, one can reduce this contrast to the dichotomous formulae of the Sony Triniton versus local Yiddish newspapers, far away liberal arts college versus textile factory on the corner. It is obvious that nowadays immigrants live with completely different expectations and demands.

During college Vladimir Girshkin dates a girl named Francesca. To please her curiosity, he purposefully mimics the immigrant with a heavy Russian accent. Also his friends – a bunch of pretentious college students – view him as an exotic creature, and he gladly takes the role. Girshkin decides to spend the summer after college with Francesca at her parents' place who are both professors and live on 5th Avenue in New York City. But soon he finds himself broke due to his lavish lifestyle:

During adolescence he dreamed of acceptance. In his brief days at college he dreamed of love. After college, he dreamed of a rather improbable dialectic of both love and acceptance. And now, with love and acceptance finally in the bag, he dreamed of money.[32]

Due to his financial difficulties, Girshkin agrees to a deal with the old man Aleksander Rybakov, father of the infamous mobster Tolya Rybakov, also known as the Groundhog. By arranging American citizenship for Rybakov Sr., Girshkin rids himself of his financial troubles. He eventually ends up in Prava, the fictional Eastern European city of the early 1990s, where he develops a Ponzi scheme for the Groundhog. Once he arrives in Prava, Vladimir Girshkin realizes that everything he futilely tried to achieve in America, comes quite easily to him there. While back in the US he had to resort to mimicking the poor Russian immigrant in order to please his girlfriend and friends, once returned to the East, he suddenly becomes an expert on America and a successful businessman (even though his business is only a scam):

In fact, he would never be an immigrant again, nevermore a man who couldn't measure up to the natives. From this day forward, he was Vladimir the Expatriate, a

---

32 Shteyngart, Gary. *The Russian Debutante's Handbook.* London: Bloomsbury, 2004. 112.

title that signified luxury, choice, decadence, frou-frou colonialism. Or, rather, Vladimir, the Repatriate, in this case signifying a homecoming, a foreknowledge, a making of amends with history.[33]

By returning to the East, Vladimir Girshkin eventually achieves his dream of climbing the ladder of success. As a hybrid of East and West, he can only be regarded as a respectable person and businessman of high account in his former home, the East. While he was considered an insignificant Russian immigrant back in the US, he is regarded as a sophisticated American in Prava. This curious reversal of migration and assimilation finally allows him to achieve the desired social status, at least for a short period of time. Towards the end, however, he returns to America once again. At the end of the novel, we find out that Girshkin has moved to Cleveland, Ohio with his American wife Morgan who's expecting a child. Eventually even his mother is satisfied: "Oh, what a healthy American boy you will have."[34] Although his mother wishes that Girshkin's wife was "a little blonder,"[35] her hopes are up to be awarded with an assimilated "healthy" American grandson.

5.3 ELLEN LITMAN – THE LAST CHICKEN IN AMERICA

Just like her peer David Bezmozgis, Ellen Litman also uses her own experiences of immigration in her fictional short stories. In her story collection *The Last Chicken in America* (2007) she tells the story of Masha and her parents who just recently immigrated to the US, more precisely to Squirrel Hill, a residential neighborhood of Pittsburgh.

One month after their arrival, the family meets Alick, an immigrant from Moscow, who is a business student at the University of Pittsburgh but also works at Rosenthal's Pizza, which is popular among the Hasidic community because of its kosher pizza. On one night, Alick brings leftover pizza to Masha's family and they talk about the religious men "sweating in their heavy jackets and hats, their beards and *payess* slick and unclean.

---

33 Ibid. 170.
34 Ibid. 450.
35 Ibid. 449.

They leave miserable tips or sometimes no tip at all. Goddamn Jews [...]."[36]

They clearly pick up the ancient anti-Semitic prejudice of the greedy and avaricious Jew, who hoards his money and thereby becomes so very wealthy. The whole situation becomes even more absurd when it is mentioned that Alick, just like Masha and her family, is Jewish himself: "He is, like the rest of us, unmistakably Jewish, with his squiggly looks and black curly hair. We don't like Hasids either."[37] Later on she explains that Alick and she are alike, that they "are the Moscow intelligentsia, the kids from good Jewish families."[38]

After a while Alick asks Masha out on a date. Since they live in America now, they have dinner at Burger King and he teaches Masha how to hold a burger: "You hold it with both hands, like this [...]. Then you bite into it."[39] She is the newbie immigrant, who needs to be taught American customs and Alick gladly takes over this part of the more experienced and assimilated man who has been around the block a few times. When Masha experiences problems in her relationship with Alick, a friend suggests that she should read the Cosmopolitan magazine, in order to learn how to act as hard to get and make the man beg for her.[40] This seems to be the complete opposite of what Masha thinks Russian women are like:

A Russian woman is all about hardships, guilt, and endurance. She waits and forgives and then waits some more. But the American woman doesn't wait: she puts on a push-up bra and has meaningless sex whenever she feels like it.[41]

Although Masha is not from a religious background, she still has a certain conservative picture in mind of how women should behave. Just like Deborah Feldman, she is fascinated by the (secular) American women depicted in the magazines. But *The Last Chicken in America* is also a story

---

36 Litman, Ellen. *The Last Chicken in America.* New York: W.W. Norton & Company, 2007. 12.
37 Ibid. 12.
38 Ibid. 25.
39 Ibid. 15.
40 See: Ibid. 27.
41 Ibid. 28.

about the pressure and the burdens which are imposed upon the young girl. Arriving in the new country with its new language and culture, is clearly more difficult for her parents than for Masha herself. In a reversal of roles, the parents become the ones who rely on their child in a strange new world:

I hate being with them [her parents] at all times, everywhere they go – classes, welfare, dentist's office, supermarket. I translate forms and letters, I interpret. This is my job and I'm required to go along.[42]

Masha is soon disillusioned, because she has expected more from their new life in America:

I used to have this confused idea, this delirious noble dream – we come to America and I immediately begin to work, an unglamorous, hard job. I support the whole family and they are grateful, grateful and also proud of me because I go to school at night. But things are different. I can't get a job because of the welfare thing, and I can't go to school because of the financial aid thing. So instead I translate and interpret for my parents.[43]

Accordingly, Masha finds herself not only falling behind her own expectations, but also held back by her own parents who rely on her. Curiously, while she cannot help this increasing alienation from her parents paired with her growing anger at them, at the same time she is well aware of how other people are separated by a similar dynamic:

This is what's wrong with immigration. Those who could be your friends at home here become cautious competitors. Parents envy their children. Sisters become dangerous – all that private information they can unleash at a strategically chosen moment. It's about surviving. Immigration distorts people. We walk around distorted.[44]

---

42 Ibid. 17. We see a similar situation in Bezmozgis' *Natasha*, in which the young Mark Berman becomes some sort of an ambassador and translator for his parents. See: Bezmozgis, David. *Natasha And Other Stories*. London: Vintage, 2005. 22-26.
43 Ibid. 20-21.
44 Litman, Ellen. *The Last Chicken in America*. New York: W.W. Norton & Company, 2007. 19.

Eventually, when Masha and Alick break up, the family comes closer again, the parents comfort their child, just like it is supposed to be, even if this feeling lasts only for one night.

In another story from the collection, called "Charity," Ellen Litman continues to tell the daily struggles of Masha and her family after their arrival in America. The story picks up some time after Masha's break up with Alick. She is now 18 years old and a college student at the University of Pittsburgh. Recently she started taking a job as a nanny for a wealthy Jewish family with two children, a boy in the first grade and a two-year-old. When the boy inquires whether Masha keeps kosher, she tries to explain that it was not easy to do so back in Russia. The young boy's precocious and hard-bitten answer to this is: "Jews have to keep kosher."[45] Another time she witnesses how Pamela, the mother of the children, prepares the house for *Shabbat*. Masha is fascinated:

I loved to watch the preparations. The dinner itself. The moment when she closed her eyes, lit the candles, recited a blessing. [...] I thought it was a beautiful tradition [...].[46]

Like the Bermans in Bezmozgis' *Natasha*, her own family seems to have no connection to their Jewishness whatsoever. After their arrival in Pittsburgh, they were taken care of by the Jewish Family & Children Service, which also covered their rent for a while. When the High Holidays came, they were told to embrace their religion and attend services at the nearby synagogue. Everything feels uncomfortable and foreign to them:

We walked to Beth Shalom on Beacon Street. The entrance was crowded. My father was handed a spare yarmulke and something that looked like a towel. [...] The service had already started. It was mostly in Hebrew, which neither of us knew. I had a hard time concentrating. I waited for it to feel meaningful. [...] My father sat shriveled under an unfamiliar prayer shawl. They were filled with stifling discomfort.[47]

---

45 Ibid. 57.
46 Ibid. 60.
47 Ibid. 60-61.

Accordingly, Masha's family experiences the same awkwardness and embarrassing ignorance as the Bermans in David Bezmozgis' stories. Masha feels envy for American Jews who seem to feel comfortable and proud of being Jewish:

> American Jews had it easy. They all seemed well-off, and except for Hasids, they weren't too conspicuous; in the proverbial American melting pot they could pass for Italians or Greeks. Not that they had any worries. They took pride in their Jewishness, they celebrated it by building community centers and synagogues, and by sponsoring immigrants from Eastern Europe.[48]

Masha becomes ashamed that there is no Jewish heritage left in her family. She blames this on her parents and stops eating with them at home, instead rather sneaking allegedly kosher Asian food and other leftovers from her employers' fridge. One time, when she is out on errands with Pamela and they run into Masha's parents, she feels awfully ashamed for their striking Russian looks and for the obvious fact that they are unemployed.

Soon the time of Passover comes and Masha hopes to be invited to join the *Seder* at her employers', even though her own family has never celebrated the occasion back in Russia. But Pamela asks her only to help with the preparations and to accompany her and the children to a children's pageant at Beth Shalom. On the way there, Pamela asks her children why the Jews celebrate Passover and her boy gives the educated reply that it is about the Exodus from Egypt. What follows is an awkward comparison of the enslaved Israelites to the Russian Jews who could not celebrate Passover in Russia and who had been rescued by the American Jews. Kevin, the first grader, does not seem to be very convinced: "Has Masha been recused? [...] She doesn't seem very grateful."[49] But his mother knows the answer to this: "I'm sure she's grateful. She just hasn't learned what it means to be Jewish yet."[50]

Of course Masha feels ashamed and upset during this naïve conversation about her fate. While mother and child easily talk about Masha

---

48 Ibid. 61.
49 Ibid. 68.
50 Ibid. 68.

over her head, she feels disempowered and wronged. Her impression is that she knows very well what it means to be Jewish from her own experiences:

I wanted to tell them I knew what it meant. It meant classmates calling you names. It meant a line in your passport, schools that would never accept you, jobs you couldn't have. It meant leaflets and threats and a general on TV promising pogroms in May. It meant immigration.[51]

Obviously Masha has a very strong understanding of what being Jewish means, namely what it had meant in Russia: being stigmatized and discriminated. Being Jewish had been like an inevitable birth defect causing you harm, that could only be escaped by immigration. However, once arriving on the other side, being Jewish turn into a problem yet again. Like the Berman's Masha is made to feel inferior in her Judaism, not quite Jewish enough (yet). Significantly however, Masha herself is left out of the conversation about her own identity, which is therefore yet again imposed on her as a label from outside: 'Russian refugee,' 'imperfectly Jewish,' 'needs correction,' 'should be grateful.'

When they finally arrive at Beth Shalom, disconcerted and humiliated by this conversation, Masha feels again completely out of place with her lacking knowledge of Judaism and the two ill-bred children at hand to take care of. Soon after this episode she decides to leave her job as a nanny. Ellen Litman's short stories are infused by a pessimistic and bitter insight into what immigrating to America and trying to make it in a new society might really feel like. Even more than in Bezmozgis' or Shteyngart's fictions, the stories about Masha's life give us a glimpse of the feelings of confusion, shame and inadequacy that many of the immigrants seem to have with regard to their Jewish identity.

The last story in Litman's collection is called "Home." It picks up at a later point in Masha's life, now as an adult woman. She has just quit her job at an insurance company, moved to Boston, and enrolled at Harvard graduate school in Slavic Languages and Literature – in short, the biggest nightmare of every (immigrant) parent. Masha returns on a trip back home to Pittsburgh because of her old friend Lariska's wedding, although she is not very eager to attend this social event. She finds herself in a constant

---

51 Ibid. 68.

conflict with her father about her liberal opinions. "We'd argued in the past about poverty and race, his opinion being that the problem was people's laziness, and that liberals like me were to blame."[52] To escape this conservative mindset and the narrow world of her family, Masha had moved away, just as her friend Lariska, who is about to get married, had once done. Masha is disappointed, however, when she realizes that Lariska plans on moving back to Pittsburgh and even picked up on her own parents' narrow-mindedness, which they both used to call "immigrant mentality."[53]

Clearly, Masha and Lariska represent characters that try to distance themselves from the world of their parents, the immigrant milieu, but nevertheless find themselves returning inevitably. Masha tries to break free from her overbearing and chronically displeased parents by assimilating – or what she thinks is assimilating – into American society. This seems to contradict with Adrian Wanner's following assumption:

Unlike Russian Jewish immigrant writers from the beginning of the twentieth century, such as Mary Antin, who advocated and celebrated the process of assimilation and Americanization, these writers show little desire to become "normal Americans."[54]

However, I would argue that the situation is indeed more complicated, and the new immigrants seem to harbor contradictory feelings: a desire for remaining distinct *and* the old aspiration for assimilation. By enrolling in university again and by deliberately avoiding such subjects that other immigrants seem to favor (accounting, computer science, engineering, etc.), instead choosing the Humanities, Masha obviously chooses what she is really interested in, rather than choosing a subject with good career opportunities. Clearly this is a thorn in her parents' immigrant flesh. When Masha expresses doubts about her friend's marriage, her father makes fun of her: "I give it six months," I said. My father said, "Like you know." "I know enough to avoid Russians." "Sure," he said. "You study them in

---

52 Ibid. 223.
53 Ibid. 223.
54 Wanner, Adrian. "Russian Jews as American Writers: A New Paradigm for Jewish Multiculturalism?" *MELUS* 37. 2 (Summer 2012): 171.

college."[55] Thus it becomes evident that Masha cannot let go of her Russian descent despite all efforts. Her own father has to point out to her that despite trying to put a maximum distance between herself and everything Russian, she nevertheless ends up studying Russian culture in graduate school.

It becomes obvious that in Masha's view, her parents are the eternal anchor that is keeping her from fully assimilating and diffusing into American society. During conversations between father and daughter, he continues to blame his child for not keeping in touch with family and friends and for denying her origin:

I told him to leave me alone. "You're already alone," he said. "You can't even talk to your parents. Is it the Russians' fault? Is it their fault you're not good enough for Americans?"[56]

Although Masha is bothered by her father's disapproval and wishes for nothing more than to prove him wrong, she starts to reflect on his words and comes to admit that there might be some truth in his them:

I watched CNN, I ate out, I read American books. I'd quit my job and gone back to school, which was something most Americans admired. But I lacked their boldness and fluency, their flippant resistance to gloom. My father said I'd *never* be quite like them.[57]

It seems that even though Masha technically belongs to the first generation of immigrants and should therefore be well aware of her alien status in American society, she keeps struggling with her background, tries to break free from it, only to find herself inevitably returning. This zeal for breakout and assimilation is typically associated rather with second generation immigrants, as I have repeatedly discussed before. Like the American born sons and daughters of earlier immigrants, Masha desperately tries to adapt to American behavior, only to discover that she still appears as an outsider

---

55 Litman, Ellen. *The Last Chicken in America*. New York: W.W. Norton & Company, 2007. 224.
56 Ibid. 228.
57 Ibid. 229.

who is trying to fit in. At the same time, she has detached herself from her Russian family and friends so that she seems to float between these two worlds without a steady guideline. She has deliberately chosen to enroll in graduate school where she studies the very culture that she tries to escape from, thereby showing that her situation can be understood as a transitional state which is much more complex than the simple three generation model or a simple dichotomy between assimilation and embracing otherness.

5.4 ANYA ULINICH – PETROPOLIS

As the last author in this chapter on the new immigrant authors, I would like to introduce Anya Ulinich, who emigrated with her family from Moscow to America at the age of 17. In her satirical novel *Petropolis* (2007), she tells the story of Sasha Goldberg who lives with her mother in a remote Russian town quite tellingly called Asbestos 2.[58]

When the girl is 14 years old, her mother Lobov Alexandrovna Goldberg decides that it is time for her daughter to pursue a leisure activity that suits a girl of her social status: "Children of the intelligentsia don't just come home in the afternoon and engage in idiocy," declared Mrs. Goldberg.[59] After enrolling her in an art class, she tells her daughter on their way home that her new art teacher made a comment on Sasha's looks, about how she resembles her mother, but that there is also something else. The girl knows immediately what her mother is referring to – her never mentioned father and his gene pool:

---

58 The town was built in 1937 and initially called Stalinsk. It had two streets, Stalin Street and Lenin Street. When asbestos was found in the ground of the town and the name Stalinsk became kind of outdated, it was soon decided to rename the town as Asbestos 2, the number attachment in honor of a larger town in the Ural Mountains already named Asbestos. See: Ulinich, Anya. *Petropolis*. New York: Viking, 2007. 42.

59 Ibid. 3.

Sasha knew she didn't look anything like her mother, who was an archetypal Russian beauty. Thanks to "something stronger," Sasha Goldberg had yellow freckled skin, frizzy auburn hair, and eyes like chocolate eggs.[60]

A few years earlier, her looks had precluded her from participating in the Winter Pageant that was held at school, in which all her class mates played snowflakes since they were all blond and blue eyed. However, Sasha was assigned to do something else. She is devastated at the time and consults her father Viktor Goldberg, who is afraid to tell his daughter that some of his ancestors were from Africa, and that he himself was adopted by a Jewish family.

The motif of 'passing' is nothing new to American literature, however, being Russian, Black and Jewish is indeed a rather complex constellation. Lori Harrison-Kahan points out that being Jewish adds to the

[...] black-and-white schema of US race relations [...]. Occupying more than one position at once, Jewishness simultaneously signifies whiteness and racial otherness.[61]

Jewishness, according to Harrison-Kahan is usually understood as both whiteness and racial otherness in America. However, others have considered Jewishness to be even more on the 'whiteness-side,' rather than racial otherness, assuming that Jewishness has become part of the white mainstream in America:

Jews today, rightly or wrongly, are perceived to be part of the white mainstream. Their formerly marginal position is now occupied by the people of color. Their literature now rivals the Wasp one in prestige and sales.[62]

---

60 Ibid. 12.
61 Harrison-Kahan, Lori. "Passing for White, Passing for Jewish: Mixed Race Identity in Danzy Senna and Rebecca Walker." *MELUS 30.1* Indeterminate Identities (2005): 22. 26 May 2015.
62 Solotaroff, Ted. "The Open Community." *Writing Our Way Home. Contemporary Stories by American Jewish Writers.* Solotaroff, Ted and Nessa Rapoport. Eds. New York, NY: Schocken Books, 1992. xx.

Whether in America Jewishness has fully dissolved in whiteness or not, with or without traces of racial otherness, certainly in Russia neither would be the case, and Jewishness is still looked upon as otherness. Considering that for Sasha's father, being black *or* being Jewish would similarly be looked at as complete otherness in Russia, it does not even seem to make a big difference to him. Indeed, nothing indicates that he deliberately tried to 'pass' as Jewish rather than being black in Russia. Still, his circumstances bring Philip Roth's novel *The Human Stain* (2000) to mind, that tells the story of a black man who passes as white and Jewish after serving in the army during World War II. He marries a Jewish woman, for "that sinuous thicket of hair that was far more Negroid than his own,"[63] so that there will be no doubt about their children's heritage and becomes a professor at a liberal arts college in New England, "in the bastion of white America."[64]

However, as I have pointed out, the story of the Goldberg's does not seem to be one of deliberate passing, and as long as the family still lived in Russia, quite possibly there would be equally much racism to be expected for being Jewish as for being black. Nevertheless, the child is looked at as Jewish in school and also her darker skin complexion is attributed to her Jewishness. Accordingly, Sasha's father is worried that his daughter will be exposed to anti-Semitism, as soon as her class mates find out what the family name Goldberg means.[65] The anti-Semitic environment in Russia eventually drives him to leave his family behind and immigrate to America. Like her father Viktor had expected, while growing older, Sasha soon starts to encounter the same stigmatization and anti-Semitic hostility as he himself once had. As a young teenager, Sasha gets invited to the 18th birthday of her friend Katia's older brother and drinks Vodka there for the first time in her life:

"That's enough, take it easy. Your people don't do this, you can get sick." Here it was again. Sasha's "people" vs. Katia's "people". A while ago, Sasha had decided

---

63 Roth, Philip. *The Human Stain*. London: Vintage, 2005.136.
64 Glaser, Jennifer. "The Jew in the Canon: Reading Race and Literary History in Philip Roth's 'The Human Stain.'" *PMLA* 123.5. (Oct. 2008): 1468.
65 He himself has experienced such anti-Semitism – both verbal and physical attacks of the worst kind – when he was drafted into the army. At that time, he even attempted to commit suicide as we find out in the course of the novel.

that when she turned sixteen and got her passport, she would take her mother's maiden name and become Alexandra Victorovna Nechaeva. To hell with Goldberg.[66]

Obviously, Sasha is unnerved by constantly being stigmatized, being looked at and treated as different, even by her own friends. In her mind, this has to do mainly with her name, Goldberg. She knows that other parents in similar cases took measures of precaution and gave children their mothers' maiden names instead of their fathers' Jewish surnames. However, her mother had not done that, so Sasha feels doubly stigmatized by her dark skin and her Jewish family name. Obviously, Sasha's discrimination is mainly due to her looks and name. Other than being called out as a Jew by others, there seems to be nothing else even faintly Jewish about Sasha and her family. The father who brought the name into the family is gone, religion is completely absent, and not even the faintest cultural trace of Judaism – a custom or the relic of a holiday – exists in Sasha's family. She knows that she is a Jew only because she has been called so by classmates and peers since childhood. Similarly, Adrian Wanner points out:

Sasha Goldberg's Jewishness has no foundation in either genetics or religion. Essentially, it is a function of her adopted last name as well as of certain African physical features (dark complexion, curly hair) that are misread as Jewish racial markers.[67]

In the following chapters the novel keeps telling how Sasha's life unfolds: While Sasha's mother seems to know quite early that her daughter will eventually need to leave Asbestos 2 in order to have some kind of future, Sasha only realizes this slowly. The teenager she is, she starts to fool around with a boy and finds out soon that she is pregnant. Immediately after giving birth to her daughter Nadia, Sasha is sent away to Moscow to attend High School there. She feels out of place and keeps longing for her child and eventually Sasha starts skipping classes and spends her days in bed reading old magazines. In one such magazine she comes across an

---

66 Ulinich, Anya. *Petropolis*. New York: Viking, 2007. 47.
67 Wanner, Adrian. "Russian Jews as American Writers: A New Paradigm for Jewish Multiculturalism?" *MELUS* 37.2. (Summer 2012): 162.

article about a Russian girl who has met an American husband through a bridal agency and decides to call this agency. Soon she sits down with a woman working at the agency and sets up a profile. Although the woman seems to be disappointed because Sasha is not the typical Russian beauty, she comes up with a proper tagline: "Passionate Dark Beauty."[68] After a speed dating event hosted by the bridal agency, an American man named Neil is interested in Sasha and asks for a date with her. Their date goes so well that he proposes to her on the spot. While Neil returns to Arizona, Sasha's paperwork needs to be arranged, and in the meantime she decides to go and see her mother and daughter in Asbestos 2. Sasha's baby daughter Nadia does not even recognize her mother anymore and keeps crying for the grandmother. Sasha cannot endure this and steals off in the night, quite like her own father had once done. Soon thereafter – Sasha is still not older than the age of sixteen – she flies off to Phoenix, Arizona.

In Phoenix, Sasha attends an English language class where she meets Marina, another Russian girl with whom she makes friends. Marina is also Jewish and came to America with her whole family. It is quite obvious that she does not know much about Jewish traditions and customs, just like Sasha Goldberg. When Marina offers Sasha a matzo and peanut butter sandwich, the girl does not know what a matzo is. Marina explains:

Matzo is a big Jewish cracker, [...]. That's what we've been mostly eating since April. We eat everything in season. Jewish Easter is in April, and afterwards we get leftover matzo from our synagogue.[69]

The fact that Marina speaks of Jewish Easter instead of Passover, speaks volumes; her family has obviously never celebrated Passover. Despite being quite ignorant about Judaism herself, Marina seems to be some steps ahead of Sasha and tries to explain to her what Judaism means:

"Jews have their own religion, Sasha." "What, they go to church?" Sasha had asked. She'd never seen a religious Jew. "No, a synagogue, and the priest is called a rabbi," explained Marina. "My grandma remembers her grandma going to one. Now we go, too, with our benefactors. We sit there, and then they give us food and stuff." "You

---

68 Ulinich, Anya. *Petropolis*. New York: Viking, 2007. 109.
69 Ibid. 98.

pray to Jesus?" "No, to God." "To a different god? What's his name?" "How would I know?" Marina shrugged. "It's all in Hebrew. In their English prayer books, they sometimes replace the o with the dash. So I call him Gd. Sounds sort of Vietnamese."[70]

This exchange seems to depict the typical way of how Russians dealt with religion. Not only Russian Jews who were denying, ignoring, and often even hiding their Jewishness, but also many Christian Russians found a way back to their religion only after the Iron Curtain came down. Also the parable of the Baal Shem Tov reverberates in this dialogue. Marina tells how her grandmother remembers her own grandmother going to a synagogue, which seems to be a similar double deferral as the apple pie story in Bezmozgis' *Natasha*. Nevertheless, Sasha proves once again to be completely ignorant of Judaism. She does not even know what 'kosher' means. "You know, it has a meat side and a dairy side?" "What for?" "It's a Jewish thing. 'Don't boil a kid in its mother's milk…'"[71]

When the girls are asked to write an essay about their families, Marina tells Sasha about what had happened in her grandmother's hometown during the war. The Germans forced the mothers to hold up their babies, so that they could be shot simultaneously. Sasha seems to be disturbed by this story, not only because of its brutality but also because of something else:

She feels stripped of all the immunity she's build up over the past months, and it makes her angry. "Why do you go on about this stuff? Is your life so boring you need to dredge up dead babies you've never ever seen? Peanut butter on matzo isn't tragic enough for you?" "Well, it *is* my family's history," Marina says.[72]

It seems that Sasha's approach to her own identity, especially with regard to being Jewish is the complete opposite of turning to the past. She does not want to lean on the past in order to create her own story. She wants to start anew without remembering any tragic experiences in her family. Quite the opposite, it makes her uncomfortable to hear of such stories as told by her friend Marina. However, we do not find out whether this discomfort is

---

70 Ibid. 158.
71 Ibid. 168.
72 Ibid. 99-100.

because she never knew about her own family's background or because she deliberately prefers not to remember.

One day Sasha decides to leave Arizona.[73] After some detours, she finds a job near Chicago working as a maid for a wealthy Jewish family called Tarakan, with whom she can also move in. When she arrives, Mrs. Tarakan gives her a tour of the house and also hands her a neckless with a Star of David, which she wants her to wear.[74] On the first evening at her new home, a charity event is hosted called 'operation exodus.' Sasha and two other women are supposed to act as exemplary Soviet Jews who have been rescued from their oppressing home country and can now enjoy their Jewishness in freedom and safety, at least this is the version the Tarakans are telling. Accordingly, while living with the Tarakan family, Sasha experiences almost identical events and situations as Masha in Ellen Litman's stories when working as a nanny for a similar wealthy Jewish family.

When Sasha is invited to attend the *Shabbat* diner with the family and light the *Shabbat* candles, she imagines a huge chandelier and is profoundly disillusioned to find only two regular candlesticks.[75] Her misconceptions continue when she hears the Shabbat blessing for the first time: "'Baruch atah Adonai...' She thought about adenoids and long winter colds, the smell of tiger balm in stuffy rooms."[76] Mrs. Tarakan offers her the chance to learn more about Judaism and hands her children's books to study. This highly encouraged if not enforced attention to religion makes Sasha feel like she is taking on a job assignment by learning more about her religion. Nevertheless, she begins to study Judaism every afternoon in exchange for being excused from her household chores. After reading the Torah for a

---

73 She breaks into the room, where her husband Neil keeps her passport and papers such as the bridal agency's brochure "After the Honeymoon: How to Get a Russian Wife and Keep Her Too," packs her things and leaves.
74 This is reminiscent of the scene in Bezmozgis' *Natasha*, in which Mark Berman is made to wear a similar necklace when the family is invited for *Shabbat* dinner by the Kornblum family. The Star of David seems to be the crucial feature and symbol one has to wear to be identified as Jewish. See also: Bezmozgis, David. *Natasha And Other Stories*. London: Vintage, 2005. 31.
75 See: Ulinich, Anya. *Petropolis*. New York: Viking, 2007. 171.
76 Ibid. 173.

while, Sasha remains unsure whether religion is something for her. "Sasha felt that God had gotten to her too late, that she was missing whatever nerve endings were responsible for taking Him in."[77] So while she does not really feel comfortable with religion, she nevertheless tries her best to meet Mrs. Tarakan's expectations. The youngest son of the Tarakans even sarcastically calls her his mother's latest toy and a "captive of the Talmud,"[78] a remark that hurts Sasha deeply.

After a while, Sasha leaves the Tarakan family, moves to Brooklyn and finds a job. She manages to come into possession of a US green card and sufficient savings allowing her to travel back to her hometown Asbestos 2. Her own daughter thinks that she is her sister and her mother is too proud to leave the deserted town. Sasha cancels her original plan of taking her daughter back with her to New York and leaves the house in disappointment in order to meet the ex-boyfriend and father of her child who is now married. His mother and his wife start questioning Sasha about her new life in the United States and Sasha feels like she is caught with her pants down:

Sasha realizes that by not having a cell phone she has further undetermined her American authenticity in the Kotelnikov's eyes. She is amazed by how much it bothers her.[79]

Here it becomes obvious again that for the new generation of eastern European immigrants it is not only about making it *to* the New World but rather making it *in* the New World. Although Sasha can afford a shared apartment in Brooklyn and has a decent job, she feels shame about these questions concerning her friends back in Siberia. She must realize that in their eyes, success in America is only about the material things, such as owning a cell phone or a car.

The novel skips four years after this encounter. Sasha meets her boyfriend Jonathan. He tries to introduce Sasha to American pop culture, to Star Wars, Nintendo and Atari, but she never seems to see the sense or importance in these things and disappoints him with her indifference.

---

77 Ibid. 183.
78 Ibid. 185.
79 Ibid. 282.

Somehow, Sasha does not seem fully willing to embrace either Jonathan or the culture he tries to introduce her to: "Loving him could have been Sasha's final conquest of America, its culture, its geography as far as Michigan."[80] However, she continues to antagonize him. One of their fiercest arguments arises when they talk about their different upbringings, and it is once more about the question of being Jewish:

When he talked about growing up the only Jewish kid in his town, Sasha hurried to explain that she had it worse. "But you aren't Jewish!" protested Jonathan, provoking a screaming, breathless lecture. Angrily, Sasha revisited the subject again and again. She even used the phrase "the core of my identity," though it set her ears on fire.[81]

Jonathan's comment that Sasha is not Jewish is based on the assumption that according to the Halacha, the Jewish law, only the child of a Jewish mother is considered to be Jewish herself. Clearly, Sasha's mother is not Jewish. However, in Sasha's own experience this fact has never played a role before, much the opposite, everything that supposedly defined her as Jewish seemed to stem from her father. Sasha might not be Jewish by any Halachic standard, but in the eyes of her Russian classmates and neighbors, her last name Goldberg and her looks were plenty enough to coin her as Jewish. Growing up in a non-Jewish world, she had always been the Jewish girl, who was mocked because of it. Understandably, it aggravates Sasha that for the longest time in her life she was called out as Jewish, stigmatized and discriminated against by the choice of others. And now, years later in America, at a time that she might finally come to embrace Jewishness as something positive, this right is denied to her and again she gets defined by the standards of others. One might say that Sasha is trying to be a Jew-by-choice, even though she does not observe any Jewish traditions or religious customs. However, she is reduced to something else once again by the outside gaze and by the standards and definitions of people around her. These people reject her claims to being Jewish, similarly as her claims to being Russian were rejected as a child.

---

80 Ibid. 294.
81 Ibid. 294.

Towards the end of the novel, Sasha finds out that her mother is dying of cancer. She knows that she has to bring her daughter to America now and thereby cut the last remaining threads to the Old World. Despite the distance that she has deliberately brought between herself and Siberia, she feels that something essential about herself is going to be missing once her family loses all ties to the place:

> My daughter is probably the last child there. When she leaves, Asbestos 2 will be gone. And who am I without it? When I'm cleaning houses, I do these little compulsive mental exercises, trying to picture things *exactly* as they were. Every time I see less and less. [...] I feel as if I'm forgetting who I am, as if I'm going crazy.[82]

Just like the *shtetl*, whether imagined or real, Sasha's home town Asbestos 2 will disappear from her mind and also from the map. Although Sasha has always dreamt of getting out of her home town, now that it becomes clear that it will really vanish and be forgotten, she is scared that she will also forget where she came from, forget all the memories of people and places that once meant something to her. Asbestos 2 is part of her identity, even if she tries to break free from it, and it scares her that this part of her identity is fading, both in her memories and in reality. She also worries that her daughter Nadia will not remember where she came from, that she will just say "Eastern European somewhere,"[83] without knowing what Asbestos 2, Siberia had meant to Sasha, what it had done to her. But this fear of rootlessness also goes the other way:

> I feel like a forefather already, [...]. I feel like I'm a thousand years old. I worry that my kid will fill her head with cartoons that I haven't seen and music that I don't understand.[84]

In this key passage Sasha admits that she fears not only the fading of her memories of the old world but also that she will never truly arrive in the new world, forever be caught somewhere in between these worlds. She

---

82 Ibid. 310.
83 Ibid. 311.
84 Ibid. 311.

knows that her own daughter will arrive young enough to master the transition easily, and quickly diffuse into American society. Filling her head with cartoons and popular music, the emblems of American adolescent culture, will be easy for her. Sasha knows that despite all efforts, she herself will to some extent remain an outsider to the future world of her own daughter. Therefore, she feels like a forefather already, somebody belonging to the old world, who is out of place and antiquated in the new world. Interestingly, Sasha herself implies the cultural dynamic of immigration here that I have repeatedly outlined before: The second generation will assimilate and thereby detach from their immigrant parents who remain foreigners to America for the rest of their lives. Nadia will arrive in America young enough to be such a child of the second generation, unlike her mother Sasha who arrived at the age of sixteen, thus spending her adolescence in transition between the two worlds.

5.5 CHAPTER CONCLUSION

I have gone through some length in summarizing Ulinich's *Petropolis* here, because the novel seems to exemplify but also complicate some of the arguments that I have so far made about this third group of new Jewish-American authors, the recent immigrants from the former Soviet Union. Their novels are a mixture of awkward coming of age stories combined with mildly tragic tales about immigration, quite often – as the case in *Petropolis* – with a sarcastic or comic undertone. The adolescent heroines and heroes of these stories have to adapt to a new culture, new language, new surroundings, and usually they cope with this situation much better and faster than their parents. However, while they struggle with getting by in the new world as children and teenagers, their specific stories reveal that the act of immigration and the subsequent transition to their new socio-cultural surroundings raises time and time again the question of their own (Jewish) identity. It has become clear throughout all the novels and story collections I have analyzed here, that the young immigrants ask themselves all the time who they are and where they belong. And more importantly, in most cases they are forced to ask themselves these questions by their new surroundings.

The first question they ask is with regard to their national identity: Are they Russians, are they Americans, or are they Russians becoming Americans? Throughout the texts that I have discussed, all protagonists had a broken relation to their homeland, and a decisively negative opinion about it. Nevertheless, they find out soon after arriving in America, that by spending their childhoods or parts of their adolescence in Russia, something Russian has inevitably diffused into them. Even if it is only the Russian accent when speaking English, the immigrants remain marked as Russians in America. However, their home country keeps looming above their heads not only in the shape of a receding Russian accent in their speech, but rather because their own memories force these young immigrants to revisit Russia in their minds – and in some cases even in person. Sasha Goldberg in Ulinich's *Petropolis* openly admits to her fear of losing an essential component of herself, her identity, if she turns her back on her home town Asbestos 2 for good. She knows that the real town is decomposing and feels that the same is happening to her as her memories of the place begin to fade. Early in her immigration process, during her first year in America, she even felt the need to travel back to Asbestos in person, only to realize that this does not console her either. Her situation is complicated by the fact that she is still underage herself, yet has a daughter left behind in Asbestos 2. In the end, Sasha cuts all remaining ties by bringing her daughter to live with her in New York. The novel does not continue to tell us how she feels about this final departure later in her life, however, during the time that is covered, Sasha's feelings for her home town and home country have at all times been mixed. On the one hand she is repulsed by the place which made her emigrate in the first place. On the other hand, she feels a compulsion for return – imaginatively or in person – and sadness for the loss.

A quite similar case is presented in Ellen Litman's *Last Chicken in America*. Masha is also an adolescent at the time that her family immigrates to America. Later she tries desperately to escape the immigrant milieu of her parents which she despises. Nevertheless, she is aware that she is and will forever remain different from her American peers. She envies American girls for their supposed self-confidence, carelessness and ease in going through life. Also Masha is drawn back to her Russian heritage, not only by visiting her parents in Pittsburgh. As her father manages to point out to her, she counteracts her supposed hate of everything Russian by returning to graduate school and choosing of all things Slavic Languages and Literature. Apparently, Masha suffers from a similar love-hate relationship as Sasha Goldberg, a mixture of revulsion and attraction to Russia.

Mark Berman from David Bezmozgis' *Natasha* on the other hand is much younger at the time of his arrival – 7 years old – and therefore almost belongs to the second generation after immigration. His experience in Canada is less determined by a childhood and early adolescence spent in Russia as in the case of those who immigrate as teenagers. Therefore, we do not find the same obsession with Russia in him as in the case of the female characters of Litman and Ulinich.

However, Vladimir Girshkin from Gary Shteyngart's *The Russian Debutante's Handbook* shares the same feelings of inadequacy in America that Masha and Sasha have felt respectively. Having been considered a Russian foreigner in America for all his adolescence and early adult life, he chooses to return to the East where he takes on the complex role of the American expatriate or rather Russian-American repatriate. Significantly, for Girshkin it was only back in the East that he was finally perceived and accepted as American. During his time in the fictional city of Prava, he takes on the role of the successful Western businessman, thereby boosting his own ego before eventually accepting his hybrid immigrant state (not quite American, not quite Russian) and returning – like Sasha Goldberg – to America once again and for good. As mentioned before, towards the end of the novel he is expecting to become a father, and declares with pride: "An American in America. That's Vladimir Girshkin's son."[85] This is the last sentence of the novel which thus ends on a note that rests all hopes of true naturalization on the next generation. Shteyngart calls his unborn son – a future native of Ohio – "an American in America," which can be understood as an allusion to Saul Bellow's famous first sentence "I'm an American, Chicago born."[86] By bowing to the beginning of Bellow's novel at the very end of his own, he seems to imply that a future sequel might one

---

85 Shteyngart, Gary. *The Russian Debutante's Handbook*. London: Bloomsbury, 2004. 452.
86 Bellow, Saul. *The Adventures of Augie March*. Trowbridge: Redwood Burn Limited, 1985. 7.

day be written by his son who will then get to tell a different story, the story of a true 'American, Ohio born.'

Apart from the relation to their home country, there is another identity question the young immigrants from the former Soviet Union seem to raise with considerable consistency in their literary works, as I have discussed throughout this chapter, namely the question of what being Jewish means to them. Similar phenomena of cultural misunderstanding and conflict about what it means to be Jewish, can be found repeatedly in the cases of all four protagonists that I have analyzed here. Stigmatized as Jews in their home country, they are suddenly confronted with the fact that they are perceived as Russians now – the very identity that in most cases they had been denied before. In their new surroundings, however, they are not regarded as Jewish, the very identity that had been forced upon them in the past, whether they wanted to or not. It is a perfidious paradox that now they are not regarded as Jewish or Jewish enough anymore, whether this is due to Halachic rules or simply because the outside world does not see them as observing any Jewish traditions. Lara Vapnyar, another Russian-Jewish immigrant and writer, portrays her own experience of this paradox quite concisely:

But once in the United States, I realized that I couldn't be either American or Jewish. My Jewish identity [...] seemed to have existed only in the eyes of my Russian compatriots. Compared to American Jews, I felt no right to be called Jewish at all. What exactly was it that was Jewish about me? My nose? My hair? The nationality in my abandoned Soviet passport? [...] I knew that with my atheist upbringing, I would never be able to accept any kind of religion, including Judaism.[87]

In the eyes of American Jews, accordingly, the new immigrants seem to have no connection to their Jewishness except for having been called Jews in the past. However, Vapnyar also hints at the fact that the new Russian-Jewish immigrants were brought up as atheists and usually did not even desire a stronger connection to religious Judaism. In her article "The Writer

---

[87] Vapnyar, Lara. "On Becoming a Russian Jewish American." *Who We Are. On Being (and Not Being) a Jewish American Writer*. Ed. Rubin, Derek. New York: Schocken, 2005. 297.

as Tour Guide" she stresses that before arriving in America, she had desperately wanted to get rid of her Jewish nationality. After arriving in America, however, she was made to feel inadequate and ashamed exactly for having felt this way about her Jewishness in the past:

> Being Jewish, in sum, meant not being able to be proud of your heritage. [...] While growing up, I experienced shame, resentment, and anger, but not pride. I longed to get rid of my Jewish nationality, to forget that I'd ever had it, but this too wasn't allowed. [...] I had been ashamed of my nationality ever since I realized that I was Jewish, and now I became deeply ashamed of being ashamed.[88]

Accordingly, Vapnyar reports of a similar sentiment that we have also encountered in the texts of Ulinich, Litman, Shteyngart and Bezmozgis, namely shame. Shame in Russia for being Jewish in the first place, and shame in America for not being Jewish enough and having been ashamed before. Except for the negative associations due to discrimination and stigmatization, the immigrant writers report of no deeper rootedness in Judaism. As told in all of these stories, the young immigrants arrived in the new world quite astonished that there could be more to being Jewish than they had formerly known. They all encounter awkward moments during which their ignorance of Jewish traditions and religion becomes apparent and thus they feel inadequate. In response to the expectations of their benefactors, but also in order to shake off these feelings of failure and inadequacy, the young immigrants start to study religious Judaism, attend Jewish schools and synagogues, and get more acquainted with Jewish traditions, such as the celebration of holidays or the *Shabbat*. Yet, they keep feeling alienated and uncomfortable with this newly discovered religion.

At the beginning of this chapter I have made the argument that these new immigrants from Russia and other former Soviet Union states should be considered as part of a new generation of Jewish-American writers, not only because they are of the same age as their American born peers, but also because they share their curiosity for Judaism and similarly deal with

---

88 Vapnyar, Lara. "The Writer as Tour Guide." *The Writer Uprooted. Contemporary Jewish Exile Literature.* Ed. Rosenfeld, Alvin H. Bloomington: Indiana University Press, 2008. 100.

the complex question of what it means to be Jewish in America in the late 20th century. However, a closer look throughout this chapter has revealed that for the new immigrants this interest in Judaism seems to be more like a necessity, or at least a reaction to expectations, and less a deliberately and freely chosen identity question as for the other writers. In retrospect, I have to concede that despite certain similarities between the new Russian-Jewish immigrant authors and their Jewish-American peers, there also seem to exist strong contrasts. Especially the stories of Litman and Ulinich reveal how different their protagonists feel about being Jewish as compared to their self-conscious American born peers. They share the fact of making the question of being Jewish – what this means and how it feels – a central theme of their literary works. Nevertheless, the conflicts as reported by Litman, Ulinich, Vapnyar, Bezmozgis and others are quite obviously not the same self-propelled curiosity and interest in Judaism and family tradition like other Jewish-American authors. Rather the whole question of Jewishness seems to a large extent to be forced upon them, obtruded exactly by those third generation American Jews who can naturally feel confident and strong about being Jewish. The Russian authors may share their generations' obsession and quarrel with the question of what it means to be Jewish, but somehow they emerge on the other side of it, not so much raising and answering such questions for themselves, but rather being once again – in America as before in Russia – the ones being defined by others.

Conclusion

As I have discussed throughout this thesis, I strongly believe that young Jewish-American writers – in contrast to the pessimistic beliefs of some authors and critics of the previous generations – have what it takes to lead Jewish-American literature further into the 21st century. They consciously turn to their Jewish heritage, thereby creating tales that depict the complexity of Jewish life in contemporary America. At the same time, they also show that Jewish literature does not always need to come in a package with Yiddishkeit and *shtetl* nostalgia, as we can see for example in the writings of Shalom Auslander, Allegra Goodman, Lisa Schiffman and others.

To [Irving] Howe, authentic American Judaism was fundamentally tied to the lost "world of our fathers" – the urban, working-class, Yiddish-speaking immigrant culture of the Lower East Side, the East Bronx, and other Jewish enclaves in which American Jews existed apart from American culture rather than as a part of it. In Howe's view, Jews could be socially dynamic, but authentic Jewishness was fixed in time, place, and language.[1]

Obviously this specific immigrant milieu and the Lower East Side scenery do not exist anymore. Still, we have seen how authors like Jonathan Safran Foer and Dara Horn pursue the classic path of exploring family histories, taking their search even beyond the immigrant milieu of New York and

---

1 Rovner, Adam. "So Easily Assimilated: The New Immigrant Chic." *AJS Review* 30 (2006): 316.

back to Eastern Europe. While this group seems to find its Jewish heritage in the past, there is a second group of authors taking completely different and new trajectories.

These are authors such as Shalom Auslander and Deborah Feldman who have left their ultraconservative religious communities, but also their families, in order to start a new life on their own terms. The chapter about such 'new beginnings' also showed us stories about young Jews searching for their Jewishness and choosing from a full plate of options of living a Jewish life in America; returns to religious observance, experimental New Ageism, Jewish pilgrimages – there seem to be no boundaries for this generation in taking Jewishness into the next century. However, this can also be seen pessimistically as a lack of orientation. Lisa Schiffman points out this disoriented state of mind in her book *Generation J*:

"I never have the feeling of being sure. Being Jewish means feeling conflicted. There's no certainty about it for me." [...] This is the predicament of nonreligious Jews: we can neither claim nor escape our Judaism. We have a problem in self-perception.[2]

By searching for their Jewishness, young authors like Schiffman eventually arrive at a point of uncertainty that is close to nihilism. While some can handle this fluidity and elusiveness of a Jewish heritage and identity that are *not* clearly defined, others feel a desire for stronger guidance. The story of return to religious observance in Allegra Goodman's *The Family Markowitz* is an example in this latter regard.

In the last chapter of this thesis, I have explored the literature of young immigrants from the former Soviet Union, such as Gary Shteyngart's *The Russian Debutante's Handbook* or Anya Ulinich's *Petropolis*, where stories are told about Jewish immigrants having to deal with acculturation into American society all over again. Besides delivering a 21st century update on the old immigrant story of making it in America, these authors share – despite their different background – the obsession of their American born peers with 'Jewish matters.' In other words, they have to deal with the same problematic question about their Jewish heritage, about what being Jewish means to them. However, after analyzing and comparing all these different

---

2 Schiffman, Lisa. *Generation J*. New York: Harper San Francisco, 1999. 40-41.

literary texts, different 'sounds' as I have called them, I must come to the conclusion that there remains a crucial difference in the case of the new immigrants, namely that they do not seem to feel the same freedom, self-motivation and joy towards asking these questions. Rather, they are forced into the contemplation of their complex identities as 'Russian-Jewish-Americans' due to feeling inadequate and misunderstood under the gaze of others.

Although there are significant differences between the texts that I have discussed throughout the chapters of this thesis, in sum they seem to prove my case that there is a new and young generation of Jewish-American writers speaking to us. All their texts deal quite unanimously with the exploration and negotiation of a Jewish heritage, as I have undertaken to show on the basis of my selection and discussion of sample texts. Their individual voices might differ in this or that regard, but they certainly all share a common curiosity in their Jewish heritage which is the common denominator of this generation. Their various sounds harmonize, because – each in their own way – they all deal with this central question of what being Jewish means to them. It has been my argument that we should call these contemporary writers a new generation, the 'third generation' of Jewish-American literature. Not only because they share the same age, and not only because most of them are the grandchildren of immigrants, but *because* this new curiosity for a Jewish heritage defines them and distinguishes them from the previous generation of writers. This previous (second) generation usually considered their family backgrounds and their Jewishness as a burden, which was often ignored and sometimes even tried to be completely cast away. They saw their heritage as a shortcoming and made an effort to become completely assimilated as Americans. The third and current generation of Jewish authors, however, is rooted entirely in American society – the new immigrants confirming this rule by offering a deviating perspective – and thus has a completely new starting point for exploring their Jewish heritage. This exploration turns out to be the dominant feature in the writings of those American Jews who grew up in the 80s and 90s of the 20th century, the sound of a new generation. Thus they provide us with new approaches and new Jewish stories, thereby showing us how diversely Jewish life can be lived and interpreted in America today.

Bibliography

AARONS, Victoria. *A Measure of Me   orytelling and Identity in American Jewish Fiction.* Athens: versity of Georgia Press, 1996. Print.
---. "The Covenant Unraveling. The Patho   Cultural Loss in Allegra Goodman's Fiction." *Shofar: An Interdisc   linary Journal of Jewish Studies* 22.3 (2004): 12-25.
---. *What Happened to Abraham? Reinventing the Covenant in American Jewish Fiction.* Newark: University of Delaware Press, 2005. Print.
---. "The Orthodoxy Unbound, or Moses in Suburbia: Allegra Goodman's The Family Markowitz." *What Happened to Abraham? Reinventing the Covenant in American Jewish Fiction.* Newark: University of Delaware Press, 2005. 104-131. Print.
ANTIN, Mary. *The Promised Land.* Boston: The Riverside Press Cambridge, 1912. Print.
ARCHDEACON, Thomas J. "Hansen's Hypothesis as a Model of Immigrant Assimilation." *American Immigrants and their Generation. Studies and Commentaries on the Hansen Thesis after Fifty Years.* Eds. Kivisto, Peter and Dag Blanck. Urbana: University of Illinois Press, 1990. 42-63. Print.
ASSMANN, Jan. *Das kulturelle Gedächtnis. Schrift, Erinnerung und politische Identität in frühen Hochkulturen.* München: Verlag C.H. Beck, 2005. Print.
AUSLANDER, Shalom. *Foreskin's Lament. A Memoir.* London: Picador, 2009.

AUSTERLITZ, Saul. "The Hidden One of N.J.: Why Dara Horn Is The Best of the New Breed of Jewish Novelists. *Tablet Magazine.* 9 September 2013. Web.15 June 2015.
BABYLONISCHER Talmud, Vol. XII, Nidda III, vii, Fol. 30b. Trans. Goldschmidt, Lazarus. Frankfurt am Main: Jüdischer Verlag im Suhrkamp Verlag, 1996. Print.
BARTHES, Roland. "Der Tod des Autors." *Texte zur Theorie der Autorschaft.* Eds. Jannidis, Fotis et al. Stuttgart: Reclam, 2000. 185-193. Print.
---. *Über mich selbst.* München: Matthes und Seitz, 1978. Print.
BELLOW, Saul. "Starting Out in Chicago" *Who We Are. On Being (and Not Being) a Jewish American Writer.* Derek Rubin. New York: Schocken Books, 2005. 3-11. Print.
---. *The Adventures of Augie March.* Trowbridge: Redwood Burn Limited, 1985. Print.
BERNDT, Frauke and Lily Tonger-Erk. *Intertextualität. Eine Einführung.* Berlin: Erich Schmidt Verlag, 2013. Print.
BEZMOZGIS, David. *Natasha And Other Stories.* London: Vintage, 2005. Print.
---. "The End of American Jewish Literature, Again." *Tablet Magazine.* 17 September 2014. Web. 22 September 2014.
BLOOM, Harold. *A Map of Misreading.* New York: Oxford University Press, 1975. Print.
---. *The Anxiety of Influence. A Theory of Poetry.* New York: Oxford University Press, 1975. Print.
BOYM, Svetlana. *The Future of Nostalgia.* New York: Basic Books, 2001. Print.
BRINKMANN, Tobias. "Jewish Migration." *EGO European History Online.* Institut für Europäische Geschichte, 3 December 2010. Web. 29 June 2015.
BROICH, Ulrich and Manfred Pfister. Eds. *Intertextualität. Formen, Funktionen, anglistische Fallstudien.* Tübingen: Max Niemeyer Verlag, 1985. Print.
BUDE, Heinz. "Qualitative Generationenforschung." *Qualitative Forschung. Ein Handbuch.* Eds. Flick, Uwe et al. Reinbek bei Hamburg: Rowohlt Verlag, 2010. Print.

BUKIET, Melvin Jules. "Machers and Mourners." *Tikkun Magazine.* (Nov./Dec. 1997). Web. 19 December 2012.

BUKIET, Melvin Jules, and David G. Roskies. Eds. *Scribblers on the Roof. Contemporary American Jewish Fiction.* New York: Persea Books, 2006. Print.

COHEN, Steven M. and Arnold M. Eisen. "All in the Family." *The Jew Within. Self, Family, and Community in America.* Bloomington: Indiana University Press, 2000. 43-72. Print.

COX, Christopher. "A Sense of Direction: Six Questions for Gideon Lewis-Kraus." *Harper's Magazine.* 21 June 2012. Web. 15 June 2015.

DICKSTEIN, Morris. "Ghost Stories: The New Wave of Jewish Writing." *Tikkun Magazine.* (Nov./Dec. 1997) Web. 19 December 2012.

---. "Questions of Identity. The New World of the Immigrant Writer." *The Writer Uprooted. Contemporary Jewish Exile Literature.* Ed. Rosenfeld, Alvin H. Bloomington: Indiana University Press, 2008. 110-132. Print.

---. "The Complex Fate of the Jewish-American Writer." *The Nation.* 4 October 2001. Web.27 September 2012.

DINER, Hasia R. *A New Promised Land. A History of Jews in America.* New York: Oxford University Press, 2000. Print.

---. *A Time for Gathering. The Second Migration. 1820-1880.* Baltimore: The Johns Hopkins University Press, 1992. Print.

---. *The Jews of the United States. 1654 to 2000.* Berkeley: University of California Press, 2004. Print.

ENGLANDER, Nathan. *For the Relief of Unbearable Urges.* London: Farber and Farber, 2000. Print.

ERLL, Astrid. *Kollektives Gedächtnis und Erinnerungskulturen. Eine Einführung.* Stuttgart: Verlag J.B. Metzler, 2011. Print.

FEINGOLD, Henry L. *The Jewish People in America.* Vol. I-V. Baltimore: The Johns Hopkins University Press, 1992. Print.

FELDMAN, Deborah. *Unorthodox: The Scandalous Rejection of My Hasidic Roots.* New York: Simon & Schuster, 2012. Print.

FOER, Jonathan Safran. *Everything is Illuminated.* New York: Houghton Mifflin Company, 2002. Print.

FOUCAULT, Michel. "Was ist ein Autor?" *Texte zur Theorie der Autorschaft.* Eds. Jannidis, Fotis et al. Stuttgart: Reclam, 2000. 194-229.

FRANCO, Dean J. "Being Black, Being Jewish, and Knowing the Difference: Philip Roth's 'The Human Stain'; Or, It Depends on What the Meaning of 'Clinton' Is." *Studies in American Jewish Literature* 23 (2004): 88-103. Web. 12 June 2015.

FRIEDMAN, Thomas. "Back to Orthodoxy: The New Ethic and Ethnics in American Jewish Literature." *Contemporary Jewry* 10.1 (1989): 67-77. Web. 15 June 2015.

FURMAN, Andrew. *Israel through the Jewish-American Imagination. A Survey of Jewish-American Literature on Israel 1928-1995*. Albany: State University of New York Press, 1997.

---. "The Russification of Jewish-American Fiction." *Zeek*. April 08. Web. 10 April 2015.

GASSER, Peter. "Autobiographie und Autofiktion. Einige begriffskritische Bemerkungen." "...all diese fingierten, notieren, im meinem Kopf ungefähr wieder zusammengesetzten Ichs." *Autobiographie und Autofiktion*. Eds. Pellin, Elio, and Ulrich Weber. Göttingen: Wallstein Verlag, 2012. 13-27.

GLASER, Jennifer. "The Jew in the Canon: Reading Race and Literary History in Philip Roth's 'The Human Stain.'" *PMLA*. 123. 5 (Oct. 2008): 1465-1478. Web. 2 June 2015.

GOGOS, Manuel. *Philip Roth & Söhne. Zum jüdischen Familienroman*. Hamburg: Philo, 2005. Print.

GOLDSTEIN, Rebecca. "Against Logic." *Tikkun* 12.6 (1997): 42. Web. 3 July 2015.

GOODHEART, Eugene. "The Jewish Writer in America." *The Sewanee Review*. 116, 1 (2008): 93-107. Web. 16 June 2015.

GOODMAN, Allegra. *The Family Markowitz*. New York: Farrar, Straus and Giroux, 1997. Print.

GRAUER, Tresa. "Identity Matters: Contemporary Jewish American Writing." *The Cambridge Companion to Jewish American Literature*. Eds. Kramer, Michael P. and Hana Wirth-Nesher. Cambridge: Cambridge University Press, 2003. 269-284. Print.

GREEN, Peter S. "Jewish Museum in Poland: More Than a Memorial." *The New York Times* 9 January 2003. Web. 19 January 2015.

HAGE, Volker. "Interview with W.G. Sebald." *Akzente. Zeitschrift für Literatur*. Ed. Krüger, Michael. München: Carl Hanser Verlag, 2000. Print.

HALBWACHS, Maurice. *Das Gedächtnis und seine sozialen Bedingungen.* Frankfurt am Main: Suhrkamp, 1985. Print.
HANDLER BURSTEIN, Janet. *Telling Little Secrets. American Jewish Writing since the 1980s.* Madison: The University of Wisconsin Press, 2006. Print.
HANSEN, Marcus Lee. "The Problem of the Third Generation Immigrant." *American Immigrants and their Generation. Studies and Commentaries on the Hansen Thesis after Fifty Years.* Eds. Kivisto, Peter and Dag Blanck. Urbana: University of Illinois Press, 1990. 191-203. Print.
---. "Who Shall Inherit America?" *American Immigrants and their Generation. Studies and Commentaries on the Hansen Thesis after Fifty Years.* Eds. Kivisto, Peter and Dag Blanck. Urbana: University of Illinois Press, 1990. 204-213. Print.
HARRISON-Kahan, Lori. "Passing for White, Passing for Jewish: Mixed Race Identity in Danzy Senna and Rebecca Walker." *MELUS* 30.1 Indeterminate Identities (2005): 19-48. Web 26 May 2015.
HENDERSON, Heather. "The Travel Writer and the Text: 'My Giant Goes with Me Wherever I Go.'" Ed. Kowalewski, Michael. *Temperamental Journeys: Essays on the Modern Literature of Travel.* Athens: The University of Georgia Press, 1992. 230-248. Print.
HIRSCH, Marianne. "The Generation of Postmemory." *Poetics Today* 29.1 (Spring 2008): 103-128. Web. 10 June 2015.
---. "Objects of Return." *The Generation of Postmemory. Writing and Visual Culture after the Holocaust.* New York, 2012. 203-225. Print.
HOLLANDER, John. "The Anxiety of Influence." *The New York Times.* 4 March 1974. Web. 13 June 2013.
HÖPFINGER, François. *Generationenfrage – Konzepte, theoretische Ansätze und Beobachtungen zu Generationenbeziehungen in späteren Lebensphasen.* Lausanne: Réalités Sociales 1999. Web. 11 June 2015.
HORN, Dara. *In the Image.* New York: W.W. Norton & Company, 2002. Print.
---. *The World to Come.* London: Hamish Hamilton, 2006. Print.
HOROWITZ, Sara R. "Mediating Judaism: Mind, Body, Spirit, and Contemporary North American Jewish Fiction." *AJS Review,* 30.2 (Nov. 2006): 231-253. Web. 3 June 2015.
HOWE, Irving. "Immigrant Chic." *New York Magazine,* 12 May 1986. 76. Print.

---. Ed. *Jewish-American Stories*. New York: A Mentor Book, 1977. Print.
JUREIT, Ulrike. *Generationenforschung*. Göttingen: Vandenhoeck & Ruprecht, 2006. Print.
KADISH, Rachel. "The Davka Method." *Who We Are. On Being (and Not Being) a Jewish American Writer*. Ed. Derek Rubin. New York, NY: Schocken Books, 2005. 277-292. Print.
KIRSCH, Adam. "David Bezmozgis' Brilliant Alt-History of an Adulterous Shransky Who Never Was." *Tablet Magazine* 17 Sept. 2014. Web. 20 June 2015.
KIRSHENBAUM, Binnie. "Princess." *Who We Are. On Being (and Not Being) a Jewish American Writer*. Ed. Rubin, Derek. New York: Schocken Books, 2005. 217-226. Print.
KLINGENSTEIN, Susanne. "Jewish American Fiction, Act III: Eccentric Sources of Inspiration." *Studies in American Jewish Literature* 18 (1999): 83-91. Web. 10 June 2015.
KRAMER, Michael P., and Hana Wirth-Nesher. Eds. *The Cambridge Companion to Jewish American Literature*. Cambridge: Cambridge University Press, 2003. Print.
---. "Beginnings and Ends: The Origins of Jewish American Literary History." *The Cambridge Companion to Jewish American Literature*. Eds. Kramer, Michael P., and Hana Wirth-Nesher. Cambridge: Cambridge University Press, 2003. 12-30. Print.
KRAUSS, Nicole. *The History of Love*. London: Penguin Books, 2005. Print.
KREMER, Lillian S. "Post-alienation: Recent Directions in Jewish-American Literature." *Contemporary Literature* 34.3 (Autumn 1993): 571-591. Web. 20 June 2015.
KRISTEVA, Julia. "'Nous deux' or a (Hi)story of Intertextuality." *Romanic Review* 93.1-2. (2002): 7-13. Web. 12 June 2015.
---. "Bachtin, das Wort, der Dialog und der Roman." *Literaturwissenschaft und Linguistik. Ergebnisse und Perspektiven*. Ed. Ihwe, Jens. Frankfurt am Main: Athenäum Verlag, 1972. Print.
KÜNEMUND, Harald and Marc Szydlik. Eds. *Generationen. Multidisziplinäre Perspektiven*. Wiesbaden: VS Verlag für Sozialwissenschaften, 2009. Print.
LEJEUNE, Philippe. *Der autobiographische Pakt*. Frankfurt am Main: Suhrkamp Verlag, 1994. Print.

LEV, Raphael. "Writing Something Real." *Who We Are. On Being (and Not Being) a Jewish American Writer.* Rubin, Derek. Ed. New York: Schocken Books, 2005. 190-201. Print.
LEWIS-Kraus, Gideon. *A Sense of Direction.* London: Penguin Books, 2012. Print.
LIEBAU, Eckart. "Generation – ein aktuelles Problem?" *Das Generationenverhältnis. Über das Zusammenleben in Familie und Gesellschaft.* Ed. Liebau, Eckart. München: Juventa Verlag, 1997. Print.
LISLE, Debbie. "Looking back: Utopia, Nostalgia and the Myth of Historical Progress." *The Global Politics of Contemporary Travel Writing.* Cambridge: Cambridge University Press 2006. 203-259. Print.
LITMAN, Ellen. *The Last Chicken in America.* New York: W.W. Norton & Company, 2007. Print.
MANNHEIM, Karl. *Wissenssoziologie. Auswahl aus dem Werk.* Ed. Wolff, Kurt H. Berlin: Luchterhand Verlag, 1964. Print.
---. "Das Problem der Generationen." *100(0) Schlüsseldokumente der deutschen Geschichte im 20. Jahrhunderts.* Bayerische Staatsbibliothek. Web. 15 June 2015.
MARTINEZ, Matias and Michael Scheffel. *Einführung in die Erzähltheorie.* München: C.H. Beck, 2002. Print.
MEYER, Adam. Abstract. "Putting the 'Jewish' Back in 'Jewish American Fiction': A Look at Jewish American Fiction from 1977 to 2022 and an Allegorical Reading of Nathan Englander's 'The Gilgul of Park Avenue.'" *Shofar: An Interdisciplinary Journal of Jewish Studies* 22.3 (2004): 104-120. Web. 19 April 2015.
MÜLLER Nielaba, Daniel. "Die alten grossen Meister. Generationsfolge als literarische Ursprungserzählung." *Generationen. Multidisziplinäre Perspektiven.* Eds. Künemund, Harald and Marc Szydlik, Wiesbaden: VS Verlag für Sozialwissenschaften, 2009. 135-147. Print.
PALEY, Grace. "The Immigrant Story. *Enormous Changes at the Last Minute.* New York: Farrar Straus Giroux, 1986. 169-176. Print
PARKER Royal, Derek. "Unfinalized Moments in Jewish American Narrative." *Shofar: An Interdisciplinary Journal of Jewish Studies* 22.3 (2004): 1-11. Web. 15 May 2015.
---. "Tugging at Jewish Weeds: An Interview with Steve Stern." *MELUS* 32.1. (2007): 139-161. Web. 20 June 2015

PINSKER, Sanford. "Post-holocaust Literature." *Tikkun Magazine* (Nov./Dec. 1997). Web. 20 June 2015.
PRUSHER, Ilene R. "Talking with Nathan Englander. From Hempstead to Jerusalem." *Newsday.com* 17 April 1999. Web. 20 June 2015.
RAPOPORT, Nessa. "Summoned to the Feast." *Writing Our Way Home. Contemporary Stories by American Jewish Writers.* Eds. Solotaroff, Ted and Nessa Rapoport. New York, NY: Schocken Books, 1992. xxvii-xxx. Print.
ROSENFELD, Alvin H. Ed. *The Writer Uprooted. Contemporary Jewish Exile Literature.* Bloomington: Indiana University Press, 2008. Print.
ROSS, Tova. "How Ex-Frum Memoirs Became New York Publishing's Hottest New Trend." *Tablet Magazine.* 7 January 2014. Web. 9 January 2014.
ROTH, Henry. *Call It Sleep.* New York: The Noonday Press, 1995. Print.
ROTH, Philip. *The Human Stain.* London: Vintage, 2005. Print.
ROVNER, Adam. "So Easily Assimilated: The New Immigrant Chic." *AJS Review* 30 (2006): 313-324. Web. 10 April 2015.
RUBIN, Derek. Ed. *Promised Lands. New Jewish American Fiction on Longing and Belonging.* Amsterdam: Amsterdam University Press, 2010. Print.
---. *Who We Are. On Being (and Not Being) a Jewish American Writer.* New York: Schocken, 2005. Print.
RUBIN, Steven J. "American-Jewish Autobiography, 1912 to the Present." *Handbook of American-Jewish Literature. An Analytical Guide to Topics, Themes, and Sources.* Ed. Fried, Lewis. New York: Greenwood Press, 1988. 287-313. Print.
SALARIO, Alizah. "Former Yeshiva Boy Nathan Englander Grapples With His Place As a Jewish Writer in America." *The Times of Israel* 13 August 2012. Web. 20 June 2015.
SAX, David. "Rise of the New Yiddishists." *Vanity Fair*, April 2009. Web. 16 June 2015.
SCHECHNER, Mark, et al. The New Jewish Literature. *Zeek.* 15 May 2014.Web. 20 June 2015.
---. "Is This Picasso, or Is It the Jews? A Family Portrait at the End of History." *Tikkun Magazine*, 1 Nov. 1997. Web. 13 June 2015.
SCHIFFMAN, Lisa. *Generation J.* New York: Harper San Francisco, 1999. Print.

SCOTT, A.O. "In the Shadow of Stalin's Foot." *The New York Times* 30 June 2002. Web. 29 April 2014.
SHALIT, Wendy. "The Observant Reader." *The New York Times*. 30 Jan. 2005. Web. 4 Oct. 2012.
SHAPIRO, Edward S. *A Time for Healing. American Jewry since World War II*. Baltimore: The Johns Hopkins University Press, 1992. Print.
SHTEYNGART, Gary. *Super Sad True Love Story*. New York: Random House, 2010. Print.
---. "The Mother Tongue Between Two Slices of Rye." *The Threepenny Review* (Spring 2004) Web. 13 January 2014.
---. The Russian Debutante's Handbook. London: Bloomsbury, 2004. Print.
SIEBALD, Manfred. "Jüdisch-amerikanische Literatur im 20. Jahrhundert zwischen upward mobility und ancestral grief." *Jüdische Literatur und Kultur in Grossbritannien und den USA nach 1945*. Vol. 3. Ed. Neumeier, Beate. Wiesbaden: Harrassowitz Verlag, 1998. 95-121. Print.
SOLOTAROFF, Ted. "The Open Community." *Writing Our Way Home. Contemporary Stories by American Jewish Writers*. Solotaroff, Ted and Nessa Rapoport. Eds. New York, NY: Schocken Books, 1992. xiii-xxvi. Print.
SOLOTAROFF, Ted and Nessa Rapoport. Eds. *Writing Our Way Home. Contemporary Stories by American Jewish Writers*. New York, NY: Schocken Books, 1992. Print.
SORIN, Gerald. A Time for Building. The Third Migration, 1880-1920. Ed. Feingold, Henry L. *The Jewish People in America*. Baltimore: The Johns Hopkins University Press, 1992. Print.
STAVANS, Ilan. *The Inveterate Dreamer. Essays and Conversations on Jewish Culture*. Lincoln: University of Nebraska Press, 2001. Print.
STERN, Steve. "After the Law". *Who We Are. On Being (and Not Being) a Jewish American Writer*. Ed. Derek Rubin. New York: Schocken Books, 2005. 130-138. Print.
---. *The Frozen Rabbi*. Chapell Hill: Algonquin Books of Chapel Hill, 2010. Print.
STERNLICHT, Sanford. "Lower East Side Literature." *Jews and American Pop Culture. Vol. 2. Music, Theater, Popular Art, and Literature*. Ed. Buhle, Paul. Westport: Praeger Publishers, 2007. 213-227. Print.

---. *The Tenement Saga. The Lower East Side and Early Jewish American Writers.* Madison: University of Wisconsin Press, 2004.

STILL, Oliver. *Zerbrochene Spiegel: Studien zur Theorie und Praxis modernen autobiographischen Erzählens.* Berlin: Walter de Gruyter, 1991. Print.

ULINICH, Anya. *Petropolis.* New York: Viking, 2007. Print.

VAPNYAR, Lara. *Broccoli and Other Tales of Food and Love.* New York: Pantheon Books, 2008. Print.

---. "On Becoming a Russian Jewish American." *Who We Are. On Being (and Not Being) a Jewish American Writer.* Ed. Rubin, Derek. New York: Schocken, 2005. 293-299. Print.

---. *There are Jews in My House.* New York: Pantheon Books, 2003. Print.

---. "The Writer as Tour Guide." *The Writer Uprooted. Contemporary Jewish Exile Literature.* Ed. Rosenfeld, Alvin H. Bloomington: Indiana University Press, 2008. 92-109. Print.

WADLER, Joyce. "Seeking Grandfather's Savior, and Life's Purpose." *The New York Times* 24 April 2002. Web. 13 June 2015.

WAGNER-Egelhaaf, Martina. *Autobiographie.* Stuttgart: Metzler Verlag, 2005. Print.

---. "Einleitung: Was ist Auto(r)fiktion?" *Auto(r)fiktion. Literarische Verfahren der Selbstkonstruktion.* Bielefeld: Aisthesis Verlag, 2013. 7-21.

WALDEN, Daniel. *On Being Jewish. American Jewish Writers from Cahan to Bellow.* Greenwich: Cited as Fawcett Publications, INC., 1974. Print.

WANNER, Adrian. "Russian Jews as American Writers: A New Paradigm for Jewish Multiculturalism?" *MELUS* 37.2. (Summer 2012): 157-176. Web. 20 June 2015.

WEIN, Berel. „Remorse and nostalgia." *The Jerusalem Post.* 17 June 2014. Web. 17 June 2014.

WEISBROD, Bernd. "Generation und Generationalität in der neueren Geschichte." *Aus Politik und Zeitgeschichte 8. Bundeszentrale für politische Bildung.* (2005): Web. 16 June 2015.

WIESEL, Elie. *The Gates of the Forest.* New York: Schocken Books, 1982. Print.

---. "The Holocaust as Literary Inspiration." *Dimensions of the Holocaust. Lectures at Northwestern University.* Eds. Wiesel, Elie et al. Evanston: Northwestern University Press, 1996. 5-19. Print.

WINDSPERGER, Marianne. "Narrative Nacherinnerung. Spuren Galiziens in der amerikanischen Gegenwartsliteratur." *Chilufim* 12. (2012): 93-114. Print.

WIRTH-Nesher, Hana. "Language as Homeland in Jewish-American Literature." *Insider/Outsider. American Jews and Multiculturalism*. Eds. Biale, David, et al. Berkeley: University of California Press, 1998. 212-230. Print.

---. Ed. "Defining the Indefinable: What Is Jewish Literature?" *What Is Jewish Literature?* Philadelphia: The Jewish Publication Society, 1994. 3-12. Print.

WIRTH-Nesher, Hana and Michael P. Kramer. "Introduction: Jewish American Literature in the Making." *The Cambridge Companion to Jewish American Literature*. Eds. Kramer, Michael P. and Hana Wirth-Nesher. Cambridge: Cambridge University Press, 2003. 1-11. Print.

WISSE, Ruth R. "American Jewish Writing, Act II." *Commentary* 61.6 (June 1976): 40-45. Web. 20 June 2015.

---. "Jewish American Renaissance." *The Cambridge Companion to Jewish American Literature*. Eds. Kramer, Michael P. and Hana Wirth-Nesher. Cambridge: Cambridge University Press, 2003. 190-211. Print.

---. "The Immigrant Phase. American Jewish Fiction from 1900 to 1950." *The Modern Jewish Canon. A Journey through Language and Culture*. New York: The Free Press, 2000. 267-293. Print.

---. "Writing Beyond Alienation. Saul Bellow, Cynthia Ozick, and Philip Roth." *The Modern Jewish Canon. A Journey through Language and Culture*. New York: The Free Press, 2000. 295-322. Print.

YERUSHALMI, Yosef Hayim. *Zakhor. Jewish History and Jewish Memory*. Seattle: University of Washington Press, 1996. Print.

ZAKRZEWSKI, Paul. Ed. *Lost Tribe. Jewish Fiction from the Edge*. New York: HarperCollins Publishers Inc., 2003. Print.

ZALEWSKI, Daniel. "From Russia with Tsoris." *The New York Times*. 2 June 2002. Web. 10 December 2012.

Literaturwissenschaft

Stephanie Bung, Jenny Schrödl (Hg.)
Phänomen Hörbuch
Interdisziplinäre Perspektiven und medialer Wandel

2016, 228 S., kart., Abb.
29,99 € (DE), 978-3-8376-3438-9
E-Book
PDF: 26,99 € (DE), ISBN 978-3-8394-3438-3

Uta Fenske, Gregor Schuhen (Hg.)
Geschichte(n) von Macht und Ohnmacht
Narrative von Männlichkeit und Gewalt

2016, 318 S., kart.
34,99 € (DE), 978-3-8376-3266-8
E-Book
PDF: 34,99 € (DE), ISBN 978-3-8394-3266-2

Stefan Hajduk
Poetologie der Stimmung
Ein ästhetisches Phänomen der frühen Goethezeit

2016, 516 S., kart.
44,99 € (DE), 978-3-8376-3433-4
E-Book
PDF: 44,99 € (DE), ISBN 978-3-8394-3433-8

Leseproben, weitere Informationen und Bestellmöglichkeiten
finden Sie unter www.transcript-verlag.de

Literaturwissenschaft

Carsten Gansel, Werner Nell (Hg.)
Vom kritischen Denker zur Medienprominenz?
Zur Rolle von Intellektuellen in Literatur und Gesellschaft vor und nach 1989

2015, 406 S., kart.
39,99 € (DE), 978-3-8376-3078-7
E-Book
PDF: 39,99 € (DE), ISBN 978-3-8394-3078-1

Tanja Pröbstl
Zerstörte Sprache — gebrochenes Schweigen
Über die (Un-)Möglichkeit, von Folter zu erzählen

2015, 300 S., kart.
29,99 € (DE), 978-3-8376-3179-1
E-Book
PDF: 26,99 € (DE), ISBN 978-3-8394-3179-5

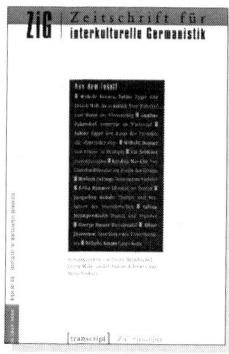

Dieter Heimböckel, Georg Mein,
Gesine Lenore Schiewer, Heinz Sieburg (Hg.)
Zeitschrift für interkulturelle Germanistik
7. Jahrgang, 2016, Heft 2: Transiträume

2016, 220 S., kart.
12,80 € (DE), 978-3-8376-3567-6
E-Book
PDF: 12,80 € (DE), ISBN 978-3-8394-3567-0

**Leseproben, weitere Informationen und Bestellmöglichkeiten
finden Sie unter www.transcript-verlag.de**